Since training at LAMDA Harriet Walter has worked extensively in theatre, television, film and radio. She began working with theatre groups such as Common Stock, Joint Stock, 7:84 and Paines Plough, and then moved on to the Royal Court, the National Theatre and the Royal Shakespeare Company, where she received the Laurence Olivier Award for her performances in *Twelfth Night*, *Three Sisters* and *A Question of Geography*. Harriet has twice won the Sony Award for Best Actress on Radio, in 1988 and 1991. She is an Associate Artist of the Royal Shakespeare Company and was made a CBE in 2000. She was made an Honorary Doctor of Letters at the University of Birmingham in 2001.

Her most recent theatre work includes *Much Ado About Nothing* (RSC, Stratford-upon-Avon and Haymarket, London); *Dinner* by Moira Buffini (National Theatre Loft); *US and Them* by Tamsin Oglesby (Hampstead Theatre); *The Royal Family* by Kaufman and Ferber (Haymarket, London); *Life x 3* (National Theatre and the Old Vic); and *Macbeth*, playing Lady Macbeth opposite Antony Sher (RSC).

Harriet has appeared in a variety of TV drama including *George Eliot: a Scandalous Life*, *A Dance to the Music of Time*, *Unfinished Business*, *Norman Ormal* (with Harry Enfield), *The Price*, *Lord Peter Wimsey*, *Ashenden* and *The Men's Room*. Her film credits include *Bright Young Things*, *Villa des Roses*, *Onegin*, *Bedrooms and Hallways*, *The Governess*, *Keep the Aspidistra Flying*, *Milou en Mai* and *Sense and Sensibility*.

As well as *Other People's Shoes*, Harriet has written *Macbeth* for Faber and Faber's 'Actors on Shakespeare' series.

Other People's Shoes

Thoughts on Acting

HARRIET WALTER

NICK HERN BOOKS
London
www.nickhernbooks.co.uk

A Nick Hern Book

This corrected and updated edition of *Other People's Shoes*
first published in Great Britain in 2003 as a paperback original
by Nick Hern Books Ltd, 14 Larden Road, London w3 7st

Reprinted 2005, 2006, 2009

Originally published in 1999

British Library Cataloguing Data for this book
is available from the British Library

Cover design by Ned Hoste, 2H

Typeset by Country Setting, Kingsdown, Kent ct14 8es
Printed in Great Britain by the MPG Books Group, Bodmin and King's Lynn

isbn 978-1-85459-751-9

For my family
(*they know who they are*)

Contents

Acknowledgements

The publisher gratefully acknowledges permission to quote from the following: *The Persecution and Assassination of Marat as Performed by the Inmates of the Asylum of Charenton under the Direction of the Marquis de Sade* by Peter Weiss, published by Marion Boyars Publishers of London and New York, English version by Geoffrey Skelton, verse adaptation by Adrian Mitchell, 1965; *Cloud Nine* by Caryl Churchill, published by Pluto Press Ltd and Joint Stock Theatre Group, 1979, reissued by Nick Hern Books, 1989, copyright Caryl Churchill; *Old Times* by Harold Pinter, published by Faber and Faber, 1971; *Hedda Gabler* by Henrik Ibsen, adaptation by Helen Cooper (Judy Daish Associates Ltd), 1996 (produced for the Chichester Theatre); *La Musica* by Marguerite Duras, this translation copyright Calder Publications Ltd, translated by Barbara Bray, 1962; *The Seagull* by Anton Chekhov, translated by Thomas Kilroy, by permission of the translator and the Gallery Press, Loughcrew, Oldcastle, County Meath, Ireland, published 1993; *The Castle* and *The Bite of the Night* by Howard Barker (Judy Daish Associates Ltd), published by Calder Publications Ltd, 1985 and 1988; *The Jail Diary of Albie Sachs* by David Edgar, first published by Rex Collings Ltd, 1982, reissued by Methuen Publishing Ltd, 1997, copyright David Edgar.

The author would like to thank Faith Evans, Kate Jones, Antonia Till, Lesley Levene, Geraldine Cooke, Cathy Courtney, Nick Hern, Jane Maud, Caroline Downing, Nick de Somogyi, Matt Applewhite and Alex Peake-Tomkinson.

[ix]

Prologue

Books by actors are usually presumed to fall into one of two categories: autobiography or instruction manual for theatre practitioners. This book is neither. My life story would make dull reading, and others have written brilliant craft books which I wouldn't presume to supplant. What prompted me to write this were the numerous questions I and other actors are so frequently asked by members of the public who are curious about what we do and how we do it. These questions vary from the gossipy to the profound and I felt that they deserved more thorough elucidation than the usual sound-bites in celebrity profiles.

Answering some of these questions in a book set me a test which I began to relish and although I set out to write for the audience, I increasingly felt that I was writing as much for myself and my fellow actors, trying to pin down this elusive craft/art in as practical a way as possible. Many actors I have met are grateful to be reminded of the purpose which first fuelled their career choice, being as they are bombarded by media pressure to subscribe to misleading criteria for success; star quality, theatre dynasty connections, a traumatic childhood, a newsworthy romantic partner. When this media fog clears we can get down to the real business of acting, which in some sense is only a study of human motivation, behaviour and interaction.

Besides exploring the job of acting, this books touches on some of the challenges of being an actor. Actors, second only to politicians, are the most interviewed and talked about people in the world, and yet misconceptions still abound. Most societies throughout history have had a schizophrenic attitude towards the acting profession. We have been thought of as priest and as parasites, idols to be emulated and self-obsessed misfits to be scorned. In many parts of the world actors have been the focus of political dissent and have spearheaded revolutions. In this country the media likes to keep actors in their place – the gossip columns. If we stray into more serious territory we risk being called pretentious. If we back a political party we are at best set-dressing, at worst seeking publicity. Despite this climate I meet people all the time who, unless they are merely being polite or are better actors than I will ever be, express a great interest in, and appreciation of, our work.

Many actors have been invited to write about acting and have refused, protesting that it is impossible. (To my mind Simon Callow's wonderfully lucid book *Being An Actor* proves them wrong.) A few of my colleagues seem slightly threatened by my attempt, as though I were intending to give away trade secrets or destroy their mystique. I couldn't do that if I tried. There will always be an element of acting which is inexplicable and which we do not understand ourselves.

Instinct and inspiration are indefinable but, when an actor builds a performance, there are many things at work besides those more mysterious ingredients. Emotional recall, clinical study, intellectual choice, personal taste all play a large part in the process, and these I have tried to anatomise. I have also attempted to point up the connections between acting and any other human endeavour and to demonstrate how drama is part of life, not an esoteric extra on the side. To do this I draw mostly on my own career for examples since mine is the only career I have the right to pry into. In that sense alone this is an autobiography. Whether I like it or not, I shall expose more of myself in and between the lines of this book than I have ever done on stage. In writing about acting I inevitably say much about myself, because acting is what I do with who I am.

HARRIET WALTER

Part One
WHY DO IT?

1

'One's Real Life Is the Life One Does Not Lead'

[OSCAR WILDE]

They say we only have one life, but some people make a career out of resisting that idea. Everyone starts with a blank page, but all too soon the biographical data creep up on us: where and when we were born, to whom, in what order and of what gender, who taught us, who loved us and who did not. The facts crowd in and shape our options. Actors, bigamists and conmen are some of those who keep grabbing for a fresh sheet of paper on which to reinvent their lives.

Actors are parasites. We function through other people's inventions and borrow other people's lives. Protected by the camouflage of character, we can express our truest selves and yet avoid detection. We are moving targets. We are reflections, but which is more 'real' – the light or the reflected light?

A Memory

I am about five years old. I am wafting Isadora-like round the drawing room of our London home to Chopin's Nocturnes on the gramophone. I wallow in the melancholy as only the young and basically hopeful can bear to do. The hugeness of my yearnings threatens to burst my little seams. My aspirations are as deep as the music, as high as the sky. And yet I cannot name them.

Now I am eleven. I have been taken to Covent Garden to watch Rudolf Nureyev dance. As he spins and leaps he takes me with him. The Nameless Aspiration is within groping distance. I want to dance like him? No. I want to *be* him? No, not exactly. I want to *be* the music? That's getting nearer but still not right. I would just have to carry on groping.

Meanwhile, there was childhood to get through.

[3]

An Early Lesson

In reality I was an unexceptional child, the younger and weedier of two girls being brought up in uneventful comfort in London in the 1950s. I juggled those irreconcilable opposites that go with the job of growing up. I was both massively important and totally insignificant at the same time. I was shy but desperate to shatter my shell and be heard.

I was surprised to hear my mother and sister say very recently that they remember me as being very funny as a child. According to my own memory, my sister was unbeatably hilarious (to this day no one can make me laugh like she can) and deserved the limelight every time.

At my first school, I was the one who ducked under the desk when they were looking for volunteers to be in the play. I suspect this had more to do with cowardice and pride than modesty. Already acting was too important for me to be seen doing it badly.

However, in the safety of my own home I do recall the sweaty exhilaration of being given my head in the 'entertainments' which my sister and I would knock up from time to time. One evening, my act in front of the grown-ups seemed to be going pretty well when suddenly, by some adult yardstick which totally bewildered me, I must have tipped over a limit.

'Now you're just showing off. . .' said by a friend of the family. Jam on the brakes. Screech to a halt. Then an interminable huff. I had been a star for a few minutes, now all of a sudden I was a worm. There never seemed to be anything in between.

We have all been there. But why can I still feel the sting of that slap in the face? In a way it was my first acting lesson, delivered in a teacher's voice, stern and witheringly gentle. Learning through shame, is that the deal? Fair enough. Swallow hard.

The thing was to learn to anticipate that point of going 'over the top' and temper the act myself.

Playing

Acting is an instinctive human ability. Children say, 'Let's pretend,' and, hey presto, it is true. As children we close our eyes and we can be anyone, anywhere. We test ourselves in safety and enter crises under our own control. We collaborate, initiate and compromise with others in creating parallel worlds. Play is a rehearsal for the real world, in which grown-up people conduct serious business, and spend their leisure time watching others doing what they have forgotten how to do.

Many actors only pretend to grow up. The child in them goes underground, but is always accessible. At school I continued wanting to invent dramatic games long after my best friends had started sneering at them. Outwardly I succumbed to convention, and it was not until I was a 'grown-up' at drama school that I was allowed to play again. By then, paradoxically, it was called 'work'.

Meeting Demons

In my year at drama school there were two mountaineers. They were good amateur rock-climbers and could have made that their life instead of acting. They were torn between their two ambitions. In those early days I could not see a link, but now I think I can. In both activities there is an element of facing one's demons, of testing oneself.

Some people feel safer avoiding their fears, while others prefer to meet them and beat them. For this reason, one often finds pilots who started with a fear of heights, doctors who are hypochondriacs and actors who are terrified of people.

How Can Actors Be Shy?

'You get up there in front of all those people!' they say. 'Yes, but as somebody else,' we reply. For 'shy' we should perhaps read 'self-conscious'. After all, self-consciousness is a prerequisite of the profession. We have to be conscious of our every move on stage, where a fist too tightly clenched or a quivering lip can give the whole game away.

For 'shy' also read 'fear of being judged', 'fear of not living up to our own standards of perfection', 'fear of being pinned down', 'fear of being misunderstood', even perhaps 'fear of being understood'.

Actors are of course not alone in feeling discontented with themselves (and I am certainly not suggesting that all actors do), but we have a particular way of dealing with that discontent. We can pretend to be someone else for a short while, and be paid and professionally licensed to do so. People who believe themselves to be deep-down horrid can become the nation's favourite cuddly comic. People who fear they are spineless can play kings and heroes. Angst-ridden introverts can project themselves on to outrageous out-spoken alter-egos. This resourceful compensation for our inadequacies keeps many an actor off the streets, out of prison and away from the psychiatrist's couch.

Containing Monsters

It is not just the people watching us whom we fear, it is human interaction itself – the unpredictability of other people, and perhaps the monsters in ourselves. All these fears can be contained and controlled in a drama, as they cannot be in life. In a drama we know what our opposite number will say next and we are ready with a fluent answer.

In the real world, if we give rein to our passions the conse-quences can ripple down the rest of our lives, so we suppress them, and can grow to fear them as unvisited caged animals throbbing at the back of our brains. But in a drama these monsters can be temporarily let out. Aggression, Vulgarity and Vulnerability can rampage round the stage. We have learned how to use them there and we know that the conse-quences will finish at curtain-down.

Compared to the dangers of real life, the stage can be the safest place on earth.

The Nosy Parker

Like most actors, I am an awkward mix of shy and nosy. I have an almost insatiable curiosity about what makes people tick, but a paralysing combination of pride and tact prevents me from downright asking. I am thrown back on gumshoe techniques such as eavesdropping on buses, listening in on crossed lines (rare jewels) and just occasionally trailing someone in the street. These methods, though fun, are frustratingly limited if you want to remain unobtrusive, not to mention legal. Once, when I was much younger, I slipped into someone's house while they were helping their husband load the car. Heart racing, I found a cupboard under the stairs and crouched there waiting . . . For what? There was no spy-hole or chink in the door, so I couldn't watch the woman, and, except for one unrevealing phone call to her doctor, I never heard her speak. Then the problem was to leave without detection. '*Please* go upstairs!' I willed her, as the inevitable desire to pee came upon me. Eventually she did just that, and I sneaked out of the fruitless house.

Lacking the boldness to blatantly intrude on someone's life, I was forced to be nosy closer to home. Like one of those nineteenth-century doctors who experimented with new drugs on themselves, I put myself through various trials: 'What must it be like to . . . ?'

And, no, I didn't do drugs, but I did spend one winter night on a park bench just to see what it was like. The trouble was that I could not re-create the conditions of someone forced to spend the night on a park bench not just for a night, but for unknowable numbers of nights to come.

Why Not Me?

We are all familiar with the protestation 'Why me?', but that equally begs the question 'Why *not* me?' When I was young, I could never grasp why I was in this husk and not that. Why was I me and not you or she or that dog over there? I am sure everyone (perhaps even the dog) asks these ontological questions at various phases in their life, but maybe with some people the phases last longer.

I have never experienced a sense of reincarnation, but I do occasionally have giddying flashes of what could be called parallel or multi-incarnations. These are almost impossible to describe, since they last only a millisecond. My most recent flash happened on a November night in London, as I was trudging in the rain past a bus-stop queue. Suddenly the glare of daylight . . . heat and flying bullets . . . a dusty headscarf tied across my nose and mouth to keep out the smell of a street battle. I don't know where the vision came from, but at the time it felt as vivid as the icy pins of rain that tickled my face.

I do not put these flashes down to anything mystical. I think it is more to do with news coverage; the fact that every day on television, on the news or in documentaries, events and people on the other side of the world are beamed into our living rooms. That flood victim could be me, that mental patient, that freedom fighter, that lottery winner. Late at night our time, we can see live footage from tomorrow morning in Australia. We have even seen a moon's-eye view of the Earth, for heaven's sake. Jane Austen's folk never had to handle all that.

2

A Bit of My Own Story

Another Memory

Night-time. I'm in the back of our Hillman Husky, looking out of the small rear window. We are swirling round what is probably Leicester Square – anyway, I remember bright lights. I contort myself so that I am looking upside-down at the stars. 'I'm going to be an actress,' I say. I am ten years old and have just seen *The Parent Trap* starring Hayley Mills. Not only was the heroine blonde and pretty, but she was twins! The twins had been parted as babies when their parents split up. One had been brought up by her mother as a long-haired little lady, the other, who had known only her father, was a short-haired tomboy, and lucky Hayley Mills got to play both.

The twins meet for the first time aged thirteen and befriend one another after a hostile start. Together they plot to reunite their parents and succeed. Hayley Mills was small and young, but she was watched and listened to by millions. According to my admittedly faulty memory, my ambition was conceived and proclaimed out loud that day.

Healing the Family

My parents split up when I was thirteen years old. Unlike Hayley Mills in *The Parent Trap*, I put up little or no resistance. When my father first told me that he and my mother were 'parting' (I remember that word), he said, 'I'm sure I can rely on you to take it like a chap.' To begin with it was easy to obey. I was numb. I remember looking at myself in the bathroom mirror and thinking, 'Why aren't I crying?'

There was inevitably a delayed reaction. I started behaving oddly at boarding school, with the result that I was taken away. My father having left by now, my mother bore the brunt of my outpourings. She gave me total licence, but I did not know where to stop. I could not stem my tears. Uncertain what to do, my mother sent me to a doctor, who diagnosed a minor nervous breakdown and prescribed tranquillisers and no school for at least six months. All this infuriated my father (who rarely took a pill in his life) and drove a further wedge between my parents.

Within the year I was happily ensconced in a new boarding school where no one knew me, and I could grab that clean page and reinvent myself. No longer was I 'slightly mad' (a description I overheard at some grand party), but the faintly mysterious offspring of a rather glamorous divorce. I buried any unfinished business with my parents and sank my teeth into work, friendship and the school play . . .

It was not until much later that I began to see how much the divorce had influenced my character and the course of my life.

Quite recently, a chance observation on the part of a relative stranger happened to ring true: 'You are healing your family through your work.' I can just hear my family saying, 'We don't need healing, thank you very much!' but as I understand it the remark was more to do with the rifts and contradictions that had remained within me as a result of the divorce than a literal mending of a marriage. I have no wish to indulge in a public therapy session, but I am almost clinically interested in the routes the mind takes in order to fill gaps and repair damage, so I will try to explain the gist.

I grew up with an impression of two mutually exclusive tribes, my father's family and my mother's family, each attached to a package of opposing adjectives. The former loomed in my imagination as remote, tough-minded and eccentric, the latter as warm, volatile and gossipy. My father's clan was through and through English, my mother's of Italian descent.

Maybe I got this exaggerated picture from my maternal grandmother's habit of defining people in terms of opposites. My father was cautious, frugal and self-contained, whereas my mother was trusting, generous and needy. My father's style was minimalist, my mother's eclectic, and so on.

There was also an assumption that because I looked like my mother and my sister looked like my father we had inherited the character packages of their respective clans and therefore must be opposites: 'You take after your mother's side of the family, your sister takes after your father's.' The years would reveal how inaccurate these generalisations were, but at the time they seemed to be carved in ancestral stone.

When my parents' marriage started to founder (politely and privately and definitely *pas devant les enfants*), it seemed to me as though my sister and I were being split into warring camps, and when my father finally left, I felt so twinned with my mother that I too became the rejected wife. In my adolescent confusion, I linked my budding femininity with being unacceptable. If I could pull back from the brink of womanhood, I might regain my father's approval.

I dusted down my tomboy act from an earlier phase, reckoning that I could just about hack it for the length of our now rare meetings. I knew my father was uncomfortable with real closeness, so I protected him from my need for it and stuck to the safe territory of jokes. I slipped up once, when he was seeing me off to school. When I hugged him that bit too vehemently on the platform, he stiffened and gently pushed me away. 'Now you're not going to get soppy, are you?' It was not unkindly meant, he was merely wishing on me some of the armour-plating that had got him through life since he was sent away to school aged seven.

I continued sifting through my character, trying to eliminate 'mother' features for my father's benefit, and trying to disguise the attempt for my mother's benefit. My self-imposed task of being all things to all people was proving difficult. In my father's sphere I felt inauthentic, in my mother's a traitor. All my disguises were wearing thin and I felt see-through.

Not so at my new school, where I continued to fashion my personality (it never occurred to me that I already had one for free). I started to capitalise on my versatility, being one thing to one person, another to another. For this please-all strategy to work, the more incontinent aspects of my nature had to be sent into exile and were allowed to return only much later, when they could safely be called artistic temperament.

Through the process of acting, over the years I have confronted and embraced the various 'contradictions' in my nature, and laid them bare in front of my family. I have been victim and leader, neurotic and clown, and in playing out these extremes have settled on my true mien. I have quietened those ancestral voices and united the tribes. I have matured from boy parts via Shakespeare's androgynes to the full-bodied Duchess of Malfi, and belatedly become an adult who is relatively happy in her skin.

A Detour

In my late twenties I wanted to give blood but was told I was underweight. I was referred to a GP, who pronounced the magic word 'anorexia'. This is not the time or the place to go into details. but suffice to say mine was a fairly mild case and I came through the worst of it with the help of some rather toe-curling little 'chats' with the GP.

After a few of these sessions, I began to suspect that the GP was fixated on the theory that gender-confusion was at the heart of my problem. He had been digging over and over the rather unyielding ground of my relationship with my father, and his eyes almost did somersaults when I told him of the numerous boys I had played on stage. From then on I had my work cut out trying to get him off the Closeted Lesbian track. (Not that I didn't give it due consideration, and not that I would have been ashamed to admit it if it were true. I was just as sure as anyone ever is that it wasn't.)

One year on, I was rehearsing Caryl Churchill's *Cloud Nine* at the Royal Court, when one of the actors injured themselves. The doctor was called and promptly turned up. And which doctor did that just happen to be? You guessed it. And what was I playing? Edward: a sailor-suited Edwardian boy who likes to play with dolls, does naughty things in the woods with Uncle Harry and whom Caryl specifies must be played by a woman. As the GP bathed me in his knowing gaze, I tried desperately to demonstrate how my now more feminine figure was straining at the confines of my sailor-suit. Oh, how I batted my lashes and flirted with the guys, but I felt I was over-acting, protesting too much. 'How are you,

Harriet?' asked the GP in his best bedside voice. 'Fine,' I squawked. I even sounded as though my voice was breaking.

And Many Years Later. . .

As I approached the age my parents were when they split up, I became more curious about their lives. When my mother was ten, her own parents divorced. When I asked her why, she replied that she never really knew. 'One simply didn't ask.'

My parents' generation are reluctant to talk about themselves, they see it as a weakness or self-indulgence, but my persistent questions seemed to arouse a similar curiosity in them. Not long before he died, my father and I were sitting in a restaurant when he suddenly asked me, 'Do you know why your mother and I divorced?' My jaw dropped with astonishment. I waited to hear the answer to what all of us (my mother included) had not dared to ask at the time. The waiter came over. 'More wine, sir?' Go away, go away pleeease, I beamed out. Left alone again, I nudged my father on. 'So . . . why did you divorce?' (Toes curling under the table.) 'What? Oh, I'm not sure. I was thinking you might tell me.'

The School Play

I cannot for the life of me remember the title, but there was bound to have been a vicar and a postmistress in it, and there were definitely some french windows, a standard lamp and a sofa set at a jaunty diagonal in the French's edition diagram. I played Cowslip, the farm girl, and my first scene went something like this:

Enter Cowslip, the farm girl, carrying a basket of eggs.
SOMEONE: Good evening, Cowslip. What have you got there?
COWSLIP: Baa-sket.
SOMEONE: Yes, I can see that, but what's in it?
COWSLIP: Eggs.
SOMEONE (*becoming impatient*): What sort of eggs?
COWSLIP: Yourn.

(I remember that 'yourn'!)

Apart from those few lines, all I recall is a feeling. Several analogies come to mind: teasing a baited fish on the end of a line, tugging a kite string, catching a wave. I lobbed each line into the arena like a pebble into a pond, waiting for the ripples of laughter to nearly but not quite die before chucking in the next. I had discovered timing. My instincts were probably as pure and uncluttered then as they have ever been since. I sat back like a passenger and let them take over the wheel.

I was cheered as I went into supper that night and the headmistress called me 'a natural actress'. I was a heroine for at least a day and had clinched my identity. I know, the performance lives only in my memory, and it probably wasn't *that* great, but the point is I had the sensation for the first time that I didn't just long to act, I might actually be able to do it.

My school acting career culminated in a performance of *Le Malade Imaginaire* in French (now I *am* showing off), as we were doing it for A-level. I played Argan, the eponymous hypochondriac, and as Maurice Chevalier was the only old Frenchman I could think of I basically did him. My mother claims to have seen through my gruff-voiced 'hon hon hon's and Gallic shrugs to the budding actress beneath. According to her, she came to the play wondering whether I had anything of 'what it takes' and left relieved to think that I had.

How can one really tell, though? Even with fully fledged professionals, one can be unsure how good or bad someone is. Kids can show a natural aptitude which they lose in later life, and besides there is more to acting than putting on accents and funny walks, and more to succeeding in the acting profession than being good at acting.

I am incredibly grateful to both my parents that, with so little to go on, they took my ambition seriously. They neither pushed me nor put me off, although they quite sensibly impressed upon me the tough and insecure nature of the game. They knew something of the profession through my mother's brother, Christopher Lee, whose own career, though relatively blessed, has never been anxiety-free. To a certain extent my uncle had already absorbed any shock-waves that might have been caused by having an actor in the family, so I had one less battle to fight.

[14]

A Funny Way of Showing It

In their heyday, my parents shared a sense of humour and were both exceptionally good-looking and fun. They had more style than money and a wide, cosmopolitan circle of friends. What they also shared was a well-concealed but deep lack of self-confidence. Both had a dominant parent who had given them a sense of failure. They had dealt with these things in opposite ways, which determined their style as parents. My mother lavished her children with praise to make up for what she had lacked. My father's style was not to impose, which I misread as indifference.

Then, on my thirtieth birthday, he showed me a letter he had received from his father. It was dated 1968, the year I left school and the year before my grandfather died. The gist of the letter was that I had a good brain and should go to university to study languages or law. I quote: 'She could obtain an interesting and well-paid post in some organisation like UNO.' He ends the letter by writing, 'All girls want to be actresses at some time or another. If you allow yourself to be diverted into the pursuit of this will-o'-the-wisp you will land yourself in endless trouble.'

Although my grandfather was ninety-four when he wrote this and the last of the old Victorians, it is interesting that he was not against a girl having a career. 'In these precarious times it is absolutely necessary for girls to be in a position to earn some money both before and after marriage.' But then, as the letter is typed and my grandfather's signature looks like the trail of a drunken ant, my father may have been right in thinking that my step-grandmother was breathing heavily in his ear.

The touching point about the letter is that my father paid it no attention and kept it for me to read until I was already well on the road.

A Joke

Q: *How do you get an elephant out of the theatre?*
A: *You can't. It's in their blood.*

3

Changing the World

'To change the world you must first change yourself.
You must become the change you want to see in the world.'

[REG BIRCH, ABORIGINAL ELDER]

My parents' cool-headedness was severely challenged when I
turned down a place at Oxford, preferring to get straight on
to drama school, at a point when no drama school would
have me. Gentle reasoning was brought to bear, but I was not
to be sidetracked. In the end I got the best of both worlds by
spending a year acting in Cambridge. I had been short-listed
by LAMDA (the London Academy of Music and Dramatic
Art), and told basically to go away for a year and learn a bit of
life. A male undergraduate friend of mine suggested I come
to Cambridge, where the college drama societies were always
short of actresses. In the days before mixed colleges, there
were about four men to each woman at the university, and
those women were too busy working twice as hard as their
brothers in order to 'deserve' their privileged place.

'There, but for the grace of whatever, go I,' I mused, as I
cycled past Newnham on my way to some rehearsal room. I had
made the right choice. Life in a women's college seemed too
like boarding school all over again. I went home each night to
a freezing bedsit, high on my new-found independence and my
certainty that I was on the road to Where I am Meant to Be.

Until that year in Cambridge, I had seldom seen a play
and I certainly had no sense of politics. By the time I left, I
had felt the power of theatre, I wanted to change the world
and I had glimpsed a possible connection between the two.

A South African Adventure

One day I was tipped off that one of the college drama
societies was planning a three-month tour to South Africa.

They were to do Shakespeare's *All's Well that Ends Well* and Peter Weiss's *Marat/Sade*. I had just seen Peter Brook's film of the latter and been knocked sideways by it, so I rushed to audition.

I got the parts of Charlotte Corday in *Marat/Sade* and the Widow in *All's Well that Ends Well*, and with two and a half months to go before the start date I had plenty of time to bask in carefree anticipation.

Or so I had hoped. In fact the National Union of Students launched a nationwide campaign to stop the tour. There were letters of protest in every major newspaper, accusatory insults flew through the air and I had a crash course in why. I had never really noticed the word 'apartheid'; I always switched off in Current Affairs lessons at school. Nor had I paid much attention in Geography; to me South Africa was just the bit at the bottom of Africa.

Many people withdrew from the tour, and I thought of it but was persuaded not to by the director of *Marat/Sade*. He explained to me that the drama tour was to be a cover for a small film unit making a documentary about the evils of apartheid. It was hoped that, if successful, the film would not only spread the story but also make some money for the exiled South African opposition. Obviously none of this could be made public knowledge at this stage.

I was taken along as a discreet observer to a meeting of representatives from these opposition groups with the film crew. I felt very meek and out of my depth, but left convinced that I should weather the NUS storm, keep my mouth shut and go.

Nothing could have prepared me for the surrealism of South Africa. From the moment I touched down at the airport to the day I straggled back to London three months later (and one stone lighter), there was no let-up in the onslaught on my moral and physical senses. It was as though someone had taken hold of my brain and was wrenching its bits apart, shifting them around like on a Rubik's cube.

In my guise as undercover sound-recordist, I attended the trial of a newspaper editor accused of bias in his exposé of prison conditions for blacks, I witnessed a mass arrest and, sneaking behind the set-dressing of the show-case miners' living quarters, I saw the rat-infested human zoo that was the reality. There was, I confess, an element of the spy thriller about all this, but the thrill soon wore off. I started to have nightmares, and one night I was woken up by a policeman sitting on my bed. (Luckily he turned out to be looking for someone else, not for the reels of film footage which I kept in the bottom of my suitcase until a safe moment arose to send them on to London.)

Secrecy was of the utmost importance, and for the other members of the crew the stakes were extremely high. One of them was on a wanted list for previous activities in then Rhodesia and had a passport with a false name. Another, a hirsute thirty-year-old, was hard pushed to pass himself off as a Cambridge undergraduate (even when called upon to act as a background lunatic in *Marat/Sade*).

Such was their well-founded paranoia that I was only just tolerated as an occasional addition to the team, and we operated entirely without the knowledge of the rest of the Cambridge group. After all, it could not be taken for granted that they were all 'on our side'. The tour had been facilitated in the first place through one member whose parents had friends in high (and obviously white) places.

However, by the six-week mark, when we had travelled half-way round the country, played in tin shacks in the townships and made black African friends, our varied political shades were forced into line. We had made a promise to Peter Weiss that we would play *Marat/Sade* only to mixed or black audiences. The big night came when we were to perform at Fort Hare, the most important of the very few black universities in the country.

The Fort, as it was dubbed by the students and locals, was in those days a mockery of a university. An entirely white staff imposed their views on students who were not allowed to leave the premises, hold meetings, talk to the press, visit other universities or receive visitors without the Rector's permission. As we passed through the main gate, a sign read: 'No unauthorised person may enter the college grounds. By Order.' This, together with the sound of a wailing siren signalling the end of a lecture period, combined to give me the impression I was entering a prison camp.

Having started to set up shop in the theatre, we inquired how the show was selling, only to find that over sixty per cent of the tickets had already been sold to the white staff and population of the town. The black students had known about the performance for just twenty-four hours, whereas the whites had been preparing for it and booking their tickets for the last month. Feeling rightly affronted, the students were refusing to come. The whole purpose of our visit had been sabotaged and turned into a white PR campaign: Cambridge University (and by implication the British establishment) endorses apartheid. I could already hear the NUS back home crying, 'We told you so.'

Even the most dithery fence-sitters among us were galvanised into action. There was a multiracial religious seminary up the hill which we used as neutral ground for a meeting with representatives of the African students. It emerged that the students were on strike in protest at the expulsion of some of their leaders. These young men had earned the right to study where many of the continent's most prominent statesmen had trained (including Mandela himself), but now, due to their political activities, they had been thrown back to scratch a living in the Bantustans, the arid areas allotted by the state as African 'homelands'.

It took time for us to prove our sympathy and our prior ignorance of the situation. We vehemently denied any association with the university staff or their propaganda. We suggested that the students turn up at the theatre that night, when we would oust the whites and make way for those we had originally intended as our audience. Brave talk. I think the students knew better.

Half an hour before the show there was still no sign of the students. Meanwhile, the whites in their furs and jewels were tripping in. Suddenly there was a stirring outside our make-up tent. A large crowd of students had assembled in the dark and anyone who was ready in costume was sent out to talk to them.

I will never forget it. Each cast member stood alone, encircled by a group of forty or so students. We spoke in simple terms as we knew that one in three of them was an informer (a role it was hard to refuse when the government was paying your fees). 'If you want to see the show, we will tell that audience to go away and we will let you in instead. If you don't want to see the show, we will not perform at all and we will leave.' A silent sea of unreadable faces. 'We understand it is difficult for you to answer as individuals, but as a group you could take a step forward if you want us to perform.' A long pause. Not a shoe shuffled. 'We understand from this that you do not want us to perform, so we will leave.'

Hardly had we turned to go when the Dean of the university leapt to a microphone in the auditorium and announced, 'Due to the intimidatory tactics of certain ringleaders among the students, our Cambridge friends are being forced to abandon the show. We are ashamed and sorry . . .' At that moment our tour leader, who if anything had been the most right-wing of us all, grabbed the mike and gave our side of the story. He was rewarded by a smack on the jaw from a well-swung handbag.

From then on our little group became more and more embattled. The Dean's side of the story was headline news in the next day's papers. We struggled to redress the balance, but made only a small column on page ten several days later.

Back in England, the *Observer* gave us a half-page to tell our version of the story and, thanks to some underground network, many of the Fort Hare students read it. I received several letters from them thanking me (mine was the name on the article) for telling it like it was. I was embarrassed by their gratitude. They risked so much more in writing to me than I ever did in fronting the article.

Apart from this feedback, it was hard to quantify the effect of our visit on the people we met, and even harder to assess their response to the plays, but when we played *Marat/Sade* in Soweto and such places, and sang:

> Why do they have the Gold
> Why do they have the Power
> Why Why Why Why
> Why do they have friends at the top
> Why do they have the Jobs at the top?

> We've got nothing
> Always had nothing
> Nothing but Holes and millions of them.

Living in holes, dying in holes
Holes in our bellies, and holes in our clothes . . .

the political resonance rang round the tin-roofed hall. We
had no follow-up survey with which to check it out, but nine
hundred African people standing up at the end of the show
and singing 'Nkosi Sikelele Afrika' is something to behold,
and is good enough for me.

New Allegiances

The documentary film achieved what it set out to do. It
raised money through sales all over the world and was shown
on television and in the cinema. I returned from South
Africa a tentative marxist – I only mumbled the label, and
even write it here with a small 'm'. I had extrapolated from
the extremes of apartheid the far subtler mechanisms of
oppression nearer home. I may just have swapped one pair of
blinkers for another, but at least I was being shown a different view of the world.

I sought political educators in pubs and in books, but I
lacked the intellectual rigour to take up any cut-and-dried
stance. Politics was not in my blood. Come the revolution, I
would never be able to trust my gut instincts as my working-class friends could. One friend I particularly envied. To
her it was so simple: all toffs were bastards and communism
was a Totally Good Thing.

I decided that only first-hand experience could determine
or shift my political point of view, so I grabbed any opportunity to taste other people's lives. I joined picket lines at
dawn and slept on floors with striking dock workers, but, as
with my park-bench interlude, these could only ever be a taste.

At drama school, where I formed my first close friend-
ships with people from different backgrounds, it was at least two
terms before I confessed to my own. In England more than in
any other country, as soon as we open our mouths a whole set
of assumptions are made about us based on the way we sound.
I wanted to make friends first and then be judged if necessary, not the other way around. So with my slippery accent
I kept them guessing, and I never invited anyone home.

But this dishonesty soon began to pall. Drama school was supposed to be a place of trust and honesty, and my own fear of judgement was making me cheat. I remember one group improvisation where we had to go back to our schooldays. The task was to recall and re-create as accurately as possible how we interacted with our peers at different stages in our development. Our teacher would set the scene: for example, 'It's morning break, the playground, and you're five years old.' He would let the improvisation run for a while, as we fought, played or clung to the outer edge sucking our thumbs, then he would snap his fingers and announce, let's say, 'School bus outing. You're in the fourth form,' or 'Exams are over. You're in the canteen.'

Not having experienced life in a state school, I was bound to slip up and give myself away. What were the playground crazes? How old was one in the fourth form? What did one eat at school dinners? I opted to hide behind a very mousy persona and not join in the games. It was a lie, and I resented my own cowardice that prevented me from playing honestly like the others.

In another group session we were invited to tell something of our life story. One girl described how her parents had not spoken to each other directly for several years. Hers was a large family and the atmosphere at meals was unbearable, with her mother saying to one of the kids, 'Tell your dad to pass the gravy,' or the father saying, 'You can tell your mother I'm off out.'

'Why don't they get divorced?' I asked after we had recovered a bit. 'Divorced?!' The girl almost choked with disbelief at my stupidity. 'Most people can't *afford* to divorce.' She looked at me with new eyes for a flash, but our friendship survived, as bit by bit I came clean.

Although there was some cowardice involved in my masquerade, there were other good reasons for it. Throughout the 1960s working-class playwrights and actors had flourished, and in the early 1970s theirs was the most challenging and interesting work. Scenes from these new plays were put on by the students at LAMDA and I wanted to be in them. If I couldn't venture beyond the facts of my upbringing at drama school, where could I?

As it was, I played rough parts, mad parts, old and young parts, which was just how I wanted it. It was not until our final year that one or two members of staff tried to box me into a 'classy' mould. One of them, an actor/ playwright with working-class origins, had written an autobiographical play about his marriage to a posh Kensington girl. He cast me as his wife, and this was the first posh girl I had had to play. I could not get a handle on her, and had little interest in doing so. I remember the writer cornering me one day in order to tackle my resistance. 'But she's a Kensington girl, you can do that standing on your head.' Now, standing on my head I wouldn't have minded!

It is not that there is anything intrinsically wrong with posh parts, just that in this case the character's poshness was her only function. Besides, like my fellow students, I was interested in the exotic. We were all trying to transcend our autobiographical data, and in a sense LAMDA was the inter-section of our respective journeys.

Not for All Markets

If I had conformed to the posh-girl type, I might have had a speedier start in the mainstream of the profession. As it is, I do not regret one inch of the circuitous route I actually took. When I came out of LAMDA, my light was still quite well hidden under the bushel, and although this was not a conscious tactic, it helped narrow down any job offers to those that would suit me best. On the whole, if your message is hard to read, you can trust that those who 'get' you will be good for you, and that those who do not will not.

Plunging In

One of the few people to read my message when I auditioned for various drama schools was Frank Whitten. He was Vice-Principal of LAMDA, and the teacher who has had the most lasting influence on me. He took us for improvisation classes and would never explain the purpose of an improvisation or acting game before we got up to do it. He was confident that the 'meaning' would reveal itself retrospectively. We were to leave behind reason and intellect, like socks and shoes at the edge of the swimming pool, plunge in and play. The more uncritically we took part, the more certainly the point of the lesson would get through, and because it was experienced first-hand, it would stay in the memory far longer than any lecture or verbal exposition. Through Frank's skilfully devised improvisations I experienced a sample of every acting principle or problem that would come up in my professional life and I constantly refer back to him.

My Circuitous Route

In my final year at LAMDA there was a philosophical split among the staff. There were those who believed that drama school should give students a taste of the ideal work model, which would remain as something to strive for in the outside world; and there were those others who took the view that ideals were all very fine, but there was no room for them in the Real Commercial World and students had better get used to that now. For me, the latter had nothing to offer but the legacy of their own disappointment. I knew who would get my vote.

The group I favoured left LAMDA and formed a company of their own, Common Stock Theatre, where they continued their pursuit of the ideal working model. Meanwhile, we students gritted our teeth and submitted to the final year's polish-up (for that was all it was).

On our last day at LAMDA, we rushed out of the school, caught the tube to St James's Park and, in an excited gaggle, signed on at the Chadwick Street dole office. Being an out-of-work actor was a definite promotion from being a drama student.

That was a Friday and on the Monday I got a phone call. Someone had dropped out of Common Stock, would I like to join? In those days, you couldn't work without an Equity card, and you couldn't get an Equity card until you were offered a job. Each repertory company could give away one or two places a year to an apprentice actor or acting ASM. If you won a place, you would get provisional Equity membership and then have to clock up forty-two weeks' work in order to earn your full card.

Common Stock was a newly formed fringe company which hadn't the means to pay Equity wages or dish out Equity cards, so I explained to them that I would love to join, with the proviso that if I was offered a 'proper job' I would have to leave them. I felt very guilty about this, but their swift agreement made me see that anyone else would have done the same.

One does not leave drama school with a diploma saying 'Now I Can Act', just a basic alphabet of acting and a smattering of the vocabulary. Although I was longing to be a real actress, I wanted to go on learning (and still do). Among my favourite classes at LAMDA were Jane Gibson's mask work and Frank Whitten's improvisations; I also loved Chattie Salaman for setting such high standards and giving me such a hard time. All three were founder members of Common Stock and continued to teach me there.

My social/political education was also continuing. Common Stock was a community theatre, which meant that it drew its material from and played it back to certain targeted groups, on their own territory rather than in a theatre building. The company was run democratically, which is to say that all decisions were shared, but people with particular aptitudes (e.g. book-keeping, set-building, directing) would specialise in those areas.

Writers were part of the cooperative, but they developed the plays in cahoots with the target group (kids under twelve, teenagers, single parents, OAPs, whatever). Thus it was that my first professional role as a squirrel who gets baked in a pot and my second as a horrid Sweetshop Lady who is magically turned into a sweet and stuck in one of her own jars (Big Prop) were conceived by a gang of under-tens from Whitechapel.

We performed all over London, from housing estates to sandpits, under the M40 and on disused railways. We visited a famously rough youth club, where a favourite pastime of the kids was to throw darts at human targets, and managed to distract them from their sport with a play devised with the help of kids from another youth club on the other side of town.

I was doing what I loved best, and in a good social cause, but eventually (several ignored letters and some failed auditions later) the lure of the Equity card summoned me away. I had read in a trade paper about a small young company based at the Duke's Playhouse in Lancaster. Their blurb emphasised their community work and work in schools, but they also played a more regular repertoire of Shakespeare, Pinter and panto. It was this variety that attracted me, so I wrote to them, detailing my 'career' so far. The attraction was mutual. I joined in time for the panto, served my forty-two weeks to get my card and stayed on for at least forty more.

In Lancaster I learned the practicalities of my trade, but was still sheltered from the Real Commercial World. After every show we would meet the audience in the bar. Lancaster was a small community; they got to know us and we them. There was no snobbish or mystifying divide. I learned to play the flute, even to compose a bit, to clog-dance and to do stand-up comedy in pubs. I discovered the energy it takes to play the lead (in this case Huckleberry Finn, living out all my childhood tomboy fantasies), and when I played Elizabeth Proctor in Arthur Miller's *The Crucible* I discovered the eloquent power of plays set in the past to elucidate the present.

One morning I woke at dawn and decided it was time to move on. This decision was based on nothing more than itchy feet and on the surface it was an unwise one. I had been offered a good line of parts in the next season and the alternative was the great unknown. The most likely scenario was unemployment in London, but that would happen anyway, so why not face it now?

When I hit London I made an impulsive phone call. I had met John McGrath when his company, 7:84, performed in Lancaster and was immediately attracted to their unusual package of humour, music and hard-hitting politics. John had seen a show I was in and we expressed a mutual interest in working together. He had given me his phone number and here I was six months later ringing it. 'Gi' us a job' was the gist of what I said, and the gist of his reply was that he hadn't got one to give right now but he'd certainly bear me in mind for next time.

A few months later, when I was close to despair, on the dole and, as I saw it, futureless, I got the summons. A message on the pad beside the phone: 'Please ring John Negrar.' A bit of guesswork, then a return call and I was in.

In 7:84 I had to coarsen up my act, broaden my humour, put over a rowdy song and load and unload vans on one-night stands up and down the country. A 7:84 gig was not just a performance, it was a rendezvous. Whether in a pub or a working men's club, the debates after the show were as important as the show that provoked them. I also had a crash course in politics through the microcosm of the company meeting. 7:84 was a broad church, embracing Marxist/Leninists, Maoists, the CP, the SWP and the non-aligned like me, and the arguments ranged from what to do about China to who should make the tea.

Touring with 7:84 I saw an alternative map of my own country and met impassioned, self-educated working people whom I might never otherwise have come across. It taught me new performance skills, with no threat of losing those which I already had, and it led me on to other points on the circuitous route – most notably Joint Stock, of which more anon.

Ancient Wisdoms

'Walk a mile in my moccasins and you will look with my eyes.'
[NATIVE AMERICAN PROVERB]

People don't change, they say, but I have staked my career on the belief that we can shift one another's point of view. True, human beings will always pursue and safeguard their own interests, but those interests can change. Changed circumstances bring new allegiances. We can travel beyond the clans and class groupings of our birth, even if we cannot ditch all of the luggage we started off with. We can embrace new people and with them new ideas.

To change yourself you must first see yourself, and theatre can show us ourselves. The ancient Greeks understood that. Through music, language and spectacle they engaged the audience's emotions, not just their minds, because it is hard to change the mind alone. A whole society would sit and watch its own drama played out. They felt implicated in humanity's crimes and moved by their own vulnerability. They left the theatre changed by the event. It was called Katharsis, a purging: not the kind of lip-service purging where you confess your 'sins' on a Sunday and behave as usual from Monday to Saturday, but a true change of intention brought about by undergoing a complete experience. That's the aim anyway.

Within this grand scheme actors perform a specific service. Their palpable humanity is the bridge between the stalls and the stage, and leads the audience into the world of the play.

The relationship between stage and spectator has shifted according to the social and political climate of the day, and especially in this century radically alternative theories of performance have been put to the test. Bertolt Brecht, for instance, devised a performance philosophy designed to distance the spectator from the events of the play. Instead of an emotional immersion *in* the characters and their predicament, Brecht hoped to provoke in his audience a critical anger *towards* them. But whatever the differences in approach, the aim has always been the same: to affirm the possibility of change.

Beating Indifference

Unlike any other animal I know of, human beings have the ability to empathise. We wince when we see someone in pain as if it were happening to us. We say, 'Wouldn't you hate to be him?' and, 'What must she be feeling?' Identifying with others broadens our intelligence, and compassion can spur us to action. The trouble is that, unless we are saints, our empathy is forced to be selective. Stories of human cruelty and stupidity come at us from every direction every day and we feel powerless. It is a painful state to be in and one way of easing the pain is to cease to care. We batten down the hatches and get on with our own little lives. We comfort ourselves with phrases like, 'At least they're not our boys,' or 'They're probably used to it,' and the empathy muscle falls into disuse.

Art has the power to reverse that cycle. It can steal up and jolt the muscle back into action. Suddenly we are weeping for 'their boys', and the feeling is a good one. Sitting in a theatre among others who have been stirred gives us hope and courage. We disperse in the street, but we are left with a hint of our collective power.

Indifference allows atrocities to happen. It is vital that we dare to care.

And Then There is Joy

There are few things better for our mental health than laughter. A balanced dose of steam-letting irreverence and taboo-busting satire keeps a society sane. Nor is the transcendent power of big bands, high kicks and dazzling scenery to be sneered at. In the pursuit of changing the world, there is still room for sheer mood-lifting, brow-soothing entertainment. The trouble starts when it takes up too much room. Sit Back and Enjoy It is great as part of a varied diet; on its own it can degenerate into Lie Back and Let It All Wash Over You While We Numb Your Mind.

Doing What You Do Best

Acting is not the most direct way of changing the world. The writer wields a more effective weapon, and in my idealistic youth, when my life's sheet of paper was still blank-ish, I fancied I might write the definitive play. I sat down to try, but found I had nothing special to say. The definitive film then. I got as far as sending off for the brochure of a film school, but an acting job came up and swept me off that particular course. My acting CV was beginning to sprawl over that once-blank page. I would have to decide whether to go with it or scrap it all.

In the end I decided that it is given to few people to be good at more than one thing. I should be grateful that I could act and channel my energies into that. If I had no momentous ideas to impart, I could at least lend my talents to others who had.

Part Two
PREPARATIONS
AND REHEARSALS

4

Early Days

'What do you do during the day?' It is a bit of an actor's in-joke that we are frequently asked that question. None of us knows much about each other's jobs. We meet someone and ask what they do for a living. 'I'm a marketing consultant,' they reply, or, 'A planning officer', 'A commercial lawyer' or 'I'm in polystyrene.' We are none the wiser. We try to look intelligent but our questions betray our ignorance. 'So what sort of polystyrene do you work . . . I mean, deal in?' Or 'Do you . . . I mean, are you *the* planning officer or do you, um . . . I suppose you work with a team.'

Once people know that you are an actor, they are often apologetic about their own job. 'You don't want to hear about this. It's so boring compared to what you do.' They are wrong of course. We do want to hear about them, but are often too embarrassed by our own stupid questions to penetrate beyond the initial 'boring' bits.

By contrast, there are many people who suppose they know all about an actor's job because it is on public display. What is more, at its best it can look so easy. The cry goes up, '*I* could do that!' After all, most people can walk, talk, wear clothes and avoid the furniture. 'Mind you, it must be difficult remembering all those lines.' In fact, line-learning can be the easy bit.

An actor's work goes on as much behind closed doors as a lawyer's, a scientist's or an engineer's. This section of the book looks at the bits of our job which are not on public display: the stuff we do during the day.

Kicking Off

You have read the play, you have talked to the director, you have got the part. Now what? It is weeks, maybe months, before the first rehearsal, but your subconscious is already at work. You read the play over and over, with no pressure to make any decisions. Dreams and instincts stir, and intellect is kept in its place.

You start to home in on your character, trying to sense their function within the play. Approaching a character is much like getting to know a friend. For some parts you will embark on a love affair, for others you will not need to get so entangled. You begin to suss out what the appropriate relationship might be.

On First Meeting a Character

Think of your closest friend. Remember the day you met. What hit you first? The look in their eyes? What they were doing at the time? What they were talking about? Their clothes? Their good looks? Their height? Their similarity to your brother? Father? Sister? Were you struck by what an idiot they seemed to be? Or by the way they treated you instantly as a soul-mate?

Whatever first came your way will have been the key, the way in to acquaintance, then friendship, probably passing through a love/hate over-close relationship before settling into an easier mutual involvement with clearly defined boundaries.

All this can be paralleled in an actor's approach to their character. During the pre-rehearsal period, you may not get much beyond the first or second meeting. You start by gathering data, the equivalent of the polite-conversation stage. 'Where do you come from?', 'What do you do?', 'What is your connection with so-and-so?' If you are getting on well and your friend/character is forthcoming, you may soon find exciting moments of overlap: 'So do I! That's just how I feel.' It is possible to get a bit deep and intimate too quickly, so you retreat, feeling it is all a bit rushed. More detailed character work is for a later stage (and a later chapter).

You go back to data-gathering, a useful and dispassionate exercise. Quite a good practice is to write four headings: 'What the playwright says of my character', 'What other characters say of him/her', 'What he/she says of him/herself' and 'What he/she does'. Then comb the play for quotes. Your character may say repeatedly, 'I have no money, I assure you', another may call her 'that mean old cow', while another calls her a 'wonderful, generous creature'. The playwright describes her 'tiptoeing round the house, turning out all the lights'. This method throws up lots of questions and clues. Mull them over; no judgements or decisions yet.

While your systematic brain is studying the text, your intuition and subconscious are busy elsewhere. It always seems miraculous how just when you are preparing *Hedda Gabler*, say, you are somehow drawn to a picture of Ibsen in a shop window, or when you are about to play Ophelia, you 'accidentally' catch a TV documentary about teenage suicide. I remember, for example, just before starting rehearsals for *The Seagull*, I had a rare impulse to clear out a trunk at the top of my house. Among the old photos, letters and Christmas cards, I found a notebook with 'Seagull' written on it. I opened it up and found notes from my first drama school attempt at the part of Nina, Chekhov's young innocent who longs to go on the stage.

I had been worried that at thirty I might have grown out of Nina's preoccupations, but reading my notes put me back in touch with my younger self, the aspiring actress I had been, and showed me that I had not changed that much. I had no recollection of writing those notes, but somehow I had discovered them at that opportune time.

Anything and everything becomes interesting and a possible way in to the part: newspaper cuttings, overheard conversations, radio programmes you would never normally listen to . . . You start to put yourself in the way of new experiences. To go back to my earlier analogy, when you are starting to fall in love with someone you want to know everything there is to know about them; you want to understand their world and be accepted in it. It is the same for an actor with a new role.

There is also the need to believe yourself in the part. If you do not believe yourself, the chances are you won't convince the audience. That is why it is important to jolt yourself off your familiar track and see yourself in another light. If my character is a gambler I must get down to the casino and learn some tricks of the trade. That is not to say I need to embark on a life of crime in order to play a criminal. Everything is relative – a little harmless shoplifting might do the trick.

I played Amy Johnson when I had only just started to drive. Many people have noticed how their personality changes and they become more aggressive when they get behind the wheel, and it is certainly true of me. However, until I was in my early thirties, the thought of driving terrified me. I simply could not see myself as a driver, as one of those people who barges through, zips across lanes and takes risks with their own and others' lives. This all changed when I joined the RSC.

One Sunday, I sat boxed into my little flat in the middle of Stratford-upon-Avon, watching the steady stream of ice-cream-licking tourists pass my window (and often peer into it). I looked ahead to the prospect of an unbroken year in this small town, working every day except Sunday, and thought, 'I have got to get out of here! I must learn to drive.' Scared though I was at the prospect, the fear of entrapment was greater.

When, eighteen months or so later, I was facing the puzzle of Amy Johnson, the girl-next-door who dared a solo flight to Australia having never flown further than London to Hull, I remembered my own first solo cross-country drive. As my battered Daf ploughed through floods with one windscreen wiper (the wrong one) trying to outpace the blinding rain, my heart was in my mouth. Everything was against me. Night fell, I lost my way and I had to change a tyre, but at the end of a five-hour journey which should have taken two, I was an altogether more formidable person. I said everything was relative.

There is a limit to how much work you can and should do alone at home, and opinions vary hugely as to where that limit lies. Clearly, if there is some special skill you have to master, like riding a motorbike or playing the guitar, you must get on with it. Otherwise, read round your subject, do some research, but keep an open mind. Personally, I aim to familiarise myself with the language and milieu of a play, rather than decide what it is about, to allow the imagery and rhythm of my character's language to soak into me, rather than learn my lines. It can be very distressing to bring your independently made-up theory into the rehearsal room, only to find it will not fit the production. No good deciding off your own bat that your character speaks with a lisp if another actor arrives at the first read-through with the same idea.

Ideally, the most important work happens in the rehearsal room, through interaction and in relation to an agreed meaning and style for the play. After thrashing away on my own, I may well find the key to my character in another actor's eyes, in the way he or she looks at me/her. Rehearsals give me time just to inhabit the character's skin. Standing around in the background of an interminable group scene with nothing to say can be turned to advantage. Drinking it all in, watching with my character's eyes, is a great way of getting to know her, and something I could not do at home.

A Caveat

I have heard of a few directors who demand that the actors 'know the score' by the first rehearsal. Perhaps they are used to international opera singers, who fly in for a quick refresher course in Carmen or Mimi, learn the geography of the stage while the chorus fits in round them and then perform in public the next night. I know that singers interpret roles, and collaborate with a conductor's phrasing or a director's concept, but on the whole they do not have the range of interpretive choices that an actor has.

Sometimes an actor's part is just so huge, it would be unrealistic to delay learning it until rehearsals begin, and some actors take longer than others to learn their lines. There are ways round the problem, which I will touch on later, but as a rule, if an actor pre-prepares their lines as a singer does a score, there is a danger of rigidity setting in. Tunes get on the brain and are hard to scrub out. If you prematurely lock into one interpretation while working in isolation, you may miss something more interesting that comes out in rehearsal.

Having said that, rehearsals are not always the well-structured and fruitful playgrounds of our ideals. Then, I'm afraid, it is a case of *'sauve qui peut'*. You go back to plotting at home, or you get in a huddle with fellow players and sort out a strategy that will get you through.

The First Day of Rehearsal

Clinging to the radiators on the edge of the room and clutching one's polystyrene cup of cold tea. Tentatively nodding at other actors one may know slightly, or else may simply have seen being brilliant in some show or other. Should I go up and introduce myself? Is that cool-looking young actress even more terrified than me? Assume that she is and approach her. Then at last someone you know quite well . . . Big hugs and nervous blurts of gossip which one regrets later.

But this is not a party and the moment can no longer be postponed. The director or stage manager calls everyone to gather round the table. A flash of schooldays – 'Who shall I sit next to?', 'Will anyone want to sit next to me?' Then the first big question: to read through, or not to read through? Time is always short and that may be a director's reason for skipping this stage. Sometimes the whole cast opts to delay the read-through until a few days in, when we should be more relaxed with one another.

For my money, there is no good moment to take that icy plunge, so one may as well get it over with. Quite apart from the benefits to director, composer, designer and marketing staff of hearing the play in its entirety, getting a general impression of its tone, atmosphere and rough length, the read-through is also likely to be the last chance the cast will get to hear the whole play before being siphoned off to rehearse specific scenes. These will necessarily dominate our focus until we start putting all the bits together at a much later stage, so it is vital to be able to refer back to the read-through, however imperfect, to restore our perspective.

Hearing one's lonely and inadequate voice hanging in the cold air of a rehearsal room is no fun. You stumble and fluff and sound totally unconvincing. You decide to go for a full-throttle rendition, then realise that your leading man is 'saving himself' (or vice versa, but whichever your choice, *you* feel the fool). You want to cry out, 'This is not how I mean to do it. I promise I will be all right on the night!' Then there is the risk that another actor will be thinking, '*I* should be doing that part. I would be miles better,' just as you are wondering, 'Is he really going to do it like *that?*' Mercifully, our common fears usually lead us to give one another the benefit of the doubt.

A Bit About the Set

The other main event on the first day of rehearsals is the revelation of the set. For pragmatic and material reasons, the design ideas are the first to be consolidated. If the set is to be ready in time for technical rehearsals (usually two or three days before the first preview), the workshop must start building it before many of the parts have been cast. The director and designer have been consulting and creating for several months before the cast get to see that cardboard model box. For the designer, the moment of revelation is an ordeal. It is their turn to perform, while we sit listening and staring, not giving anything away. Do we hate it or love it, this thing the designer has put so much time and care into? The answer for most actors is that it is too early to decide.

It is hard to avoid forming our own mental pictures while reading the play, and now we must adjust to the ones before our eyes. This is to be the world of the play. This is what the audience will see. This is the image I must be part of.

As the designer points out our doll-selves on the doll's-house set, we can only sit and gasp. It all seems so clever. How will we negotiate that huge staircase? Will the rake of the floor make it difficult to fight, dance, move? How will that chair affect my posture? These are all unknowables at this stage. On day one it is hard to formulate your arguments against Act Three being set in a corridor of distorting mirrors. It may be a genius idea or it may be a disaster, and you are in no position to know which yet; besides, those mirrors are already being bashed out at the maker's.

For all these reasons, actors are rarely in a position to overthrow a fundamental design concept, even though we may be saddled with one which blocks our creativity, and stands between the play and the audience like a billboard advertising the designer's 'genius'. We have all been there and it is a spirit-breaking experience. However, at best (and in Britain there is a lot of the best about) the design can lift you beyond your wildest hopes for a show, plug you into a believable world and inspire you to match its scope.

We love or hate sets because they have the power to make or break a show and, being the only concrete manifestation of an ephemeral art form, they can dominate the memory. 'Oh, yes', we say, long after we have forgotten the plot and the meaning of a play we once saw, 'that was the one set on a tube station,' or, 'All I can remember is that huge Buddha in the middle of the stage.' Unlike an actor's performance, a set can be re-created with the help of plans and models, and captured by photography. When all else has faded, the image of a play remains.

Immortality apart, a set has got to be workable, and that is where the actors can contribute. For the most part, actors are very practical (I have to say I am not, and will often discover too late that I have nowhere to sit, or no time for a costume change) and a few can foresee a hitch even at the model-showing stage, and suggest ways to avoid it at no extra cost.

Having said we seldom rock the design-concept boat, I do remember a rare instance when the actors got up a protest half-way through rehearsals and managed to force a rethink. Admittedly the mutiny was led by a star actor, without whom there would have been no show. Usually we confine ourselves to practical details, and sometimes an actor's forethought can save on hospital bills. It may be thrilling for an audience to watch *As You Like It* set on an ice-rink, but we could break our necks on it.

It is frustratingly difficult for actors to share the audience's experience of a play. A brilliant design can transport an audience into a perfect 3D fantasy but, except when we turn our backs to the stalls and face upstage, we seldom get the chance to savour the full glory of the illusion. Mostly, what we see are shadowy stacks of strangers in a dark auditorium dotted with green neon exit signs. When I did *A Midsummer Night's Dream* at Stratford years ago, the audience saw cobwebs and gossamer, where I remember unethereal floorboards and polystyrene. Small wonder that actors are seldom transported, but then we are not supposed to be.

An Early Disappointment

When my uncle Christopher Lee was making horror films for Hammer, we would occasionally be invited down to Bray Studios and, during a lunch break, would be let loose to play on the sets. You can imagine the heaven. I no longer had to imagine the dungeons of a castle, there they were. The only trouble was that a step in the wrong direction would give the game away. The walls were just a façade propped up by scaffolding. Dracula's fangs were removable plastic jobs which my uncle kept in a box. Sometimes make-believe is easier without visual aids. Like the boy said, the pictures are better on the radio.

Entering the Process

Rehearsals are the scariest bit of acting. It is one thing to perform to a paying public when you have consolidated your performance and had some encouraging feedback, but in rehearsals you must be prepared to stand up in front of people and do it *wrong*! You try something out that you hope might be brilliant and it flops like a bad joke. You can feel the pitying winces of the cast like a chill wind. Ideas are exposed in a half-baked state, like raw flesh without the layers of protective skin which one hopes will eventually develop. That is why generosity and trust are so important – and trust is a two-way traffic.

Job Description for Ideal Director . . .

Should be: visionary inspirer, self-effacing interpreter, fine-tuned character judge, Henry V-style rallier, ringmaster, alchemist, conductor, father, mother, nanny, child, shrink, doctor, encyclopedia, actor, designer, lighting and sound expert, gentle coaxer or stern coercer depending on temperament and attitude of actor (which he/she must assess correctly – no second chances allowed). All this and more, for the director must take critical flak, little credit, and never burden anyone with his or her personal feelings about same. No wonder a lot of them feel paranoid and inadequate. No wonder the good ones are so few.

The Use of Time

If the director has successfully communicated his or her intentions to the company, and assuming that the actors can freely operate within that framework, then we should all be able to use the time efficiently. Along with Trust, Time is a vital element of the rehearsal process. Just as the production manager must apportion the budget, the director must apportion time.

In this country, we get an average of four to six weeks from first rehearsal to first preview. When I started in rep, we had three and a half weeks if we were lucky, and we have all heard of weekly rep – those days when actors had to supply their own costumes (well, smoking jackets for boys and evening gowns for girls; presumably specialities like dog collars and police uniforms were from wardrobe stock). With that sort of pressure of time, the cast were expected to know their lines and have a pretty ready-made character by the Monday (hence jokes about Character No. 4b, etc.). Rehearsals were for practising entrances and exits, working out where to move in the space. One wonders how this exercise came to be known as 'blocking'. To me at least it has unfortunate connotations of blocked paths and blocked creative juices.

It has to be said that very good performances could come out of these strictures, and indeed that used to be an argument against expanding rehearsal time. If you can get a reasonable show up and running in a week, why waste money on five? Besides, a change of bill once a week would guarantee regular attendance by the local audience.

However, for better and for worse, times have changed. What is better is that with more time at our disposal we can go more deeply into the work. What is worse is that, for reasons too enormous to go into here, the relationship between local theatre and local audience has virtually disappeared.

So how do we use those four to six weeks? Let me get something out of the way first. The habits formed in the weekly rep days die hard. There are still quite a number of directors who see their job as Chief Blocker and they simply stretch the same old routine to fit the extra time. Briefly, their system might be:

DAY ONE	*a.m.*	read-through and design model
	lunch	
	p.m.	block Act One
DAY TWO	*a.m.*	finish blocking Act One
	lunch	
	p.m.	block Act Two
DAY THREE		. . . well, you can carry on.

Weeks two, three and four will be more of the same, going over and over the plan fixed in the first week, until the actors are perfectly drilled. Extra time will be given to set pieces like balls or battles, and actors will be reluctantly surrendered for occasional wardrobe fittings or publicity interviews. In the last week, the director will put on his (seldom her) field-marshal's cap and oversee the technical rehearsals. All that then remains is to keep an eye on the shape and speed of the show (*'Faster and louder, please'*), a rallying of the troops on the opening night and Bob's your uncle. I exaggerate, but only a bit.

Given that the Chief Blocker seldom acknowledges the existence of an acting process, it is not surprising that the highest praise an actor will confer on them is, 'At least he/she leaves you alone.' I suppose unhelpful hands off are better than unhelpful hands on, but most bad acting habits set in because the actor has been forced to work in isolation, and breaking those habits takes a lot of . . . Trust and Time.

I wanted to get the Chief Blocker off my chest, so as to set in relief the joy of working with directors who *do* acknowledge an acting process. Understandably, for the above hands-off-type actors, the words 'system', 'method' or 'process' strike a chill to the heart, but as with everything there are good and bad experiences. I have been lucky in my share of good ones, some of which I will attempt to describe in the next few chapters.

5

Joint Stock and the Workshop

In the 1970s to many people including myself the fringe was central and not peripheral as its label might imply. I do not remember having any careerist eye on the mainstream. The RSC, the National, even the Royal Court had the ring of foreign place names which I *might* visit some time in my life, but could happily survive if I did not. The pinnacle of my ambitions was to get into Joint Stock Theatre Company. The fringe was Where It Was At, and in my view Joint Stock was the crème de la fringe.

I based this on the only two productions of theirs which I had seen, *The Speakers* and *Fanshen*. The subject of the first was Speaker's Corner in Hyde Park. The audience promenaded round the action, as one soapbox after another sprang into life. Anarchist ruffians, IRA stirrers and downright nutters goaded and put us on the spot (in the way that theatre quite literally can). We shared the actor's/character's breathing space in an eyeball-to-eyeball present tense. I forgot these were actors, so well did they inhabit their characters and their scruffy coats. They were dangerous, they were tigers released from their cages – well trained, but you never knew.

Fanshen was a complete contrast. Discipline was at its heart. A uniformly dressed cast moved with schoolroom orderliness, representing members of a village in Maoist China going through the process of revolution. Emotions were channelled into constructive criticism, confrontation was framed as debate. Again the audience was caught up in the thrill of immediate affairs.

I did not analyse it at the time, but I recognised in these shows a matching of subject matter to style, and a quality of concentration and detail in performance, which I longed for after the agitprop rough-and-tumble of 7:84.

Joint Stock was able to achieve this standard for two main reasons. First, it was steered by experienced practitioners from all walks of the profession who had for various reasons become frustrated by the status quo (David Aukin, Max Stafford-Clark, Bill Gaskill, David Hare), and second, helped by their combined reputations, they had persuaded the Arts Council to fund their unusually long workshop and rehearsal periods.

In other words, Joint Stock bought time. It was recognised by the founders to be the single most essential condition for their work. They wanted to create new plays and to explore different styles and methods. They also wanted to maintain the highest possible standards of excellence and to reach a larger public than the usual fringe venues could contain. They were political with a small 'p', focusing on the un-fashionable, the outsiders, the strugglers, rather than blasting us with a world view. They had emerged from the *Fanshen* experience with a new rigour and wisdom, so that by the time I joined them they had settled on a pattern of work:

a) The collective would discuss and finally decide on a topic for the next play.

b) They would do a four-week workshop exploring the themes with the writer and designer present.

c) There would be a two-month break, during which the writer wrote the play.

d) Then everyone would reassemble for a six-week rehearsal.

e) Finally, the play would tour for three months and play in London for one.

Amazingly, the Arts Council coughed up. It was a battle, but they soon recognised the quality of the results and, at its height, Joint Stock received a grant to finance two productions a year. I remember we complained then about the annual begging-bowl round, but, looking back through the smog of the 1980s and 1990s, those were rosy days indeed.

Although we got the lion's share of fringe funding, and everyone received an equal slice of that lion's share, we were

still extremely poor relations of our continental counterparts. To give you some context: in a year when the Joint
Stock grant was £50,000, to cover two shows and about
twenty-five on the payroll, Peter Stein in West Germany
received a subsidy of £1.5 million for one show (*Summerfolk*),
with which he sustained a collective of thirty.

Here I have to confess that I am nervous of the word
Collective. I suspect it may be more of a director's ideal than
an actor's. In any case, by the time I joined Joint Stock, the
collective idea had been tried and allowed to slip in favour of
a more practicable pool of actors who would work with the
company more than once and mix with first-timers. I was a
beneficiary of this messier system, as Bill Gaskill chose a
completely new company (except for Bruce Alexander, who
had been in *Fanshen*) to work on Stephen Lowe's adaptation
of *The Ragged Trousered Philanthropists* by Robert Tressell.

The Ragged Trousered *Workshop*

What is the purpose of a workshop? In a workshop, one has
the luxury of time in which to take things to pieces, to
explore themes and techniques and to ask fundamental
questions, without the immediate pressure of an opening
night. What are the ideas that brought us all together in the
first place? What is the most effective type of theatre for
communicating those ideas? And sometimes, even more
fundamentally, do we need a writer? A director? A designer?
(Luckily, so far no one has found a rationale for a theatre
with no actors.)

The specific aim of any workshop needs to be clearly
articulated and frequently reassessed, so as to avoid too many
blind alleys (though some blind alleys, as in any scientific
experiment, can be very instructive).

Over the four or five years of its existence Joint Stock had
consolidated the horses-for-courses principle – i.e. different
subject matter could and should completely alter the nature
of each workshop. The subject matter for a show could come
from anywhere and from any member of the group. Sometimes it came from a novel, sometimes a newspaper article,
sometimes from the seed of an idea put forward by one of

the group. A technique that produces great results in one workshop might be totally unhelpful in another.

Thus for *The Speakers* the actors had practised public speaking, heckling, bumming and begging on the streets. *Fanshen*, dealing as it did with a community seeking an ideal Marxist form of self-organisation, demanded some parallel experiments from the workshop, while for the as yet untitled project which became *Cloud Nine* a group of actors were hand-picked for their varying sexual proclivities so as to throw light on the chosen subject of sexual politics.

So what was best for *The Ragged Trousered Philanthropists?* The story concerns a group of house-painters at the beginning of this century, the hardship of their lives and their eventual introduction to the early trade union movement. Put like that it sounds dull, but when I tell you that Tressell (or Noonan, to use his real name) was himself a house-painter in the early 1900s, labouring for a pittance by day while writing this six-hundred-page first novel by night, and when I tell you that the manuscript was discovered after his death from TB at the age of forty, that it has since been hailed as the first working-class novel and the socialist bible, and when I tell you that it is humane, generous, angry and funny, and is written in a refreshingly unique style, you might begin to understand its attraction.

Since physical labour was so central to the novel, it was to play a large part in the workshop. Bill had connections with Dartington College for the Arts in Totnes, Devon. The college had recently acquired an old warehouse in Plymouth which they planned to transform into an annexe for their final-year art students, and it was agreed that we were the guys for the job . . . supervised by a professional foreman, naturally.

So we all moved down to Plymouth for a month, working on the building from nine till lunch, and on creating the play from two till sometimes eight or nine.

The broad tasks of the workshop were to whittle this epic novel down to its essential dramatic scenes and to find ways of translating Tressell's idealised Fabian vision into something more relevant to our own age, while keeping faith with his variety of styles.

[48]

First, we split into groups, each with an elected director, and, using any old casting, experimented with different story-telling devices. We would then present the results to the rest of the group for discussion. Some scenes in the book lent themselves to grotesque caricature, others to gritty naturalism, others to Victorian melodrama. (All of these styles were eventually used in the final production.) On one level the book was easily dramatised, but we all wanted more than a faithful page-by-page transferral to the stage. It would make for a quaintly entertaining but essentially pointless evening. So what did we really want to say, and which scenes would best help us to say it?

The play could have turned into anything from cute comedy to domestic tragedy, depending on what was included or left out. In choosing to use six men and one woman, Bill and Stephen were clearly moving towards certain priorities before the actors came on the scene. They were not going to put women centre stage.

My feminist pride smarted, but I was in a fix. Given the context of Tressell's book, I had to agree with them. We enacted some of the domestic scenes and found few ways of lifting them out of the sentimental. That was how Tressell conceived them and that was how they remained. The women's chief narrative function was to accentuate their husbands' plight, and even if on the page one could marvel at how the wives budgeted for survival on the pittance their husbands brought home, it hardly made for exciting theatre. Nor, you may argue, does watching men paint walls, but the thrust of the story gave the men's work its dramatic point. They were soon to band together and change things.

Perhaps if there had been even one other woman in the group we might have argued a better case, but as the sole and not very confident mouthpiece I preferred to let things ride. Anyway, by now I had become one of the lads (drinking and playing darts with the best of them, even staying at the YMCA) and that was a lot more seductive than isolation.

So I threw myself into the improvisations, playing not only wives and barmaids but also Bert the apprentice lad, Hunter the sinister foreman and even Owen himself. Owen was Tressell's mouthpiece. Like Tressell, he was a sign-writer who relished the privilege of skilled work for its own sake but never allowed this skill to divide him from the other workers, whom he attempted to convert to socialism during their tea breaks.

Each member of the workshop group took a turn at one of Owen's lectures. Which, if any, should we keep in, and how could we best present them? In the book some were extremely long and preachy, many were deliberately simplified for the men's benefit, but some had a wonderful lucidity. I was given the 'Great Money Trick', which I chose to perform as a kind of party conjuror. Owen divided up a loaf of bread in order to demonstrate to the men the movement of capital; I chose to slice up a cucumber – it was quicker and less messy.

Mugsborough was Tressell's pseudonym for his own home town, Hastings, and it is a name which encapsulates the affectionate irritation which his alter-ego, Owen, feels for his fellow workers. They were all mugs for propping up a system which crushed them, the Philanthropist Poor giving their lives away to the Greedy Rich.

Occasionally Owen loses patience with their dogged blindness, but he battles on through their thick skins and eventually gains enough allies to fight against sackings and wage cuts. The story ends with them all joining the union and marching towards the glorious socialist rainbow in the sky.

Apart from that last bit, there was plenty for a modern audience to identify with. The British working class is notoriously conservative and, seventy years on from the events of the book, was about to usher Margaret Thatcher into power. It was as infuriating as it was baffling to us angry young socialists, but we knew that until that particular nettle was grasped the revolution would have to wait.

It was easier to understand the men in Tressell's book than their modern-day counterparts. In those pre-union days, a man had no choice but to accept wage cuts and longer hours. If he complained, there were plenty queuing up for his job. Thanks to the unions, things had hugely improved for workers in the late 1970s, but by now some of those unions had overstepped the mark and earned themselves a doubtful name. Conservatism was being restored as the prevailing habit of mind.

In one of our regular progress-so-far meetings, we got into a discussion on poverty. How did we each define it? Nowadays we were rich compared to the Edwardian workers, but we all agreed that poverty was relative. In the book, wages are earned in order to secure the 'necessaries of life' – presumably food, clothing and shelter. What did we consider the 'necessaries' besides these things? Some said job security; some education or health. Where did spiritual and cultural poverty fit in? Was poverty to be measured in relation to the currently agreed breadline? Was it to do with not owning your labour? Was it to do with not having choice, the aptly named poverty trap? We went on flailing around for answers.

Although on matters political and philosophical Bill flailed with the rest of us and never attempted to hide his uncertainties, it was part of his directorial acumen that he knew when to cut these flailings short. 'How can we put poverty on stage?' he asked, bringing us all to the point.

Through a series of improvisations he steered us towards an answer. We could demonstrate the economic relationship between the men and their bosses. In fact, according to Bill's story-telling framework, it was the only relationship that mattered. Individual character traits were by the by; a man did what he did because of his need for money, his need to survive.

We were working on a scene in which Hunter, the foreman, passes three unemployed men and takes one of them on at a pathetically cheap rate. The man, Newman, agrees because he has a wife and kids and has not worked for ages. Bill argued that all we needed to *see* was Newman's grovelling gratitude and Hunter's unyieldingness. From the extremity of their behaviour the audience could infer the desperation that gave rise to it. Pity and judgement were for the audience to feel and were not the actor's concern. It is a hard thing for an actor to eschew complexity and individualising character detail, but that afternoon I learned that, in the right context, this approach has its own rewards.

We worked on obsession and status, and these exercises went a long way towards unlocking the play. First we improvised situations which had nothing to do with the play. Each of us was given a slip of paper with our own private obsession written on it. This could be anything from 'You *have* to feel taller than everyone else' to 'You are terrified of chairs.' Then someone would suggest a set-up – for example, 'Monday morning at the dole office' – and one by one each obsessed character would enter the scene, with often hilarious results. But it was not pointless hilarity. The exercise demonstrated how the energy of an obsession can drive the scene, and how dramatic things occur when two opposing obsessions meet.

We moved on to scenes from the book, identifying each character's obsessional drive and pushing it to extremes. The men were obsessed by the fear of poverty and Owen by his need to convert them. The bosses and middlemen were obsessed by their fear of losing whatever small foothold they had on the system that corrupted them. Watching these scenes, I reflected that fear is the real root of all evil.

Like scientists, we were isolating different elements in order to test the whole, and a lot can be revealed by isolating the status element in human interplay. Sometimes we worked in pairs, sometimes in bigger groups. Sometimes a new person was thrown in half-way through an improvisation, as a rogue catalyst to the scene. The usual form was that we would be handed a card from a pack and whatever the number of the card that was the degree of our status. As we improvised scenes unrelated to the novel, the idea was to work out the status of the other players and fit in accordingly. From the outside, the people watching should be able to assess who was underdog and who kingpin.

Naturally it got more complex and more interesting the bigger the group. If I had a seven, I might think I was quite something, until someone else swaggered up looking down his nose at me. But was he a true-blue number nine putting me in my place, or merely a number six who thought I was a number five? True to life, the number fives were more aggressive towards their inferiors than the number tens ever needed to be, and the threes and fours might be either supportive or dismissive of the number twos. Meanwhile, the eights and nines cruised around eyeing one another warily, but exchanging polite smiles.

An Interesting Revelation

It came about through a cock-up. A couple of actors were invited to play a scene in which an outgoing managing director interviewed his successor in his office. The usual bluff bonhomie ran the scene for a while, but it began to lose its coherence. Both old and new boss lorded it equally, and each exchanged complacent smile for complacent smile. The scene was going nowhere. It turned out that both actors had mistakenly got hold of the same-number card. Each was convinced he was the superior and neither would yield his place. So like real life, I thought, where we do not always comply with someone else's hierarchical scheme.

Meanwhile, Back at the Warehouse

Every morning, in our paint-splattered overalls, we stripped wood, pulled out old nails, Polyfillaed holes and, having made good, covered the warehouse walls with two coats of white and the door- and window-frames with glossy brown. Later, the more skilled (among whom I did not number) built partitioned offices at one end of the huge space.

This was no DIY set-up, we had the professionals keeping an eye on us. In our communal imagination we found more and more parallels with the book. The men in the book lived in constant fear of Hunter the foreman's impromptu inspections. Our situation might have been less scary, but when the stooped figure of Jim, our foreman, shuffled into our eyeline, or if Pete the Paint's bosun's build loomed into view, we went into a flurry of work to prove we were not a bunch of useless townies. In my case, I had to doubly convince, and bite back my indignation when Pete said, 'I don't rightly know what I can give you to do, young lady.' This misplaced chivalry never quite disappeared.

Sometimes we worked with loving care, sometimes with overconfident slapdashery. As in the book, individuals devised ways of breaking down the time and pacing their work. 'The men work with their hands, the master works with his brains,' avers one of Tressell's bosses, but one of the men counters with, 'Your work in't made wi' your hands, it's made with your brains, planning, thinking, all the time.' A resounding 'yes' from Joint Stock. The morning passed between concentrated stretches of silence, each locked into his solo rhythm, the murmured plottings of twos and threes working in a team, and sudden outbursts of group banter and song.

The fact that all of us had been through the same sort of morning and were similarly exhausted helped the afternoon's work in an indefinable way. Maybe the physical tiredness relaxed us and released our imaginations. It became clear very soon that the realistic depiction of physical work would play a large part in the end production. Peter Hartwell, the designer, rigged up scaffolding and placed blank flats around the walls. With planks, trestles and upturned boxes, we each began to map out our workplace. Real paint was sloshed on the flats and the dramatic action was governed by the real time it took to cover them.

The book quotes several work songs and popular songs of the day, which we set about finding and learning. The songs reflected a unique cultural cocktail of temperance puritan, Edwardian sentimental and music hall which, once we lit the touch-paper and burst into song, would whip us back into a bygone age as only music can. So work lightened by song was becoming a cornerstone of our play.

One day, in Plymouth, we turned up at the rehearsal hall to find heaps of props and rows of bulging clothes-rails, lining the walls. Peter Hartwell had culled an amazing array of second-hand gear and am-dram cast-offs, and we were simply asked to dress up. We were going to work on the bosses (or the Brigands, as Tressell called them).

Like kids at a bun fight, we swooped in to grab the best garb. 'Wow, look at this!' we screeched, as we piled layer on top of outrageous layer. An admiral's hat could offset a tutu, a kettle could serve as handbag. There were no rules and no limits to our silliness. Once we were all costumed, we started the improvisation.

The only precondition of the exercise was that we were all to have high status. At first we just explored the space, getting used to our new silhouettes and dimensions, and the way these made us move. It was important not to force anything or try to be funny, but just to let the creature take shape. Bill, Stephen or Peter then started lobbing in suggestions for a scenario – 'The doctor's waiting room', 'An audition for a play' – and we would try out our 'person' in a group.

With the work on obsession fresh in our minds, it was not hard to find a manic motor for these scenes. We could make sounds and use the occasional word, but coherent dialogue was out. That was fine. This riff-raff did not need words as they snatched, barged and elbowed their way through the scene. I seem to remember a bolstered dowager – someone in a girdle, with a Christmas wreath round his head? A kitchen apron tied round an army greatcoat? Or was it just a Lewis Carroll-type dream?

From the edge of the rehearsal room, Bill orchestrated this bedlam. Just when you felt invention flagging, he would move the exercise up a gear. Now we were to be Robespierre and his cohorts in the Committee of Public Safety naming names for the guillotine. I got caught up in the bloodlust and a sort of Edith Evans voice came from somewhere within me, trumpeting the repetitive riff, 'The Duke of Bedford! The Duke of Bedford!' In choosing who was for the chop, Bill had asked us to think of someone we really hated. Poor old Duke, I knew nothing about the guy.

Now to extract some method from the madness. As swiftly as possible a tiny acting area was created with planks and trestles, and the scenario switched to the 'Brigands' Cave' in the book, a gathering of the bosses. They have names like Sweater, Grinder and Didlum, and run firms called Smeariton and Leavit. Their middlemen toadies are called Crass and Slime. Not much else need be said. Tressell is not concerned with any redeeming human traits. He blasts through the smoke screens of deference and respect that blind people to the injustice of the class system. His bosses are boorish, stupid and slavering with greed.

But greed unites them and greed gives them cunning. However much Tressell ridicules them, they run the men's lives. Our characters should reflect that. They should be funny, but also vicious and repulsive. The cartoon grotesques we created that afternoon slipped into the Brigands' Cave like ducks into water. We scoffed tea and buns and sprayed one another with crumbs as we pontificated. We were caught up in ourselves and our pretensions, and seldom listened to each other, but as we swayed and teetered on the precarious cramped stage we were forced to cling to one another for support. It was an eloquent staging and changed very little when we came to perform it.

Winding Up

The workshop time was drawing to a close. We would soon disband and then Stephen Lowe would be left on his own to pull all the strands together and write the play. It was decided to give a little private viewing of work in progress. We invited some of the Dartington staff and students to the newly overhauled warehouse, where among the scaffolding we painted, sang and re-enacted highlights from the workshop. In this semi-performance mode, we tested what was dramatic, what was funny and whether it need be boring to watch the proverbial paint dry.

The final reward for us all was the works outing. In the book, the men get one day's holiday a year. It is known as the Beano. They set out in various carriages on a pub crawl leading to a country hotel where, courtesy of the bosses, they can drink themselves stupid and generally let off steam. On our last evening, the Joint Stock group gathered for a similar celebration. Dressed in approximations of Edwardian costume culled from our second-hand clothes-rail, we set out in a minibus on our own pub crawl, which would eventually land us at Dartington Hall.

As described in the book, the Beano feast is constantly interrupted by speeches from the bosses, each one more vacuous and pompous than the last, while the men heckle or grovel according to their disposition. Suddenly Barrington, the most confirmed socialist among the men, makes a fierce retaliatory speech, but the bosses are rescued by Crass, their toady, who orchestrates an outbreak of revelry and song.

All this, plus many an ad-libbed extra, was played out that evening at Dartington. Highlights included Bill making a speech as Rushton, one of the bosses, Mark Wing-Davey's reply as Barrington, Peter Hugo Daly as the Semi-Drunk singing 'Put Me Amongst the Girls', and then accompanying all the other songs on the honky-tonk piano, which he managed to make beautiful. I was delegated to sing the wonderful and weepy 'Won't You Buy My Pretty Flowers?' (which was kept in the final show). Then people's own party pieces took over. Fred Pearson broke into a Geordie song, Kenny Ireland gave us his 'Albert and the Lion', and so we revelled on.

It was a truly happy and generous culmination to the four weeks' work and I remember nothing of the journey home.

Then there was the two-month lay-off while Stephen went away to write. It is not every writer who can participate in the workshop process and come up with a play. Some try to please everyone all of the time and end up in a mess, but Stephen survived well. He had taken the workshop to heart and preserved its essence, and with Bill's firm hand the piece continued to be cut and shaped during rehearsals.

Quite radical changes were still being made right up until the first preview, but from then on experimentation stopped and consolidation set in. I have since seen this as some sort of orchestrational ideal. It prevents ease setting in too early and turning to complacency, but by the same token it guards against a negative kind of insecurity lasting too long into performance.

The End Product

The design and staging of the production sprang directly from the workshop. The walls of the performance space were the walls of the house, with the audience incorporated within. Our work went on all around them. Sometimes a scene took place behind their heads, where an actor was painting a real wall. Further into the space, for obvious reasons, the walls became invisible. Doors freestanding in their frames marked the division of rooms, and an outer door at one end of the space marked the front door on to the street.

Other work areas were defined by planks and trestles, and an archway was set high up near the centre to mark the Moorish Room, where Bert assisted Owen in his gold-leaf decoration. In the middle of the space was a tailor's dummy wearing the overcoat and bowler hat which each actor in turn would don as Hunter.

The play began with the early morning arrival of the men, wheeling their cart up to the house, unlocking the front, unloading their equipment and setting to work. A rhythm was established. An old man scraped away at a door-frame and filled the holes with putty, the stronger younger men got into their slow, steady painting stride, while Bert the apprentice rushed about his chores – the only sign of urgency.

The action built through hirings and firings, conspiratorial two-handers, animated tea breaks and sneak visits from Hunter which sent the men into a frenzy of activity. The end of the working day was heralded by a solo whistled tune which the others then picked up as they began dismantling their gear, and finally the house was cleared to a rousing chorus of 'Work, Boys, Work'.

Suddenly, as if by sleight of hand (but actually thanks to a magical lighting change by Andy Phillips), the set turned inside-out. The dusty interior became a sunny pub garden. The cacophony of clanking buckets and lusty song faded out, to be replaced by the gentle twittering of birds.

Now came my moment of truth – the quickest change I have ever known (and certainly the quickest sex-change ever). Bert, wearing cloth cap, too-large jacket and heavy boots, slipped unnoticeably into the boisterous stream of workers, darted behind the door, doffed cap, donned M&S wig with mobcap stuck on it, rolled up trousers, chucked on skirt-and-apron-in-one, picked up folded tablecloth and a tray of cutlery, and floated unhurriedly (!) back on stage as Elsie the barmaid, just as the last ragged-trousered leg disappeared from view.

Out in the pub garden another sleight of many hands had turned planks and trestles into a long table aslant the stage. Weighting down one edge of the tablecloth with the help of the tray, Elsie took hold of the other edge and with one tug (if I was lucky) pulled it from its concertinaed folds into a high, billowing arch which floated down to cover the table in brilliant white. It was a spectacular and swift effect, for which I have to thank David Hare, who had used the concertina trick before – another example of the benefits of accumulated company knowledge. And as Elsie started to lay the table, the same men who seconds before had exited so boisterously now crept back on in their Sunday best, caps in hands, to gasp at the Beano spread before them.

Nor was that the end of my quick-change exploits. Once the men had eased up, had a few pints and were about to play cricket, Bert bounded on to sample his first taste of beer before rushing off to go fishing. Seconds later, Elsie reappeared (phew) and bestowed her girlish smiles all round. (The boots were the only giveaway, if some spoilsport cared to notice.)

After the speeches and songs the same Cinderella touch which had conjured the Beano dismantled it. In a blackout the table was divided into two and when the lights came back on they had become the two carriages which recklessly raced one another home, piled high with their drunken charges. Elsie had evaporated for good and Bert took the reins of one carriage, whipping the horses along. A momentary animated tableau, then a snap blackout and lights up again on the empty house.

Back in their rags, the men plod about their work in an atmosphere of anticlimax. There is one quick blast of cartoon energy while the Brigands stage their tea party, but from then on naturalism takes over from theatricality as harsh reality kicks in. The men are being threatened with a further cut in wages and the word 'union' is whispered for the first time.

The final scene is the only one to take place in one of the men's homes. Stephen Lowe has taken up Tressell's baton and condenses, conflates and urges the play to its conclusion. A union banner is being prepared in someone's back room. Bert is in the corner making a wheelbarrow for a child. Owen and the Barrington character argue over their visions of socialism. In their differences, Stephen showed the roots of division in the labour movement which were to grow into strong trees by the time the play was performed.

In the last beat of the play, the glorious finished banner was raised centre stage, as we formed a group beneath it. Barrington begins his address to the rally: 'Brothers . . .' Our group froze in a tableau of expectation, as the light went from white to blinding white, and just when you thought if it went on any longer there would be a nuclear explosion, the stage was snapped into blackness.

I had spent most of the evening under a table scraping out paint tins and yet I remain prouder of *The Ragged Trousered Philanthropists* than of most other shows I have been involved with. The reason for this is simple. We had time. Every idea in the show had been discovered through group work, rather than imposed. The show belonged to us all. Every shared experience in the last six months, whether ordeal or treat, had bound our imaginations together and this informed the quality of the work.

The show was a resounding success and in my own case brought huge openings in my career, but the most important thing about the experience was that it taught me for life that the best achievements of a good ensemble can far outstrip any virtuoso display an actor might pull off alone.

6

Rehearsal-Room Diplomacy

Demarcation of Roles

In a workshop a group of people with different skills are equally involved in exploring material with a view to creating a piece of theatre. To this end, everyone does a bit of everything. Actors direct, writers act, lighting technicians do research, directors move the set around.

To me it is a good thing for members of a team to have as much understanding of each other's areas of work as possible. It gives me nothing but confidence to learn that a director or writer has done a bit of acting. In a workshop, before we are cast in a specific role, actors gain an objective insight into the aims of a piece and how it works, but we must be tactful with our new-found know-how when we are in more conventional rehearsal situations. There is no point upsetting the 'I don't tell you your job, don't you tell me mine' brigade, but by all means suggest, demonstrate, sneak ideas in unnoticed, do deals, negotiate. Diplomacy is the name of the game.

Many actors make excellent directors, but that is when they are deliberately wearing a director's hat. Directing *while you* are acting is not a good idea. It is a rare person who can be in a scene and outside it at the same time. It comes down to subjectivity – necessary for acting but incompatible with directing. Besides, supposing all the actors were to chip in with their brilliant but conflicting ideas? Whose are rightest and best? We have to elect and trust one outside eye, otherwise it's a case of too many chiefs.

The demarcation line cuts both ways. Most actors hate it if a director starts 'doing' their character for them, or giving line-readings to show how they want things to be. Then there are those directors who trample over the actor's territory, telling them what their character feels or needs. which is the bit the actor invariably knows already. There are directors who judge your character, summing them up in adjectives before you have had a chance to explore; and there are directors who talk only in terms of results not processes. They know the desired effect, but cannot help you get there.

In over-simplified terms, the actor can be dead hot on the who and the why of a character, and the director (even the Chief Blocker) can usually handle the where and the what. Where everyone can flounder is with the how, and that is often what the actor most needs from a director.

A Nightmare

ACTOR (*to Director*): I have all this going on inside me, but it does not seem to be getting across. Help me. Focus me. How can I tell my story?

DIRECTOR: Just remember you're very upset at this point . . . Remember you're in love.

ACTOR: I know *that* but . . .

DIRECTOR (*interrupting*): Remember she's a ballbreaker.

ACTOR: Well actually, I'm not sure that she –

DIRECTOR: Look, just Do That Thing You Do and you'll be fine. I *must* work on the special effects.

ACTOR: Aaaaaagh!

> *Actor falls in a spiralling plunge down well-shaft. Director's wicked cackle builds to crescendo. Then . . .*

> *Actor wakes up in a sweat. The bedside clock reads 3.05 a.m. Actor grabs script from bedside table, pores over it till dawn and with any luck gets An Idea.*

A Lesson in Minding My Own Business

As soon as we are cast, we become partial. As time goes on, we become more and more subjectively involved. We argue passionately from our character's point of view, and to a certain extent that is our job.

The word subjectivity gets confused with self-centredness, and as such has negative associations. Many actors are hypersensitive to the charge and lean over backwards to accommodate their fellow players. But what is a virtue in real life is not necessarily one on stage. Voicing your needs and making demands may make for better results in the long run. To use an analogy, a patient who can give a detailed account of their pain is more helpful to a doctor than a silent stoic.

It is a paradox, but in certain circumstances it is the actor's duty to be selfish. I learned this during rehearsals for *The Ragged Trousered Philanthropists*. We had split up into groups of two or three, each working on different scenes simultaneously. We were directing ourselves, while Bill Gaskill moved unobtrusively between us, eavesdropping, questioning and guiding, like a benign version of Hunter on the prowl. Mark Wing-Davey was up a ladder painting a wall, while I (as Bert) stood by with extra paint and water to thin it out. I noticed that Mark was having to crane his neck to speak to me. My immediate response was to shift my position for his benefit, even though this made it hard for me to reach the paint pot.

Bill noticed me contorting myself and, when I explained it was to make things easier for Mark, told me that this was not my responsibility. If Mark was obstructed in any way, it was up to him to point it out. He must pursue his aims and I must go all out for mine. If there was a conflict of needs, we should expose it, then the director would have something to work on and useful new light could be shed on the scene.

It was a little incident but a big lesson. In my concern for someone else's needs, I had come out of character and reverted to my own polite-female middle-class pussy-footing. If Bill had not 'caught me out' the scene would have stagnated with something artificial at its heart.

This is all very well provided you have a vigilant and skilful director around. If this is not the case, the actors must negotiate among themselves. Most of the time this works fine, but because of the nature of the job, if there is a clash of wills, it is hard not to take things personally. Why should I accept your subjective judgement over mine?

The absence of a strong director breeds insecurity and fear, which in turn bring out the worst in people. If you cannot trust the Overseeing Eye, you compete for attention. Over-acting and upstaging (that is, distracting focus from an actor by pulling faces, or by funny business, or forcing them to turn their back to the audience by standing upstage of them when you speak to them) and other undermining tricks set in at this point. It is not a question of malice towards the other so much as a fear for oneself. If you feel robbed of limelight, what do you do but steal someone else's if you can? Bad acting is often a cry for help.

Sizing Up the Director

If you think I attach too much importance to directors it is because, like it or lump it, they do have power. Imagine this as a worst-case analogy . . . You are in a foreign country. You have something desperately important to impart. Perhaps you are in a law court giving evidence, or even pleading for your life. You have one interpreter through whom to channel your message. Your instincts tell you that the interpreter has missed your point. You have been forced to wear clothes which do not help your cause. You protest, but the interpreter cajoles you (or bullies you), 'Trust me, I know these people. I know the law.' You are helpless, gagged. That is what it can feel like with the wrong director in charge, be they *ever* so *nice*.

There is an important distinction to be made between power and authority. The reason these two so often get confused is that, for various historical reasons, the director of a play is likely also to be the artistic director of the theatre, and thereby a person of influence in the profession at large. Running a theatre well and directing plays well do not necessarily go together.

The director's power in the rehearsal room lies in the fact that, more than anyone else, they can help or hinder you in getting your message to the audience. It is worth remembering that the role of director was invented only about a hundred years ago, and that actors of yesteryear were far more self-reliant. There was a tradition of actor-managers and of young actors learning the tricks of the trade through apprenticeship to their seniors. A company would learn by necessity how to get a show on the road, and perhaps some race memory of this collective ability gives actors an initial suspicion of directors.

If you equate the director in the rehearsal room with a teacher in the classroom, power comes with the position, but authority has to be earned. We *need* the director's authority, but we can be messed up by their power. By authority I mean a trustable judgement which comes from the experience of being outside the action of the play, though involved with its broadest message; an authority which allows the actor to go to the edge but not over the top.

Because we need the director's authority, we test it all the time, like kids with the aforementioned teacher, or with their parents at home. 'How far can I go?', 'How much do you know?', 'Can you protect me, save me, if it comes to it?' In schoolroom, nursery or rehearsal room, too much leeway can be as damaging as repression. Kids with no clear boundaries feel insecure, and so do actors with a mean-dering, indecisive director.

When insecurity does set in during rehearsals, it is interesting to note how often we revert to the tactics which got us through school, or which secured us our place in the family. Some become teacher's pet, others sulk. Some whip up opposition, others toe the line on the outside while secretly working things out for themselves. It is quite a good game detecting people's chosen role, be it Dad's challenger, Mum's helper, sibling rival or any other variant.

As the Chinese proverb says, 'Squeaking wheel gets oiled first', and a weak teacher/director will woo the troublemaker in an effort to get a potential ringleader on their side. This way, their energies are diverted from the job of directing the play, the attention-seeker takes over and the quiet getters-on-with-it are left feeling betrayed. (NB: None of this is because 'actors are like children'. Most people's jobs involve teamwork, and all such microcosms are in some way based on family lines, be it an office, boardroom or factory floor.)

There is also the Spot the Authority Figure game. I have often been asked what is the difference between male and female directors, and have disappointed those seeking a neat generalisation. Female directors are not necessarily better listeners; male directors are not necessarily more decisive or whatever. The only observation I have come up with so far is in the negative area, when things go wrong. Given that all directors are in a position of power, when that power is threatened male directors tend to use the paternalistic model to regain control (shouting, threatening, judging), while women will use the maternal (emotional blackmail of the 'How could you let me down?' variety).

Some directors habitually infantilise actors and then wonder why they do not take responsibility. The best directors, like good parents, steer actors towards independence. I remember asking Bill Gaskill after a preview of another play I did with him whether a certain scene was working 'any better'. 'By this stage you shouldn't have to ask me that,' was his challenging reply.

It is over to us to grow up.

Parallels and Ironies

Mirroring the labour movement at large, the socialist theatre companies of the 1970s took some time to accommodate feminism. Before Monstrous Regiment, the Women's Theatre Group and others sprang up to remedy this, companies employed far fewer women than men, and the choice of performance material reflected this. With few exceptions women were more conscientious than the men about menial tasks like clearing up the rehearsal space and about turning up on time for get-ins and get-outs (in good socialist mode, we *were* allowed to lift heavy scenery).

In these companies, power did not lie in ownership or higher wages and, if knowledge is power, in theory we all had access to the same information. The power in these mini-democracies lay in the ability to bring a majority round to your point of view. For this you needed persuasive argument and/or a loud voice. Often the loudest voice won the day. We women, few in number and still fledglings in the feminist movement, found it hard to influence things in these male bastions, and our isolation was all the more painful in the context of a self-styled democracy.

In my Joint Stock experience, there were many ironies. For a kick-off, when we reassembled for rehearsals after the break, I learned for the first time that, while Bill and Stephen Lowe had been questioning what to include in the show, my own job had hung in the balance.

CATCH-22: Male writer understands men best, so makes them more rounded and dramatically interesting. Male world of work more historically dynamic than reactive support system at home. Male writer and director seeking to cut down six-hundred page tome choose to remove entire section of female domestic life. Precisely because it is so separate from the men's working lives and relationships, it is a discrete lump that can be lifted out with little loss to the main drama. The pressures of feeding a family could be referred to rather than acted out. So what to do with Harriet?

Contractually they could have let me go and saved on one whole wage packet, but luckily for me they decided to keep me on. I was cast as Bert the apprentice and I was delighted. He might have been a skivvy, but at least he was part of the workplace, and as such included in the club.

So I was in, *but*... The knowledge of my tenuous status in the show would sneak up on me in my weak moments. Still, a lot of acting is about finding imaginative parallels, so I was able to turn my own insecurity into something positive by finding parallels between Bert's position and mine. We were both smaller and weaker than the men, and neither was quite included. Bert's job and his status among the men were much like a woman's. He was in charge of cooking the bloaters, making the tea and generally clearing up after the men. Not a huge leap for my imagination.

There was another ironic parallel for the whole cast. For all our work on the economic basis for relationships in the play, Bill, who was paid the same as us and on paper was an equal member rather than a boss, nevertheless had power over us. He might not be able directly to hire and fire us, but he had chosen us and, depending on how we played our cards, he might or might not choose us again.

Power is not simply based on money, it is based on need. If I need you more than you need me, you have power over me. Actors, like the seasonal labourers in the book, know they can be easily replaced, though the consequences for us are less dire.

The Hierarchy Confusion

It is easy for the hierarchy of characters to spill over into a hierarchy in the cast. Symptoms to watch for:

> The person playing the servant tiptoes into the canteen and whispers, 'Is it all right if I sit here?'
>
> The person playing the biggest part gets taken for Most Important Person. Their weakest jokes are greeted with guffaws. Their account of this morning's traffic jam is listened to with awe.
>
> Understudies and small-part players, who spend much time together and not much with the principal cast, become socially ghettoised through no one's fault or intention. They begin to feel like second-class citizens and this has a detrimental effect on the end product. (I remember seeing a crowd of 'guests' in Act Three of *The Cherry Orchard* who looked so apologetic about being on stage that it was impossible to believe in them as land-owning friends of the family. Result: illusion carefully built up over evening by director, designer and rest of cast greatly damaged. Disbelief not re-suspended for at least half an act.)

Another symptom of hierarchy confusion (admittedly not so prevalent nowadays) can be seen when an actor who has habitually been cast as kings and rulers starts to fancy himself as such. I once found myself at a social congregation of very senior actors. They were talking about various members of the royal family past and present. They spoke with a puzzlingly intimate knowledge. Then suddenly I clicked. They had all played them – the kings and queens, I mean – and were having a family gathering.

Another time, years ago, I happened to be invited to a cast party for *Upstairs, Downstairs*. All the Upstairs cast were at one end of the room and all the Downstairs cast were at the other. This is not to say that they were a particularly snobby lot; it was simply a case of making friends with the people you spend most time working with.

The hierarchy confusion rarely takes hold in low-budget companies with small casts. In these companies, if actors are not playing a large part, they are usually compensated with two or three smaller ones, and the pleasure of showing off their doubling skills. Not only is the workload more evenly distributed, but everyone gets the same wage packet and shares the same dressing room. However, this is not an argument for continued underfunding. The wage packet could be bigger and so could the dressing room. The virtue lies in the absence of hierarchy, *not* in the penny-pinching.

On the whole, theatre is a great leveller. Living at such close quarters, we cannot fool one another for long. Contrary to the age-old stereotype of the back-stabbing, self-obsessed diva, most actors have a wide range of interests, and are generous towards other talents. The nature of the job demands it. We work on an intimate level with people from assorted backgrounds, age groups and creeds, and must rub along together or fail. If we pull rank it may rebound on us, since today's backstage skivvy could be tomorrow's star director. In the theatre men have played women, lords have played slaves and blacks have played whites, and in that act of reaching out to an opposite role their point of view has been changed.

Back to Bert

Although there was no established pecking order in the Joint Stock rehearsal room, the fact of spending six hours or so per day running errands as Bert and trying to keep out of the way of the Important Action was working on my psyche. I kept telling myself that every part matters, however small; if it did not, the playwright would not have put it there. The trouble was that in my case he nearly hadn't.

My tasks in rehearsal were all to do with timing my work activities to the dialogue of the other actors. Could I unload the paint from the cart, distribute the cans to each man in each room and brew up the tea by the time so-and-so got off his ladder and shouted, 'Tea break!'? Could I arrive in my place up the scaffolding bang on cue for the start of Scene Six without walking through and distracting from some other important scene?

Because Bert's/my role was peripheral, I did not feel I could take up precious rehearsal time with my little difficulties. I knew that in theory I had every right to, but the practice took a confidence I had yet to acquire. This to me is the key to diplomatic negotiation in the rehearsal room. When have I the right to take up time, and how much of it?

Whatever the size of your part, it is not easy to translate a hunch or a subjective feeling into words. The usual dictum is, 'When in doubt, show 'em' – in other words, actions speak louder. Unfortunately at the half-baked rehearsal stage it is often not easy to show something you have yet to perfect, and an imperfect demonstration can spoil your argument. Talk becomes necessary. Fear of taking up rehearsal time means that you waylay the director at the end of the day. There is usually a queue of others with the same idea, only they are from other departments (technical, publicity, wardrobe, music), all with a claim on the director's time.

Ideally one should be able to incorporate acting questions into the rehearsal hours and overcome any fear that one is wasting one's fellow actors' time. It may well be that in airing your problem, you elucidate a more general one. I may have learned to do this, but I am still not great at feeling OK about it.

The *Ragged Trousered* rehearsals were early days for me and I preferred to work things out on my own. If I thought long enough, a solution would usually come up. Intent on turning negative to positive, I swallowed injuries to my pride in the interests of growing towards Bert. He had to learn his trade the hard way. He was not a child to be sentimentally indulged, but a man-in-the-making. He would never ask for help or expect recognition, and this was my big acting clue. Everything in Bert's actions and manner was designed to avoid attention. The paradox was that the better I got at 'being' Bert, the more unnoticeable I became.

The big difference was that I *did* want to be noticed, and I was ashamed of the fact. Shame is a great silencer. Bill was canny and, sensing something was up, tried to tease it out of me, but pride held my tongue. Something would have to trick me into losing my cool.

One day, after a run-through when yet another scene had been shortened, thereby throwing out my timing for the nth time, and when once again Bert/I got the blame for the chain of mistimings which ensued, I could no longer contain myself. A pile-up of grievances was about to spill out, but Bill stemmed the flow. 'Bring it to tomorrow's company meeting,' he said.

A sleepless night, a summoning of nerves and next morning out it came in my shaky girl's voice. The fact that I had heard my own voice so seldom during the last weeks (Bert had few lines) made me self-conscious. The instrument had got rusty. Other people had not been listening out for it and so had not heard me.

Now I told them how I had asked for some bits of Bert's costume early on so as to practise his boyish walk, but my request had been ignored. I told them that I felt people had fallen into the trap of confusing my status with Bert's. I told them how I had nothing to cling to but structures, timings and shapes of scenes, and that as these kept changing the rug was never under my feet.

It would be nice to report that I felt relief when I had finished. Instead I felt as foolish and isolated as I had dreaded. The reason I had not brought all this up before was that I was acutely aware of its irrelevance to anyone else. It seemed to have remained so. When I did have another go at asking for Bert's boots and jacket (this time in a firmer voice), I was told, 'You *are* a pushy lady,' but at least I got them. As another 'pushy' actress once said, 'Do you want to be star of the dressing room or star of the show?'

A Word About Bill Gaskill

His reputation went before him. The great interpreter of Bond and Brecht, one of Olivier's young Turks. To have 'given all that up' for Joint Stock only added to his authority. We were in awe of him and he was impatient of that awe.

He was sure-footed and unsentimental. He would dismiss a time-wasting idea with a word, like a lion batting away a fly with a languid flick of his paw. We were young and willingly bowed to his experience, his clarity and his not infrequent brilliance. Yes, he could be intimidating, but he was a truly great teacher, and praise from him was praise indeed. I felt proud that he bothered to test me to my limits and I learned lasting lessons that way.

Now I have come to realise that rich work can be produced without playing off one's insecurities each time and I question anyone's right, guru or not, to make me do so. But I shall always be grateful to Bill for setting high standards and for his leadership in creating one of the most perfectly realised and beautiful productions I have ever been part of.

Born Not Made?

In the early 1990s I was invited by the Gulbenkian Foundation to sit on a committee of inquiry into the training of directors. More than six hundred directors were interviewed about their training for the job and it was revealed that most of them had had none. Nothing formal that is.

One interviewee posited that good directors were born not made and therefore training was not the point. Happily for us all, the Gulbenkian committee did not think it was that simple and, thanks to their recommendations, a number of directing courses were established all over the country. Given the job description outlined on page 41, these courses were not easy to devise, but at least the stranglehold of mystique could be loosened and some practical lessons learned. I hope it is not just wishful thinking, but I am already seeing evidence of a more confident approach in the work of young directors.

As to hierarchy . . . I may have just hit lucky but the young directors I have worked with seem much more calm, more daring, more willing to say 'I don't know', and both women and men seem equally at ease with taking charge when they have to.

Ego-smoothing

In less happy circumstances, a lot of rehearsal time is taken up with working round the obstruction of a director's ego, searching for the non-threatening phrase with which to make a suggestion, laughing at their jokes and saying, 'What a great idea' a lot (especially if they nicked any from you). Some directors are so paranoid that you had best not go to them with a problem in case they take it as an accusation of incompetence.

If you do have to cross swords, you had better burst into helpless tears afterwards so that the director can feel manly calming you down. Less acceptable is cool, forceful argument, and the worst thing you can do is be right! The eyes narrow and it is best to retreat and regroup. Those who persist in their argument come to be known as difficult and this label, whether deserved or not, can jeopardise their future career. Is it any wonder that we so often take the diplomatic route and climb down? We have all been there. I still smart over some of my concessions, but at the time scoring my point seemed less important than keeping the peace.

Naturally, when it comes to the performance everyone rallies to protect the weak director from exposure and paper over the cracks in their work, because it is in all of our interests that the show be a success.

And What About Women Directors?

In the 1960s and 1970s women directors were so few that they had an impossible struggle. They were constantly on trial and it took only one failure for them to be cast out of the circle. Because of this, the female director's ego could be even more brittle than the male's, and female actors were expected to be doubly protective of them. The slightest challenge to their authority was seen as an unsisterly betrayal. If they were incompetent, the lads would pounce, but we would rush to defend them. 'How can they improve if they don't get the practice?' we protested, while desperately needing their help.

Thanks to their older sisters' struggles, there are more women directors around now than ever before and they need no concessions. Long may the trend continue, because they are still too few.

A Memory

A female director at a company meeting. The group had taken a very painful decision not to re-employ her. I had voted against this, but in my heart I agreed that she was better at committee meetings than at directing plays. I have a lasting memory of her defending herself with pure political argument while tears streamed down her face. 'Ignore these tears,' she said, fighting to keep the strength in her voice, 'just listen to my words.'

A Born Director

A born director is not an actor *manqué*, a choreographer *manqué* or an anything else *manqué*. A born director loves directing and has a particular package of talents which enables all the other areas of theatrical creativity to cohere and be revealed. They are talents which can be developed and perfected, but their roots go back beyond training. I suppose I am talking about instinct, the bit of us that works without our interference and which we cannot explain.

Personally, I cannot pick out the born directors till I work with them. I can have my hunches based on sitting in the audience, but as theatre is a collaborative process I can never know for sure who is responsible for what just by watching. Like everyone else, born directors have strengths in some areas and weaknesses in others. There are designers' directors, who create magic visually but are not so good with actors; there are writers' directors, who are not so hot on sets, and so on. I never said the born director was perfect.

For obvious reasons I am not going to start on my list of top fave directors, but I will say that those from whom I have learned the most are what I would call actors' directors. Max Stafford-Clark is one, and I single him out here because his strengths are particularly relevant to this chapter.

Max is that rare phenomenon, a non-actor who understands the acting process, and he demonstrates that understanding all the better by seldom talking about it. Instead he sets tasks, asks questions and devises games, all of which go to the heart of acting. At his best, he is confident enough of his own gifts to take on the full force of the actors' contribution. He respects the acting process and his own approach perfectly complements it. In other words, he does not cross the demarcation line.

He has an established method of work which dictates the structure of rehearsals, but he encourages daring experimentation within that structure, so that by the time the play opens and for as long as it runs each actor can push against the outer walls of possibility with confidence, knowing that neither they nor any other actor can distort or sabotage the whole.

One of Max's great strengths lies in his pacing of rehearsals. He knows when we need to talk and when to stop us, and he perfectly judges the point in rehearsal when exploration must be drawn to a close and decisions made. (Obviously, even for the born director, this sort of skill is honed by experience.)

The first week usually entails some ice-breaking games, interspersed with work on the text. At the end of the week you may feel as though you have given quite a lot of yourself away, but so has everyone else including Max, so we are quits.

Max has become an expert in managing the responsibility of all this. Group discussions must never become therapy sessions, negative judgements are outlawed, hangers-back and coppers-out are gently exposed. Self-revelation is invited and volunteered on a strictly need-to-know basis, carefully tailored to the topic of the play. Thus the cast of *Cloud Nine*, a comedy about sexual politics, found out quite a lot about each other's sexual orientation, *The Seagull* cast heard each other's confessions about being in love and for *Three Birds Alighting on a Field* we publicly exhibited our ignorance about modern art.

Work on the play begins with analysing the text in terms of 'actions'. Max did not invent actions. Like most acting methods, they are a public and systematised version of what most actors do privately and randomly at home. With actions we not only ask what our character feels or wants, or why they say what they say, we shift to a more objective position and ask what they *do* with what they say. Speaking is an action. So is a pause. At no point during a play is nothing happening.

We think of our character in the third person for as long as possible – a habit that Brecht used to encourage – and by delaying our subjective immersion in the character, we keep our clarity about the whole. This pays off in performance. In situations where this kind of awareness has not been nurtured, one actor can be sidetracked by their own psychological wallowing and the play gets becalmed. Max's actions guarantee a forward dynamic and a shared responsibility for the story-telling.

Actions in Action

First some rules:

a) An action should always be expressed with a transitive verb. Each speech, sentence within a speech and pause between speeches contains an action. In deciding what their action is, the actor should ask, 'What does my character want to *do* to the other person?'

b) The actor must speak of his or her character in the third person, and use proper names of their own and others' characters.

c) The full phrase (i.e. my character's name + transitive verb + your character's name) must be voiced aloud before each speech/action: e.g. 'Jane woos Fred: "I like your tie"'; 'Hamlet rejects Ophelia: "Get thee to a nunnery"'.

d) Do not deliberate too long. At this early stage, you cannot hope to finalise the answer, but something has to break the cycle of, 'How can I know what my character wants till I have played the scene?'/'How can I play the scene till I know what my character wants?' Start a ball rolling, any ball. If it is unhelpful, you can change it.

e) An action cannot be right or wrong, only helpful or unhelpful. What helps tell the story? What helps us get to the truth of what is *happening?*

An Example from Cloud Nine

The following is not necessarily what we used, but is simply an illustration.

An Edwardian family in some colonial outpost of Africa. A young boy, Edward (played by a woman), is struggling to become the little man of the family, despite leanings towards girlish toys and sexual proclivities. Betty is his mother (played by a man). Joshua, the African servant, is played by a white actor.

Speech	Some possible actions
BETTY: Joshua, fetch me some thread.	BETTY *commands/begs* JOSHUA.
JOSHUA: You've got legs under that skirt.	JOSHUA *obstructs/insults* BETTY.
BETTY: Joshua!	BETTY *stops/warns* JOSHUA.
JOSHUA: And more than legs.	JOSHUA *debases/overrides* BETTY.

Note that some action words are more forceful than others. With an action like 'insults', be sure that it answers, 'What does the character *want* to do to the other?' The insult is contained in the line anyway, so there may be another intention. On the other hand, a character may want to insult as an action but, because of the mind of the other character, may end up flattering instead (e.g. in another life Betty might be flattered by the mention of her legs). That does not matter. The action should always describe the intention, not the result.

The scene continues:

Speech	Possible actions
BETTY: Edward, are you going to stand there and let a servant insult your mother?	BETTY *shames/enlists* EDWARD.

EDWARD: Joshua, get my mother's thread.	EDWARD *placates* BETTY. [Note that you can do an action to one person by speaking to another.]
JOSHUA: Oh, little Eddy playing at master. It's only a joke.	JOSHUA *exposes/belittles/ challenges* EDWARD.
EDWARD: Don't speak to my mother like that again.	EDWARD *overrides/belittles* JOSHUA or EDWARD *impresses* BETTY. [Try each and see.]

Actors can pick up ideas from one another. For example, the actor playing Edward may not have thought of the word 'belittle' until the actor playing Joshua used it. Hearing one another's intentions towards us is a privilege peculiar to the rehearsal room and can have fascinating results. The scene's underbelly is suddenly exposed and you can then choose actions to play along with a meaning which you might otherwise have missed.

On with the scene:

Speech	Action
JOSHUA: Ladies have no sense of humour. You like a joke with Joshua.	JOSHUA *enlists/woos* EDWARD.
EDWARD: You fetch the sewing at once, do you hear me? You move when I speak to you, boy!	EDWARD *rejects* JOSHUA.
JOSHUA: Yes, sir, Master Edward, sir. (*Exit.*)	JOSHUA *respects/belittles* EDWARD.

Notice the pretty huge character choices which remain open to all these characters (e.g. in the gap between Joshua respecting and belittling). Actions do not preclude character exploration. If the text is the skeleton, actions are the muscles, so there is still plenty of room for flesh and blood.

As rehearsals progress, we keep checking the actions. Are they still appropriate? If an action no longer works, another one is found. The least helpful directorial notes are those framed in the negative ('Be less x', 'She shouldn't be so y'). They feel repressive and vague ('How *much* less, exactly?'). If an action needs changing, it must be for a positive alternative, because an action needs total commitment. If 'challenges' seems too aggressive, for example, instead of challenging less, I can go all out to 'test'.

The checks continue after the show is up and running. One of the hardest things for actors is to give each other notes, but with actions we can point out where a scene is going wrong without getting too personal. just remember, ~~Never Give Negative Instructions~~ . . . sorry, Always Give Positive Instructions.

All shows alter night after night and over a long run, that is what makes theatre dynamic. However, it is one thing to grow and develop, and another to go off course. Thanks to the charting of actions, Max's shows have a kind of route map and keep their original shape better than most. If the course has been mutually agreed, the show is less likely to go off it.

In addition to the actions, we locate a super-objective for our character. The dynamic tension of each scene is kept in place by the pitting of one person's super-objective against another's. Think of the above scene in terms of 'Edward wants to be a girl', 'Betty wants to leave her family', 'Joshua wants to expose them all.'

If each actor sticks to their objective, no one can hijack the play, and that assurance sets us free. Like a football team, we dodge and pass to one another differently each night, while always driving towards the same goal. No time to get stale or bored.

Actions also define responsibility. Who is driving the scene at any given moment? Max likens it to a relay race. By exposing the actions, the actor discovers when to grab the baton and run with it, and when to give it up. In less secure productions, the actors can find themselves in a free-for-all battle for their moment, and it all ends in squabbles and tears. Actions give us the diplomatic tools which allow us to be grown up.

With his strong sense of the demarcation line, Max knows when to pass on the baton himself. He begins to let go at the first preview and surrenders it entirely on the press night. If the actors are not in charge by then, he has not done his job.

7

Roots and Pathways

Making Something Happen

When Lindy Davies and I first met in 1995 we both had to make a very quick decision about one another. She had just directed Harold Pinter's *Old Times* to great acclaim at Theatre Clwyd, and now suddenly had to find a new 'Anna' and re-rehearse the show for a West End opening in ten days' time. I had just finished filming *Sense and Sensibility*, which was an unusually cushy job, and was just having my periodic muse, 'Why does anyone slog their guts out in the theatre for very little money when they could be doing a film?' when the phone call came. Would I go and meet an Australian director called Lindy Davies about taking over in a play with Julie Christie? How ironic. There was a film star returning to the boards after thirty years.

My first reaction was to throw things round the room. I had wanted a break from theatre, in fact a break from acting. It sounds churlish when so many are out of work, but I had worked non-stop for several years and was bored of my own acting. I felt like an acting machine. I was all set to try and write a screenplay, and had little enough conviction that I could do so without being tempted back to acting. Despite all this I weakened and went to meet Lindy.

Throughout our interview, despite the white dog on my shoulder whispering 'Keep an open mind', there was the constant heckle from the black dog on the other shoulder: 'You don't need this. Night after night. Summer in the West End. Too much like hard work. Unknown director. She talks of her working method. Beware of people with working methods unless they are called Max,' etc.

Then Lindy said something which shut the black dog up. She talked of the actor's facility for pretending. How expert we were at making it look as though something was going on inside us when in fact we were on automatic pilot. She had seen many well-produced, well-made plays which had left her admiring but cold. One could not pinpoint a fault in the acting. All of it was efficient but too often it was empty. 'Nothing was happening,' as Lindy put it.

A loud bell of recognition sounded in the weary acting machine's head. I had felt that too and had not dared admit it even to myself. There were enough philistine voices out there saying theatre was boring, I was not about to add to them. I listened to more of Lindy's story.

She had been an actress in Australia and had suddenly hit a patch of stage fright, of terrifying blanks when she forgot her lines. She had devised her working method as a means of clawing her way out of this darkness. Like Max's actions, Lindy's method was nothing intrinsically new. Most of it revolved round breathing and allowing time for the imagination to connect with the text.

If lines are shallowly learned, they can easily flit away. If they are absorbed in a tranquil, unhurried state and sucked deep down with the breath, they will become part of your interior landscape. Breath accesses the emotions. It is like a channel which can be choked or kept open. Keep the channel open each night and things will happen to you, shift inside you. If things are shifting in you, you stand a chance of shifting the audience.

The advantage that stage performers have over their colleagues on celluloid is that they are accessible in the present tense. Anything could happen at any time. That is where the real danger and excitement lie. Too often this unique potential is wasted in an attempt to emulate film in high-tech slickness or in shallow breathing, superficial expertise.

Lindy and I had hit it off, and each had heard good things about the other, but did that necessarily mean we could work together? Unfortunately there is no way of knowing till you try. We both decided to risk it.

We had ten days. In many cases, if an actor is replaced in a show they work with an assistant director. The other actors pretty much stick to what they always do and the new actor tries to slot in. Because of Lindy's particular method, my fellow actors in *Old Times*, Julie Christie and Leigh Lawson, would have to go back to scratch and build the new play up with me. This would involve them giving up some much-treasured moments (one of the hardest things to do) so as to leave a path clear for some new ones.

I had been told not to learn my lines. I would soon understand why.

Dropping In

The first stage of Lindy's process is known as 'dropping in'.

NOTE TO STAGE MANAGEMENT: The rehearsal room will need:

i)	some loose sheets of paper
ii)	pens and pencils
iii)	chairs to go round
iv)	overhead projector and screen
v)	one copy of the script.

NOTE TO ACTORS: You will need:

Lots of i)
one of ii)
one of iii), placed so you can relate to fellow actors,
    and see iv) at the same time
you will not need v).

The stage manager projects the script page by page on to the screen. The actors sit quietly, breathing, listening and watching, while someone else is speaking, all the time finding out what is 'happening' inside, what effect the other's words are having. When it comes to their turn to speak, they glance at the screen, catch their words in the corner of their eye, digest the first sentence or phrase (*'Breathe,' prompts Lindy*), think about what it means to them in the light of what they have heard and thought so far, wait to find the impulse, the reason to speak (*'Keep breathing'*), then speak.

(It is surprising how often Lindy has to remind us to breathe. Think about it. Think how much of the time we clamp our diaphragm in place, hold our breath and talk in

[83]

little gasps and flutters. This is because we are usually worrying about the impression we make on others, rather than opening up to them.)

So let's try that again. The line is, 'Queuing all night, the rain, do you remember?' Breathe. Let the thought drop in with the breath. A memory, a vision, an impression. Anything. Your mind is a free agent. Some people will visualise a queue, maybe at the bus stop on the way to rehearsals or for a rock concert in their youth, whatever. Images come as quick as a dream. Cold night, winter rain. Feel the rain on your face. What memories are triggered by that feeling?

Having found the image, find the impulse to speak of it – what Lindy calls the pathway to the line ('*Breathe*'). Impulses can come from without or within. Look in the eyes of the other actor listening. Take it off Leigh ('*Breathe*'). It can be wince-making to look deep in the eyes of an actor whom you only met that morning.

Drop in the situation: Anna (me) is visiting her best friend, Kate (Julie), for the first time in twenty years. She is introduced to Kate's husband, Deeley (Leigh). Lindy talks of dropping in as a means of finding out what is going on. Don't pre-plan or pre-judge. Dare to go down there with an empty mind and trust that something will happen to you . . . Suddenly I want to claim my friendship with the wife, my friend, because I sense a challenge from the husband. I speak the line to Julie. I bind her in a conspiracy (in Max's terms, Anna binds Kate): 'Queuing all night, the rain, do you remember?'

But Kate cannot be bound if she does not want to be. We cannot own another's thoughts and that is one of the play's key points. I move on to my next phrase: 'My goodness, the Albert Hall, Covent Garden, what did we eat?' My own associations with the Albert Hall and Covent Garden are as different from Anna's as they are from Julie's, or as Anna's are from Kate's. That does not matter. In a more conventional set-up, we would aim at a consensus on the characters' past, but *Old Times is* partly about the disconnections between one person's memory of events and another's, and how the characters try to colonise the past by asserting their version of it over any other. In this case, the actors' imaginative independence from one another could only enrich the texture.

We move on through the play. Remember, the old hands are having to drop in all over again, responding to the new chemistry and accordingly re-routing their pathways. It is agonisingly slow at times, but a tacit deal is struck: 'I promise not to be bored waiting for you to find the impulse to speak, if you promise not to be bored waiting for me.'

On my first day I had an added trial. Pinter had dropped in (forgive the pun) to see how things were going. I felt strangely impertinent as I groped in my subconscious for a link to his. It was like trespassing.

Not that the writer sits there knowing what each speech is about and testing to see whether the actor is clever enough to 'get it'. Most writers I know are as curious about their character's subconscious as the actor is. Evelyn Waugh is reputed to have said that he had no idea what his characters were thinking, he just wrote down what they said and did.

Pinter's work is perfect for the dropping-in exercise. Each speech is a precisely chiselled iceberg-tip floating in a sea of silence. Our job is the underwater exploration. It is almost like detective work, given that no word is an accident, no chat is idle, and that things may masquerade as ordinary but never are. I wonder now how I would ever find a way through a passage like the following without dropping in.

ANNA: You have a wonderful casserole.

DEELEY: What?

ANNA: I mean wife. So sorry. A wonderful wife.

DEELEY: Ah.

Poor Pinter, watching us weigh down his leavening eccentricity with internal logic. What must he have been thinking? (There I go.) I wanted to tell him that this was only a stage and that when it came to performing we could lighten things and speed things up. But maybe he already realised that. How could I tell? You see how this sort of thinking can get to you.

But if Pinter had his private thoughts so did I, and it was on this axis of insecurity versus strength that *Old Times* turned. That is why the play lent itself so well to dropping in. My

imagination is free to roam and so is yours, and unlike with
Max's actions, we are not privy to each other's intentions.

Consider the following seemingly innocent dialogue:

DEELEY: What month are we in?

KATE: September.

Pause.

DEELEY: (*to Anna*) We're forcing her to think. We must see you
more often. You're a healthy influence.

ANNA: But she was always a charming companion.

Imagine someone looking you in the eye and saying, 'You're
a healthy influence.' Drop in the knowledge that Deeley has
set up a rivalry with Anna over the possession of Kate and
now the line feels dangerous. You can only guess what the
other actor is thinking, but what you do know is that he has
been dropping in to his deep, dark centre. But then . . . so
have you. You return the fire: 'But she was always a charming
companion.' Anna aims to unnerve Deeley, but she cannot be
sure if she has. Maybe he suspects that Anna and Kate were
lovers. The line may send a shudder of jealousy through him.
Tickle him with it and see how he reacts.

So the actors dance around one another, hopping from
defence to attack, parallelling the characters' game. Meanwhile, Kate gives nothing away. Is she victim or sphinx? If all
the actors are dropping in, the air can become electric. We
can play on the knife-edge of ambiguity and – what is vital to
the playing of Pinter – never explain.

Prior to rehearsals, the play has been divided up into short
units which mark the end of a beat – something coming to a
conclusion, or a subject being changed. These act as staging
posts where we get our pen and paper and try to recall everything and anything that entered our heads in order to reach
the line. This is known as 'retrieving'.

We may never look back on these notes, but the act of
writing them down consolidates the memory and before too
long we find we pretty much know our lines. We have built a
very personal path connecting image to feeling to thought to

[86]

impulse-to-speak, and we can retrace that path if we get lost. Later, if something is found to be blocking the flow, Lindy might ask us to check what we wrote. We then whisper in her ear (our jottings are as private as a teenage diary), and she, as guardian of the play's overview, might discreetly suggest that ours is not a helpful pathway and nudge us towards another.

The Advantages of Dropping in

A script in your hand can be used as a shield. Without it, you are obliged to look the other actors in the eye and to engage in the situation. Dropping in also hastens the process whereby the words become your own, part of your inner landscape rather than an object out there.

Personally, if I get too used to a script, I find it hard not to remember the layout photographically for ever more. This means that even in performance a tiny bit of me is thinking, 'Here comes so-and-so's long bit. I can switch off till I hear my cue.' With Lindy's method I can retrieve on stage the thoughts that flitted through my mind on first hearing Deeley tell the story of the day he met Kate. At that point I did not know where the speech was going, or when it would end, any more than Anna. The task in performance will be to keep breathing and to drop in to that initial state of innocence each night.

One of the hardest things for an actor to do in play rehearsals is to start, to take that first step into the space, script in hand. Lindy's method acknowledges this and builds in the time it takes to become ready to act. In most situations, you simply have to jump in, simulating emotions you have not explored yet, taking premature decisions about character and the meaning of a scene, just to have something to show. Lindy puts the emphasis less on showing and more on finding out.

As you wade further into the play, you find your thoughts and images merge more with your character's. You begin to see and smell places familiar to them which you have never known. A villa in Italy, a London pub in the 1950s, a seedy hotel lobby become vivid and real to you. Lindy uses rehearsal time vertically rather than horizontally. Going through the play twice, plugging in deep Lindy-style, is worth several more conventional run-throughs. The deeper you plant the roots in rehearsal, the stronger the performance will be and the longer it will continue growing.

In case you think Lindy's work is all about sitting around, for one thing there is always a physical and vocal warm-up to start the blood flowing, and then there is play time, or the 'abstract' work.

The Abstract

This is usually stage two in Lindy's work, but due to the tight schedule for *Old Times* it was a stage I had to miss out. I did experience it later, however, when I worked with Lindy again on *Hedda Gabler*.

NOTE TO STAGE MANAGEMENT: The rehearsal room will need:

i) anything and everything . . . that is, any props, bits of costume, bric-à-brac and old tat you can find – dump whole lot in heap in middle of rehearsal-room floor

ii) slide projector and screen, and script as before.

NOTE TO ACTORS

The object of this exercise is as before, to find the pathway to the line, only this time, instead of exploring inside your head, you project the search outward, physicalising the subtext with the help of any props, clothing or stick of furniture you can lay your hands on, climb on to or into.

SOME GUIDELINES:

The person with the line runs the game. The other players must accept and go with him/her until it is their turn to speak.

Glance at your line on the screen, then search for the props, etc. which help you find the impulse to speak. Only speak when you are satisfied.

Make sure you and fellow players can see the screen at all times (e.g. not helpful putting bag over head – not for long anyway).

Think lateral rather than literal.

Do not worry about boring your colleagues. By the same token . . .

Do not show off or perform. The exercise is not to impress others with your inventiveness, but to find things out for yourself which will stay with you.

Throw inhibition to the wind, but try to avoid physical danger to self or others.

Funnily enough, it gets boring only when someone tries to be interesting. When no one is trying, it is fascinating.

How does all this help when you play the part? I hear you ask. Well, for one thing, the dropping in plants things so deep that you cannot hope to retrace them in all their detail once you come to speak your lines at performance pace. (Besides, you should not be in that state of introspection when you are performing.) The abstract throws up some memorable visual images, which are quicker to access than complicated chains of thought, and act as a kind of shorthand to trigger your imagination and memory in performance.

The abstract encourages spontaneity, and spontaneity can yield up wonderful clues. For example, one of my lines as Hedda Gabler was, 'The leaves, they are yellow and withered . . . September already.' While dropping in, I had visualised the view from my window, I had thought of the child possibly growing inside me and tried to find out how long I might have been pregnant. In real life September is the month of my birthday. I fed in 'end of summer, back to school, another year older', and so on.

The abstract work forced me to be more impulsive. I spotted a long piece of dirty lace. I draped it round me, Miss Havisham-like, and looked out at the world through the dusty veil. Suddenly everything appeared sad and tawdry. In one unplanned gesture I had found a connection between yellow withered leaves, faded bride and prying neighbours. (Hedda's fear of scandal? Or maybe Hedda herself peeking out through the grimy lace curtain.)

Watching another actor finding their pathway to a line can throw up insights and memorable images for you. When it comes to your turn, you can run with their idea, convert it or reject it, but you cannot ignore it. This game of give and take is a perfect model for the teamwork of performance.

The abstract can illustrate very precisely what is really happening with the dialogue. There was a great example when Jenny Quayle and I were working on the first scene between Hedda and Mrs Elvsted. These two had known one another at school and not met since. Mrs Elvsted is a threat to Hedda. She is not only an old flame of Hedda's husband, but recently has also developed a close friendship with Lovborg, the man Hedda loves/loved. Hedda needs to learn more about this relationship. She knows that Mrs Elvsted has always been afraid of her. If she wants any confidences, she must allay that fear.

In the abstract play, a pair of black leather gloves lined with white fleece became the focus of our interchange. I will try and reproduce it here as well as I can remember it.

Harriet picks up pair of gloves, places them together and gives them to Jenny. Then says line:

HEDDA: We used to call each other by our Christian names.

Jenny slowly and deliberately hands gloves back.

MRS ELVSTED: I'm sure we didn't.

Harriet turns gloves inside out, examines and strokes soft fleece.

HEDDA: I remember clearly.

Hedda gently kisses Mrs Elvsted's cheek.

Harriet caresses Jenny's cheek with fleecy inside of glove.

You must call me Hedda.

Mrs Elvsted presses Hedda's hand.

Jenny gently turns gloves back the right way and places them in Hedda's hand.

MRS ELVSTED: You're very kind. I'm not used to kindness.

Harriet places left-hand glove on Jenny's right hand.

HEDDA: Dear Thora.

Jenny removes glove and puts it on the correct hand.

MRS ELVSTED: Thea.

Harriet plays absently with Jenny's now-bare right hand.

HEDDA: Sorry?

Jenny holds up her begloved left hand for Hedda's inspection.

MRS ELVSTED: My name is Thea.

Harriet places right-hand glove on her own right hand and clasps Jenny's left in a firm grip.

HEDDA: Of course, Thea. That's what I meant.

Seeing this written down makes it look too calculated, but in fact we were both thinking on our feet, and were in the same state of not knowing what the other was going to do next, as the women in the play. I/Hedda made an important discovery thanks to this game. Mrs Elvsted was no pushover, and I/Hedda could never be quite sure how much or how little she knew. A shared memory of the glove game left us with a vestigial frisson when it came to the performance and throughout the run the scene retained a sense of mutual danger. Thea was always enigmatic in her quietness and Hedda was only just in charge.

The Blueprint

This is Lindy's answer to blocking. Once we have been through the play twice with the dropping in, we are ready to stand it on its feet. (By this stage we have been 'allowed' to sit down at home and learn any lines which have not sunk in anyway, provided we take time still to drop in the pathway.) The projection screen remains in place for the beginning of the 'blueprinting' and is discreetly withdrawn as we get more secure. If we cannot work on the actual set, the designer will rig up a close approximation to it, hopefully reproducing the exact width of room, height of chair backs, etc. that we will be dealing with on the night. Every angle matters.

Guided by Lindy's outside eye, the actors start to move the scene, trying to find the position which best supports their action, mood or attitude. Keeping that breath flowing, we work off impulse, trying out a line leaning on the back of a chair, sitting in it, hugging the wall or standing centre stage. We are using a kinetic intuition rooted in the character's inner life, not just their practical needs. I am not saying this never happens with conventional blocking, and many actors do all this instinctively anyway (so long as the Chief Blocker doesn't block), but for those of us for whom blocking often feels tacked on, blueprinting can be a release. It gives permission to feel things out and, being by now pretty secure in our characters, it need not take too long.

Actors are on the whole a practical and cooperative breed and are used to sorting out minor blocking problems among themselves, although speaking personally blocking has always been a weak point. For years, if I had something to say to someone on stage I found myself magnetically dragged to within an inch of their nose and there I would deliver my line. Then I would get stuck. For as long as my speeches were directed to that same person I could see no reason to move, so I remained trapped staring up their nostrils. It felt all wrong of course, but if left to my own devices I might not have budged all night.

I have become more resourceful over the years, but that just means I have learned more stagecraft. I can now execute grand swoops and impressive entrances, but they can be just an empty parade, a cover-up for a gaping hole. It goes back to an old enemy, the premature decision, which then gets irreversibly sealed in by the blocking.

Blueprinting happens at the right moment. The dropping in has centred you in your character's needs, while the abstract work has opened up your imagination. You can use the space to support an inner emotional truth, but you have also discovered a non-naturalistic dimension to the play which can inspire some bold expressionistic choices.

The set and the act of moving around in it trigger a whole new layer of thoughts and impressions, and we take the time to drop these in as we plot the blueprint. Blueprinting is not just about deciding where to move, it is also about where to look. I might access a memory by looking at the floor or even, in my new environment, an exit sign. A certain chair can become associated with a person in my mind, so I dart a sidelong glance at the chair when I talk or think about that person. In Act Two, an area of the stage resonates with the echo of something that happened there in Act One.

These echoes can be comic, poetic or sinister. The actors

need simply to be aware of them, and as long as they happen organically and are not demonstrated or contrived, there is a good chance that the audience will pick them up.

I remember standing at the window as Hedda, while Thea talked of a red-haired singer in Lovborg's life. A brief stab of anxiety went through me as I dropped in an image of the woman. The image froze like a life-sized photograph replacing Thea in the middle of the room. When two acts later Judge Brack refers to a Mademoiselle Diana throwing a late-night party for Lovborg, I had only to glance at that spot where Thea had stood earlier to make the connection. 'Has she got red hair?' Hedda asks as the stab returns.

In Act Three, as another example, Thea puts Lovborg on the spot as to what has happened to his manuscript. Hedda listens as he invents a story of tearing it in little pieces and scattering it over the fjord. She watches as he acts it out. The story fools Thea, but Hedda knows better. She has the lost manuscript hidden in her desk. The picture which Lovborg created of his shredded masterpiece drifting on the cold surface of the water stayed in my mind and helped form my pathway to Hedda's climactic act of destruction.

Having set in motion what she thinks is a clean and beautiful act by sending Lovborg off with the pistol with which to shoot himself, Hedda is left alone, unable to bear the silence. On impulse she grabs the manuscript from the drawer and, in an attempt to obliterate the cause of her pain, she rips it into shreds over the exact same spot where Lovborg had 'placed' his fjord. The image had been so vivid to Hedda that in a moment of madness she sees the pieces floating away. Then, shocked to her senses, she sees the evidence of her crime littered over the carpet. Panic. What have I done? What can I do? The stove. Of course. A frenzied scrabble for the scraps of paper. Burn it, burn it quick.

The Final Stage

If the mock-up of the set is a faithful enough copy of the real one, the transition from rehearsal room to stage should be relatively painless. Often with more conventionally rehearsed pieces, this can be quite a traumatic time. Distances and angles feel all skew-whiff. The chair is a different height or shape. It forces you to sit bolt upright when you had rehearsed a languid loll. All directors try to avoid these hiccups, but while the furniture is still in the workshop substitutes have to do. The only difference with Lindy is that finding the most exact replica possible becomes a top priority.

So we move in on the set as though into a familiar home, bringing with us all the baggage of our emotional reference points and memory triggers, and discovering new ones in performance. The set for *Old Times* was physically fairly empty – a three-piece suite, a window, a rug and a small table for Act One; two beds, a rug and a window for Act Two – but I remember it as crowded with ghosts, and incidents past and parallel, my own being jostled out of place by those of the other two whenever their characters took over the scene.

Lindy's method may seem slow to begin with, but it has built-in acceleration and ends up taking no longer than any other. In the case of *Old Times*, it took considerably less. I was ready and word-perfect by opening night, after just ten days of rehearsal, and the other two actors were secure in their subtly altered skins.

Quite often with much longer rehearsal periods I have felt rushed, almost gasping for air. 'Wait!' I want to yell. 'Give me time to have the thought. I'm just saying the line because it's in the script. I'm just moving here and sitting down because it gives me something to do.' You end up feeling cheated, with a perpetual nag of avenues unexplored. The trouble starts when this nag prompts an actor to go off and explore on their own in mid-performance, leaving their colleagues stranded. Multiply this by the number in the cast and you could have as many different side-shows and no play.

Research

Games, actions and rehearsal exercises are like ladders which help you reach your performance and eventually get kicked away. But they also deliver a bonus by-product: namely, the unification of a disparate bunch of individuals into a mutually committed team.

Group research is another useful means of pulling a company together. We are often sent out to research different topics touched on in a play, not because the playwright has not already done so, but in order to connect us with the material in a more personal way. Some small-cast plays may involve everyone in the same quest. The whole company goes on a group outing and returns with a useful common ground of information. But besides this, each person will have picked up something slightly different from the visit, according to their own interests and their part in the show, and may notice a telling detail which the writer overlooked.

If the play has a large cast and covers a wide range of subjects, each actor or small group of actors might be delegated to research the subject which most concerns their character, and then share their findings with the whole company. This is an extremely efficient use of rehearsal time.

The structure of certain plays dictates that certain actors never meet on stage, and consequently rehearse separately. This happens less in low-budget productions where there is a lot of doubling up, so that one actor is involved in many plots, but in larger companies where this is not the case, it is all the more important to find a means of welding the cast into a whole. Consider the case of *Henry IV*, with its battlefields and pub brawls, its high politics and low comedy. He who plays the king never brushes with the mob, while the lowlife are strangers to the court, so how do you ensure that the actors finally belong to the same world?

In 1982, the RSC put on the play as its inaugural production at the Barbican. Early on in rehearsals the director, Trevor Nunn (another born director), got us all going on medieval history. Every area was covered in an effort to match the epic scope of Shakespeare's play: historical, social, social-historical, medical, pastoral, lowlife and high. We researched in twos and threes, and then had to stand up in front of everyone and spout out our findings – a terrifying ordeal for actors but a great device for trust-building.

Sometimes the subject of the play is so difficult to digest that we have our work cut out even to get the gist. There is just no time to wander down other paths. This was the case with another Trevor Nunn production, Tom Stoppard's

Arcadia. The whole company sat round the rehearsal room at the National Theatre, clinging together in our confusion, the blind leading the blind through the labyrinth of chaos theory. Now you grasp it, now you don't. 'I've got it!' you shout with glee, only to find the whole thing falls apart in the telling, like last night's dream. Luckily my character, the libidinous Lady Croom, had only to cause chaos, not to understand it.

Dabbling in Art

In 1991 I was rehearsing a new play by Timberlake Wertenbaker called *Three Birds Alighting on a Field*. In its broadest sense, the play was about value. What and who do we value and why? The metaphor was the art world at the end of the 1980s, and this world brought together characters as diverse as a Greek tycoon, his Sloane Ranger wife, a lesbian painter and a New York dealer. It was a play bulging with ideas and topics to be researched.

Timberlake had naturally done her stuff and whittled down a mountain of information already, but the rest of us also needed to know about the artist's relationship with the dealer, the dealer's with the buyer, about London clubs, the preservation of Romanian churches and all the other subjects in the play. It would be impossible to do the play justice without going into what we thought of Julian Schnabel and Carl Andre, or what we felt about Englishness, or the fall of the Berlin Wall. Without these deeper connections, we could have resorted to caricature and sold the play cheap.

Books and newspaper cuttings were brought in every day by actors, members of the stage management, whoever. Time was scheduled for outings to galleries and for actors to meet painters, dealers, the head of the Arts Council, etc., and then each of us would have to give the dreaded 'talk' on our findings.

Biddy: A Personal Detour

I was cast as Biddy, an ostensibly vapid Sloane, and my area of research was the social season. I steeped myself in 'Jennifer's Diary'. I rang up a friend of the family who had been an equerry to the royals and sounded him out on questions of etiquette. My Greek husband in the play was desperate to buy social acceptance with his millions, so I researched a little on his behalf. That was how I learned that it was harder for a Jew to get into a St James's club than for a camel to go through the eye of a needle (well, not quite, but apparently it is easier for a Greek tycoon than for a Jew).

Since we were rehearsing at the Royal Court, I was lucky in that I had only to step out into Sloane Square during my lunch hour to supplement my research with observation. I followed many a 'Biddy' into Peter Jones or the General Trading Company. I dug out and brushed up the upper-class accent of my past life, and tried it out in a shop when ordering some flowers (trouble was, I forgetfully reverted to my usual sloppy tones when I went to collect them that evening).

I accepted an old schoolfriend's invitation to the sort of cocktail party I would normally have run from. Something useful might turn up, I thought, and it did. I got talking to a forty-year-old English rose. She did not work and spent most of her time alone in Yorkshire, while her children were at boarding school and her banker husband was in their London flat. So far so like Biddy. Once or twice during our conversation, her husband would remove himself from a boorish back-slapping circle of men and stake a cursory claim on his wife, otherwise he ignored her.

She confided in me (women of all classes have the ability to get intimate remarkably quickly) that she was happy that her husband seldom noticed her because it was an indication that he seldom noticed any women. Judging from his behaviour at the party, I reckoned she was right. But he should be so lucky. This woman was adorable, while he struck me as an oaf. I was amazed at her lack of confidence. The truth was that for whatever deep-seated reasons she was terrified of being dumped and had almost deliberately chosen an unsexy husband as a precaution against it.

As I said much earlier, I had always steered clear of upper-class parts because they were so often written as ciphers. But in Biddy Timberlake had written a beautifully rounded character, full of wit and compassionate observation. Meeting that woman at the cocktail party had given me a bridge towards Biddy. Like her, Biddy exemplified the insecurity of the trophy wife. The events of the play empower her and tragedy matures her. By the end, she has found her true voice (not by coincidence the accent loosened), her own opinions and a sexy lust for life. I would wish the same on her counterpart.

Keeping in Touch

They say actors don't get out much. If there is an element of truth in this, it is because the out-of-work ones are too busy looking for work, while the working ones are too busy working. When we do work it is in a specialist area and we keep antisocial hours, but then the same could be said of government ministers, hospital administrators and many others who are supposed to know what is going on out there.

But if at the silly extreme there are film stars in luxury fortresses who never go anywhere without a wall of body-guards surrounding them, most of the rest of us for most of the time have to live in the real world. For a start, any actor in charge of rearing a child or caring for any other dependant is forced to keep their feet on the ground, and even the more footloose cannot be fancy-free for long. It is in the nature of the job that they will be in that real-life dole queue sooner rather than later.

That said, I admit that when I have been working very hard for a long time, I can get tunnel vision. In particular, while filming I can go months without travelling on a bus, and several days without venturing anywhere but to the corner shop, and we all know that buses and check-out queues are essential eavesdropping venues.

So yes, at times and to varying degrees, actors live a rarefied existence, but it could also be argued that the very unpredictability and variety of the job force actors out of their little boxes and into the unknown more often than most. Suddenly an actor gets a call to play the part of a paraplegic, or a policewoman, a rent boy or a military dictator. As far as your domestic life allows, you drop whatever you are doing, put your own life on hold and dive headlong into another.

These big jumps can have life-changing effects. Actors have become religious converts or political campaigners, have emigrated, met spouses and discovered life-long passions, all because they started researching and got involved in another world. It is a privilege to be given the opportunity to learn a new skill, travel abroad and generally broaden your knowledge, but mostly there are those long stretches when no such chance comes your way.

Just as dancers have to exercise their bodies when they are out of work, actors have to keep their minds open and exercise their powers of observation. If you sense you are losing touch, a lazy but not unfruitful option is to watch a good fly-on-the-wall documentary (always remembering that the 'fly' is a big fat film crew, but still . . .). Or you can get out there and eavesdrop, becoming the fly-on-the-wall yourself (unless, of course, you're very well known – a famous fly defeats the purpose somewhat). Best of all, if you've got the nerve, talk to people.

The Joint Stock Interviews

It was a technique devised originally by Joint Stock for their show *Yesterday's News*, which I saw at the Royal Court Upstairs. Seven actors sat in a row and directly addressed the audience in monologues which had been edited from verbatim interviews with real people. The subject was the war in Angola as seen through the eyes of a journalist, a couple of British mercenaries, a soldier's wife and others. The actors re-created exactly the interviews, complete with ums, ers and pauses. What impressed me was the con-centrated immersion of each actor. It was as though the actor's own persona had been obliterated, and they were possessed by another. Each actor had gone out with a tape recorder and interviewed their 'subject', and therefore felt a great responsibility to keep faith with them.

Poverty is Another Country

One day during the *Ragged Trousered* workshop it was decided that the actors should abandon the rehearsal hall for an afternoon and instead scour Plymouth for interviewees, modern-day counterparts of the men in the book.

For various reasons, the painting trade had resisted total unionisation and a lot of lump labour still existed. What were conditions like now? What could a painter earn? How did he get his next job? Who had joined the union and who had not? We had already got some information from Jim and Pete, our supervisors at the warehouse, but there was a broader picture out there.

Meanwhile, what was I to do? I was offered the afternoon off, but I gulped down my feelings of insignificance and volunteered to do my own investigation. We wanted to know about poverty, so why should I not visit one of the poorer housing estates and look for a woman to talk to?

Off I went like an innocent abroad. It was one thing for the chaps asking man-to-man questions on the work site, but I needed to get into someone's home. How the hell was I going to approach anyone? 'Hello. I'm an actress and I want to snoop into your life'?

I went into a pub and knocked back a couple of stiff drinks for Dutch courage. I got talking to some late hangers-on, some local jobless, a hooker, a sailor who tried to pick me up. All very colourful, but I had to move on as they were not directly relevant to my task. They had told me which was the poorest area of town and I made my dream-like way towards it.

Once there, I went to the grottiest tenement I could find, climbed some urine-stained concrete steps and rang a doorbell. Bang went preconception number one. There before me stood an elegant woman with a towel round her head and long varnished nails. In deep background was a room decorated like a beautician's waiting room. I blustered something about the wrong address and legged it.

I tried more doorbells. I waited stupidly. Occasionally I caught a shadow in the frosted glass or heard a snuffling dog, but mostly nothing. One or two doors were shut in my face before I got a word out, but at last I got a response. A young woman in a stained dressing gown opened the door. 'Yes?' She heard me out – something about being an actress and wanting to find out about other people's lives. I might have been from another planet. We were interrupted by an old woman's voice shouting, 'Linda!' 'Can I come back tomorrow?' I asked. I was given an incurious, 'OK,' and left feeling ridiculous.

At the risk of sounding like some molly-coddled Milady, poor people frightened me. I imagined they all must hate me. If I was guilty of lumping 'them' all together, it was a symptom of the great divide between the haves and the have-nots. Our different circumstances had given us different preoccupations, and those different preoccupations made us almost aliens to one another. During my brief meeting with Linda, I had felt irrelevant rather than hated.

When I returned next morning, having skived off work on the building, I quite expected Linda not to open the door. However, she did, this time dressed to go out. Hardly meeting my eyes, she said, 'I've got to go to the market.' 'Can I come along?' I felt like a pushy journalist. 'All right,' came the blank-toned reply.

She let me into the flat while she tucked a child into a pram and collected a purse. As soon as I stepped into the room, what had been a murmur of chat abruptly stopped. Taking in my surroundings, I noticed a woman a bit older than Linda standing smoking in the corner. She instantly turned her back on me and looked out of the broken window. An old lady sat in the only chair, her stockings rolled down to her ankles, her skirt up above her skinny knees. A large collie dog snorted round the dirty child in the pram. Three scruffy boys played on an upturned mattress. There was no other furniture.

I had seen poverty in Africa and Eastern Europe, but was less familiar with its UK form. It was as though there were two parallel universes, the one I normally moved around in and this one, which remained invisible until you were either forced or volunteered to go there.

Linda opened up a bit as we went round the market. It turned out the children belonged to her sister, the other young woman in the flat. At the age of eighteen, Linda herself had had a spina bifida baby by her docker boyfriend. The baby had died. They wanted to try again, though they knew the risks of having a second spina bifida child were high. They were living off supplementary benefit and were saving to get married.

We passed a second-hand clothes stall and Linda held up a lacy white blouse against her chest. Her face lit up for the first time. I bought it for her with no awkwardness and she accepted it with none. 'Thanks for giving me your time,' I said, and swam back out into the other world.

The Hot Seat

Back in the rehearsal room the company met to exchange their stories. Following the guidelines of the *Yesterday's News* experience, each actor took their turn in the 'hot seat' in the centre of the space and represented their interviewee, while the rest of the group formed a many-headed interviewer.

The questions started off with the factual, sticking to things the actors themselves would most likely have asked: 'Where do you work?', 'How long have you lived in Plymouth?' Then they became more probing: 'Are you satisfied with your job?' – and more speculative: 'What would you have done if you hadn't been a painter?', 'What are your hopes for your son?' Chances are the actors would not have asked those particular questions, so they must answer as honestly as possible according to how they imagine their subject would have answered. If they think their person would simply have no answer, they must say as much.

Over the afternoon, we gleaned some useful facts and 'met' some fascinating people. Then it was my turn. Linda could not be so easily accessed as some of the men who had gone before her. I started my reconstruction with my back to the group, remembering the physical attitude of Linda's sister. The group spoke to me in hushed tones, as if sensitive to Linda's reluctance.

Internally, I visualised Linda's lack of eye contact and heard her disaffected voice. If I did not impose anything, these would probably surface to my own face and voice. I was as sticky an interviewee as Linda had been for me, but the group persevered, as I had, and learned of her family, her home (her view of it rather than mine was what I aimed at) and even the spina bifida child. However, when the questions turned to, 'Would you like to move away from Plymouth?' or, 'How do you see the future?', we all met a blank wall. I was worried I was making a judgement on Linda's limited imagination or that the group would criticise me for mine, but I knew I must not invent for invention's sake.

When I had finished, Bill led a discussion on the limits of our horizons. Life is more bearable if you stick within an appropriate range of hope. None of us can look into the full glare of life's possibilities, but Linda's expectations were so low that, in thinking for her, I had to close down the shutter to a chink.

What I had learned from the experience was not so much the facts of poverty as an attitude, and something of Linda was retained in my performance as Bert the apprentice, something in the way he looked out at the world.

Other People's Shoes

In a way, actors are vampires and voyeurs, but we can be somewhat redeemed by an honesty towards our 'victims'. While in the hot seat, we are the custodians of another person's thoughts, and must locate them and reproduce them as faithfully as possible. This has nothing to do with interpretation or imitation. Accents and mannerisms are not the point. The exercise is to quieten our own ego and let another person speak.

Writers, too, have to think and feel as other people, slip into other people's shoes. Writers have the added power to put words in other people's mouths. It is a huge responsibility, and sometimes truthfulness can go astray. For this reason I think writers might benefit from a spell in the hot seat now and then.

Just as an actor's personality can get in the way of a character, a writer's voice can drown out the character's own. A writer's wishful thinking can make a simpleton spout elaborate philosophy (usually the playwright's), and in a rush to tie up ends a writer can wrench a character into a

U-turn two minutes before curtaindown. Expediency at the expense of truth. Scrupulous testing in the hot seat can guard against these temptations.

In the best circumstances, the writer's (or actor's) own instincts will pre-empt any such tests. I remember an incident when I was in 7:84 which illustrated the limitations of writing by committee. We were putting together a play which John McGrath would finally write as *Yobbo Nowt*. The main story followed a working-class mother and housewife who is forced to take on a job in a factory when her husband suddenly leaves her. The show was to contain the usual 7:84 brew of songs, jokes and hard issues, and each of us was tossing our ideas and demands into the pot.

We wanted Stephen, the son of the family, to turn to petty crime so that the play could touch on police–community relations, but John came in one day and said, 'I'm sorry, I just cannot get Stephen to nick cars. He's too wrapped up in his hobbies.' Stephen's main hobby turned out to be weight-lifting, which he practised in the kitchen, to the audience's delight. They recognised that special brand of fanaticism that only adolescents have. Stephen was a person, not a formula.

A Bit of Initiative

Talking of adolescent boys, there is a chapter in *The Ragged Trousered Philanthropists* called 'The Pandorama', in which Bert performs a magic-lantern show for the workers' families one Christmas time. I read this chapter avidly as it showed another side to Bert – an extrovert who stood on a chair to announce 'Bert White's World-famed Pandorama' and proceeded to show the audience his own handicraft, singing out the commentary in confident tones.

I had accepted that for the purposes of the play the audience would need only to see the subdued version of Bert, but I wanted to find out what it was that was being subdued. One day I happened to find some old Royal Court model boxes knocking around the rehearsal room. (These are scaled-down cardboard models of the theatre which give the exact proportions of the stage, proscenium arch and wing

space, and are used by the designer to work out and demonstrate the set.)

I took one of these home with me and set to work
replicating the mechanics of Bert's show. In the book, the
Pandorama is described as 'a lot of pictures cut out of
illustrated weekly papers and pasted together end to end so
as to form a long strip . . .' These processed across the stage
and were back-lit by three candles. Bert had coloured in all
the pictures with watercolours, and the titles ranged from 'A
Dreadful Storm at Sea' to 'Tariff Reform Means Work for All'.
Tressell described how 'just behind the wings of the
stage-front at each end of the box was an upright roller' and
the 'long strip of pictures was rolled up on this'.

I found two rollers and fixed a handle to the top of each. I
then found a very long strip of see-through plastic and Sello-
taped a sequence of pictures on to it, keeping as faithfully as
possible to Bert's topics. Some of these I drew and coloured,
some I cut out of an illustrated *Milestones in Working-class
History*. I then wound the plastic sheet on to one of the
rollers and secured the free end of the sheet on to the other.
It would now operate like the film in a camera winding
between two spools, which is how I understood what Tressell
described. For the back-lighting I rather lazily resorted to a
bicycle lamp.

I remembered one of Bill Gaskill's on-the-nail prods:
'Let's have some initiative, Ms Walter.' The truth was I had
never lacked ideas, just the confidence to enact them. It had
been extremely helpful to me to concentrate 'with' Bert on
his task, trying to think, draw and write like him – no better,
no worse – but now I must go public. The whole point was to
see how Bert behaved when he was on top of things, when he
was proud and literally in charge of the show.

Understandably I had some difficulty getting my little
demonstration on to the rehearsal agenda. There were more
urgent things to do. However, in the last week when we were
packing up the room in preparation for the tour, I held all
the company's attention for a good twenty minutes as I
rattled off the show. It was quite a little hit, and both my
honour and my curiosity were satisfied.

In Praise of Smatterings

Dabbling can be dangerous. The director suddenly decides it would be exciting to have the cast perform circus tricks, and they all set about learning to ride a monocycle or walk the tightrope. Within days there are broken collar bones and strained backs. Is it any wonder? Why should we expect to master in three weeks what the experts hone over a lifetime?

Having said that, over the years, in the name of background research, I have tackled jazz ballet, done a bit of puppeteering, learned a smattering of different languages and skimmed various other surfaces. I have picked up just enough to briefly convince as a pianist and a pilot, and to bluff my way through many a topic, from medieval medicine to McCarthyism to plumbing in Jane Austen's England.

Usually I retain the information for just as long as it is relevant, and wipe the slate when the next job comes along. I have worked half a day in a cotton mill, spent a morning in an optician's and done an all-night shift on a soup run for the homeless. I have marvelled at the people who do these things all the time, but I no longer feel apologetic about my own dilettantism. There is not time in life to be a specialist in everything.

Anything that plugs you in must be good. There is group research and there is the individual actor's personal quest. Some actors do a huge amount of academic research which may or may not be helpful. Too much erudition can miss the point. Always leave room for the inspiration to drop in from left field. Reading books and looking at pictures or photographs are invaluable triggers for the imagination, but they won't help you actually play the part.

Improvisation

I have not really mentioned improvisation as a plugger-in. If skilfully directed, this can produce memorable results. I have taken part in useless time-wasting improvisations for improvisation's sake, and I have witnessed near-miraculous ones. I have been sent to prison for an afternoon to see what it was like, but as the whole point about prison is the loss of choice and the enduring of endless time, one afternoon in the local lock-up surrounded by courteous if amused policemen didn't quite do it for me. I have also known inexperienced directors to set up dangerous situations which then got out of control. An under-supervised 'exploration' of madness for *Marat/Sade* comes to mind. Some of us took days to recover from what seemed like a bad trip.

On the positive side, I have seen how a morning's well-guided improvisation can open up huge areas of a character's lifetime. In 1993 I did Marguerite Duras's play *La Musica* at the Hampstead Theatre Club. It is a two-hander about a couple who meet in a hotel just after they have signed their divorce papers.

The couple are alone and their intimacy is signalled by their frequent lapses into shorthand. He says, 'I haven't heard anything about you for two years.' She says, 'Valerie sometimes gives me news of you.' He asks (*'with a slight start of surprise'*), 'Are you seeing her again?' She replies, 'Yes . . . I've changed my mind about her.' They do not need to elaborate. The audience, who are no more than privileged eavesdroppers, are none the wiser.

Jo Blatchley, the director, recognised that if Larry Lamb and I had a clear joint idea of who Valerie was and what she meant to each of us (as per *Old Times*, we needn't share all of it) something extra would happen between us and thus to the audience, just a shimmer, but that in itself can be thrilling. Together we set up and improvised various scenes that were referred to in the play: Our First Meeting, the Day 'He' Proposed, a Major Quarrel (after 'She' had gone missing), the Day 'He' Left. In this way we arrived at a telescoped version of the couple's life together. Larry and I had not lived their life, but we each had a memory of the same very intense improvised scene, which gave us our own brand of intimate familiarity when we came to do the play.

So research and improvisation are means to an end. Hard work is not necessarily good work, and the best work can happen in daydreams. It is the journey not the arrival that matters, and talking of journeys . . .

Any Excuse to Travel

Travel, as we all know, shakes up the mind. It forces us to reappraise our lives, whether we set out to do so or not. We become a different person. We are thrown into situations we could never have planned, and what we do plan often goes surprisingly wrong. Travel brands strange images on the mind (we don't need our cameras nearly as often as we think), and brings about unusual meetings, which an actor can usefully store up for future recall.

To give just one random example, while visiting India in the 1970s I befriended a young Muslim woman who had been trained in a Western university but was about to enter an arranged marriage which would send her into purdah for the rest of her days. She was not happy about it, but accepted it philosophically, as she had always known this to be her destiny. Her plight, as I saw it, impressed me all the more because in so many other ways our take on life was so similar. Much later, when I was playing some beleaguered Jacobean girl forced to marry against her will, this friend dropped into my mind and provided the imaginative link I needed to make the girl real for me.

Norwegian Interlude

In the spring of 1996 I took myself off to Norway. I was due to play Hedda Gabler later in the year at Chichester and had a little gap before rehearsals started. A perfect excuse to travel.

I based myself in Oslo and went out on daily expeditions to meet people, visit the Munch museum or watch rehearsals at the National Theatre. One of the privileges of being an actor is that we have a passport to the backstage of almost any theatre in the world, and a common language with the people who work in them. The theatre is a small world anywhere, but it is even more the case in a country with as small a population as Norway has. One friendly meeting led to another, and I had wonderful invitations to see shows and even to watch rehearsals for a current production of *Hedda*.

I had been given several introductions back in England

and more were spawned once I arrived in Norway, but all conversational roads seemed to lead to one man: Stein Winge. So off I went to meet him. His *Hedda* had already been rehearsing for two months and would be opening *after* ours, which was a long way from starting! That in itself was interesting, but what was even more so was that he was working on Ibsen's prototype version of the play, called simply *Hedda*, and this threw much useful light on the play.

A major discovery for me was that in *Hedda* it is clearly stated that Hedda's father had gone bankrupt. Ibsen's own father had suffered the same fate. The whole family had been forced to move to a small house in an unfashionable district, and Ibsen had felt the humiliation acutely all his life. Many people had told me that Hedda is in many ways a self-portrait of Ibsen. Would this not help explain the terror of scandal which is such a major motivator for Hedda throughout the play?

I found it a much richer seam than simply the petty need to keep up with the Johannsens. Although in the later play the bankruptcy is not mentioned, I felt it explained why the house that the newlywed Tesmans move into is paid for by Tesman's family not Hedda's, and why she is so dependent on his fortunes to restore her to the status she thinks she deserves. I also wondered whether the bankruptcy might have driven her father to suicide, which in turn might have fed Hedda's own suicidal compulsion and obsession with his guns.

In the prototype version of the play, Ibsen hints heavily that Mrs Elvsted knows that Hedda is the woman from Lovborg's past who casts a shadow between them. Ibsen also quite directly implicates Tesman in the theft of Lovborg's manuscript. It is made clear that he knows that Hedda will destroy it, and he wants her to do so without being seen to ask. It suggests more of a Macbeth–Lady Macbeth interdependence and partnership in crime, which gave me added weight on stage when I came to the words, 'I did it for you, Tesman.'

This more spelled-out version of the play provided many explanations of (if not excuses for) Hedda's character, but the most telling thing of all was that Ibsen cut these out in his final version. If he did not wish to explain Hedda or exonerate her, neither should I. Ibsen knew what he was doing. Hedda's ambiguity is her strength.

Most Norwegian actresses worth their salt have played Hedda or will, and I met at least four of them. They came in all shapes and sizes and all had opposing views on how to play her. But it was not only people in the theatre who had an opinion to offer; I heard from many others – a businessman, a museum curator, even a couple on the train.

I listened unselectively at first, but then began to pick out some ideas. First, I would be wrong to try and think Norwegian when playing Hedda. Many people spoke of Hedda as an outsider, like Ibsen, who spent most of his life abroad. Hedda is an uncomfortable mix of petty and courageous. She despises the narrowness of society, but knows she is caught up in it by traps of her own making. She projects on to her lover all the courage for life and death that she lacks. She has grand poetic aspirations, but her feet are firmly planted in the drawing room. Ibsen apparently longed to live romantically alone by the sea, but never did. He could not altogether deprive himself of the attentions of society and his loyal wife.

I have tasted provincial suffocation in my life, every country has it, and every country has the equivalent of Janteloven (or the Law of Jante, which roughly translated means 'Don't get above your station', an attitude which helped drive Ibsen abroad). But what of the fjords and what of the trolls? These are unique to Norway and, although Hedda may never mention them, they must form part of her imaginative landscape, as for all Norwegians. So I took myself off.

After a seven-hour journey swapping trains for boats and boats for buses, I finally arrived at the edge of a remote fjord and there and then decided to spend the night. I had left the boat at four in the afternoon and had not even asked how I could get back next day. I was being deliberately impulsive, wanting to trick myself out of civilisation. I set off on a walk along a road which rose and dipped beside the fjord, my heart dancing with this unprecedented freedom.

Above me towered the mountains, giddily steep, and slow-shifting sheets of silvery waterfalls were all around. The days are long in a Scandinavian summer and at ten o'clock I was still walking, having passed only one couple the whole time. As dusk gathered I did fancy I saw the troll-like shapes I had seen in paintings in the galleries. These are nothing like those rubbery flame-haired gnome things that you see in toyshops, but enormous humanoid rocks and mounds of earth, and spirits in the shape of giant trees. It was time to go home.

'Home' was a log cabin. Throughout Norway there are little wooden huts used by tourists on walking treks and the like, equipped with blankets, kettles, soap and towels. All you have to do is leave them as you found them. I ate the peanut-butter sandwiches I had prepared back in Oslo and slept as soon as I hit the bed.

The next morning I looked out of my hut and saw a shroud of rain. Undeterred, I hiked up the hill. Not a sound except the tumbling of water from the great heights above and my own panting breath. By midday I had reached a small hotel, where I bought a late breakfast and found out about a bus that would take me to a station. It was due in half an hour and there was only one a day. The spirit of Ibsen and Hedda got a hold of me. Civilisation beckoned. There was a limit to what one could do in the rain. More importantly, I had another adventure to fit in: a trip to the Arctic Circle timed for Midsummer Night. I got on the bus with a few silent others and as we wound our way up the zigzagging road I looked back at the small dot that had been my shelter for the night until it finally disappeared from view.

Part Three
CHARACTER AND CONTEXT

8

Horses for Courses

Actors are often asked, 'What type of role do you best like playing?' 'Big ones,' I have been known to reply facetiously, balking at the 'Where do I begin?' nature of the question. The fact is that the type of role is seldom the point. Just suppose I could answer that I liked playing bossy women best, there is a huge difference between Beatrice in *Much Ado About Nothing* and a two-dimensional nag in a bad soap. There are well-written roles and badly written ones, and I'm not just talking about what the characters are given to say, I am talking about context. There are good parts in flawed plays and dull parts in great ones. There are parts which have a lot of stage time but finally amount to very little, and there are beautifully placed small parts which can be the most eloquent of all. What matters is the overall purpose of the story and the way in which my character helps to tell it.

Plays tell stories through character in action. Character and plot are a bit like chicken and egg. The character propels the story, the story in turn reveals and determines character, which propels the story ... The job of the actor is to make the audience believe in their character so as to draw them into the story. We are the bait that lures them into the fake reality of the play, the wriggling worm that must not let the fishing line be seen. Style is our camouflage. Step out of the style and your cover is blown. Your actor's truth means nothing in a vacuum; you can be true only within the context of the play.

By style I mean the chosen visual and verbal language of the play, what is left out as much as what is included. The writer (and at a later stage the director) has decided whether the story is most effectively told in bold strokes or minute detail, through naturalism or absurdism, humour or tragedy. An actor who fights against or simply has not understood the style-language of a play will neither serve it nor be served by it.

Actors can become over-reverential with certain writers' styles. There is nothing wrong with a bit of healthy rule-breaking now and then, as long as you realise that in order to break rules to good effect, it pays to have mastered them first. A Noël Coward character cannot be brought to life unless you start with the rules of Coward's style-language. This might seem like a restriction but, as with any language, once you are fluent in it you can take flight and even occasionally add to the vocabulary.

Just as there are appropriate styles for telling a story, there are ways of working on a character that fit the style. A lot of time and energy can be saved by recognising this. Building your physical athleticism is not likely to help you into a Beckett character, nor is there much sense in bringing a Marlon Brando-type Method to a Feydeau farce (though Brando could probably pull it off).

Let me admit right now that acting *can* be as easy as falling off a log. A handful of actors find it easy all of the time, most of us find it easy at least some of the time. If and when it does feel easy, don't complicate it, enjoy it. Some parts come to you in one big instantaneous flash of understanding, others have to be chipped out of the rock. If you do immediately get the hang of a part, it is best not to analyse your work (the intellect can play havoc with your instincts), but if, as is more usual, there are bits that come easily and others that just won't yield, a little intellectual tampering can help.

For the sake of argument, here is a list of possible approaches to character (they are in no particular order and I am sure there are many more). Each is more applicable to certain tasks or styles of work than others. If you think of the following as keys, you can try each one out until the lock starts to give, or test out a combination of keys. As a rule, try anything and everything out at first and eliminate the un-helpful and unnecessary later, and (here's a note to myself) always leave a channel open left field. Lateral thinking can reach places that plodding logic never can.

Physical   For physical theatre, political agitprop, characters physically unlike you.

Psychological   For naturalism (e.g. TV and film), subtext
   (e.g. Chekhov).

Language   Where the key to character is the language
   (e.g. Shakespeare, Pinter, Barker).

Personality   For 'personality'-driven roles, for underwritten scripts, film stardom.

Biographical   For people who really lived; research
   needed, also tact sometimes.

Functional   Suss out your function and stick to it –
   function can be fun once you've accepted that it's
   not about you.

In the next few chapters I will have a look at each one of these
keys, but I must stress that they are only the triggers, the
kick-off points, for a complex and mostly subconscious
process which differs for each individual and which I do not
presume to explain.

9

The Physical Key

By physical theatre I mean theatre in which the language is subordinate to the visual picture not the other way around. Examples of this would be mime and mask work, visual comedy, performance art and expressionism. For these the character kick-off point usually comes from an external stimulus which is experienced physically and, when taken through the body, engenders an inner life or state of mind. The trigger can be anything – a physical mannerism, part of a costume, a picture, a sound or even a smell. The inner state then feeds back into the next movement or gesture, thus setting up a continuous circuit. This is how I understand the term 'working from the outside in'.

The same circuit is set up by the opposite inside-out method. The character is motored by inner impulses and feelings which then work their way on to the physical surface. For example, I understand that I am about to die, I feel terrified, my breath quickens, I begin to shake. But just try out the opposite approach for a second. With no particular thought in your head, you can quicken your breath, shake at the knees, assume a mask of fear and suddenly feel panicked. At its simplest, the inside out equals 'I feel happy, so I smile,' and the outside in equals 'I shape a smile and then feel happy.'

Whichever approach you use, the performance can be manifested only physically anyway. There are brilliant technical actors who can reproduce totally believable emotions through sheer behavioural study, while others have to feel them deeply every time. The one is not morally superior to the other as long as the audience is made to believe the situation. Most actors hover somewhere in the middle. We cannot feel things every night and we cannot hold the action up until we do, so we are forced back on technique. If our preparation and study have been honest, then with any luck so will our performance be.

Some actors profess always to work from the outside in, getting the character from their shoes, their walk or by building a prosthetic nose. Other actors swear by the internal approach, but I am arguing for flexibility. Clinging to your method can become a security blanket and actors are not supposed to be secure.

It is different with clowns and stand-up comics. There are clowns whose character is their costume and they simply cannot perform without their hallmark hat or coat, as though it possesses an instant magic. They stand neutral in front of the dressing-room mirror, reach for the pork-pie hat or too-small jacket, put it on and whoosh! Instant character. The body slumps, the toes turn in, the eyebrows waggle in one instinctual nano-second. In fact, years of refinement and discardings have gone into this.

The only inkling I had of what a clown goes through was when we had a few clown and mask classes at drama school. Mask work I loved, but clowning did not come easily to me. Everyone has their personal clown inside them. To find and refine your clown requires great honesty. I thought I was reasonably self-critical, but picking out a physical trait of one's own and exaggerating it for the amusement and scrutiny of one's peers is quite a tall order for a self-conscious twenty-year-old. At that age I had less sense of humour about myself than I do now. Mask work, which involves relinquishing oneself and going off to meet a spirit out there (I can't think how else to put it), I took to much more happily.

Masks are the most ancient of our keys to metamorphosis. With a mask we can become God or evil imp, buffoon or the animal spirit of our ancestors. What is thrilling about working with a mask is that you discover primitive archetypes which you literally did not know you had in you. From nowhere that you can easily explain, you summon up a force that is physical and which seems to take you over. Suddenly your body can do impossible things. You (but it isn't you) become a repulsive old man totally credible to behold, or the embodiment of, say, Greed or Sorrow.

At LAMDA and during a couple of courses I took much later, I tried out Commedia dell'Arte masks, Basle masks and the classical Greek masks, both whole face and half. The half-mask allows the actor to speak, but I always felt my voice let the mask down. It is hard to find the voice to fit a Greek god or a Commedia dell'Arte grotesque. Sometimes the actor speaks behind a full mask, which can distort or amplify the voice to good effect, but often simply muffles it. The Basle mask is a white, full-face mask which comes in several almost abstract shapes. They have a strange archetypal purity and operate best in silence. For my money, most masks do.

Masks are hard to write about, partly because they work so quickly in the moment and partly because (at the risk of sounding mystical) there is an element of superstition surrounding them which makes me feel I should leave the subject alone. That said, I now feel free to outline the rules of the game as I was taught them.

1) Handle the mask with great care at all times. I have seen shows where masks are used purely as a gimmick. They are perfunctorily clapped on, ripped off and generally chucked about. Having been taught a mixture of respect and reverence for the mask, I am made very uneasy by such behaviour.

2) Before putting the mask on you should empty your mind. The teacher/ director may set up a simple scenario in which your mask has a clear objective, but never pre-plan your actions. Let the mask lead you and learn from its innocence.

3) The moment the mask is on, glance at your image in the mirror for no more than a second and work instantly off the impact of that image. Never impose your will on it. If you try to steer the mask, its energy will die on you.

4) Avoid touching the mask when it is on. A flesh and blood finger scratching a mask's nose only destroys the illusion.

5) Take the mask off as soon as it stops working.

We use masks more than we think we do. Leaving aside prosthetics, we can turn our own faces into a mask and instantly conjure a character by thrusting out our lower lip, scowling or fixing our eyebrows in an expression of permanent surprise. An example that comes to mind is Wilfred Brambell as Old Steptoe in *Steptoe and Son*. He seems to me to work primarily off his screwed-up Scrooge mask.

If clowns and masks depend on external impulse and a lack of self-consciousness, mime demands a concentrated inner visualisation and an almost scientific observation of the external world. A mime artist will study an object, its size, its weight, how far it travels when thrown, what it feels like to the touch. Then he/she will notice just how the body behaves when leaning against it, walking round it, sitting on it or carrying it. Exactly how far do the knees buckle under the weight of a heavy trunk and what is the exact compensatory tilt of the torso needed for carrying a bucket of water up a hill? How do the fingers grip a bar of slippery soap, a rubber ball, a gun? With this observation recalled, and re-created through the body only, the mime artist makes the audience see the invisible. With the best mimes we not only see the bucket but know how full it is, and if the artist were to mime chucking it over us, we would instinctively reach for a towel.

Mime, mask work and performance art are skills practised in specialist branches of the profession and are not obviously applicable to conventional acting jobs. Despite this and almost because of it, I think it is essential to get a taste of them at drama school. The joke about drama schools is that students stand around 'being trees' for three years and then spend a whole career in naturalistic TV, but the fact is that, having once flexed those physical and imaginative muscles, we will use them as professional actors much more often than we think.

In LAMDA movement classes we were not only trees, we were machines, we were diseases, we were fire, earth and water, and then came the animals. We would all go off to the zoo and each pick an animal to study. Once or twice we would spy a similarly engaged troupe from RADA or the Central School, and exchange embarrassed nods. Studying an animal was of necessity purely a matter of observing their

physique and exterior behaviour. Projecting human senti-
ments on to them was banned. A fish is not necessarily in a
bad mood because his mouth turns down.

Back in the classroom we would physically 're-create' our
animal. We would start off being as scientifically accurate as
possible (amazing illusions were created, birds seemed to fly
and insects to dart) and then by stages the ban on anthropo-
morphism was lifted and we could fill the room with grumpy
fish, goats with attitude, snobby camels and gossipy pigeons.
If you were feeling lazy, you could choose a lizard who had
just had lunch.

This all sounds like fun but it has a serious application
too. We each have our personal rhythm and the way our
bodies are strung together leads us to move in certain ways.
Studying an animal that is very differently constructed and
has a faster or slower pulse rate than our own allows us to
break our own physical mould. The physical variations in the
animal kingdom are extremely marked and therefore easy to
latch on to. Later we can tone down the extremes and relate
them to human beings.

As a key to character it works like this: you alter your
posture and that alters your breathing; change your
breathing and you can change your emotional state; cock
your head on one side and it changes your attitude. Such tiny
physical adjustments can take you inside a character when
the psychological approach has got you stuck.

If I had not experienced the scope of the actors' physical
imagination at LAMDA and been surprised by my own
body's elasticity, I suspect my natural bent would have led
me exclusively into the psychological school of acting, and
my career would have been the poorer. I still love psychological detective work and get the most sustained satisfaction
from emotionally inhabiting a character, but physical theatre
rewards the actor in another way. For one thing you can be
anarchic and illogical, and physical theatre can reach bits of
the audience which no other theatre can.

The Brigands in *The Ragged Trousered Philanthropists*
were found through pure physical experiment. The psychological key would have been wasted on them and would have

told the wrong story. The piece was not concerned with what made each individual brigand tick, but with demonstrating their generic awfulness. Any more detailed approach would have sidetracked the audience's focus.

For this reason physical theatre has been used for political ends, as in agitprop. Like satire or lampoon, it can exaggerate one aspect of a person and diminish all others for the sake of clarity. It is a question of proportion. That a dictator loves his own children must not be admitted as evidence to cloud the fact that he causes misery to other people's.

It is no coincidence that the strongest tradition of physical theatre is to be found on the Continent, especially in the East, where first-hand experience of dictatorships is fresh in the memory. Britain's relatively liberal tradition has allowed playwrights like Shaw, Granville Barker and David Hare to discuss politics on the mainstream stage, but in countries where that has not been possible audiences have learned to interpret the subversive codes hidden in gesture and body language. Playwrights and actors learned to duck and dive. Words can be censored but how do you police a mime?

A Russian Adventure

In 1985 I worked with Yuri Liubimov, one of Russia's most illustrious directors, on Dostoevsky's *The Possessed*. He had had a great success the year before with his production of *Crime and Punishment*, which had played at the Lyric, Hammersmith, with an all-British cast, but during the run of the play he had been refused permission to return to his country. As I said before, I will grab any excuse to travel, so I decided that a visit to the run-down tenements of Leningrad (as it was then) would help me play 'Maria the Cripple'. I asked Yuri for some contact addresses and offered to deliver messages to some of his friends.

Over tea in South Kensington he gave me a crash course in subterfuge. I was to ring only from public payphones as the hotel would be bugged. I must say I was Anya from Paris and profess an interest in theatre design. The danger was not to me, but to Yuri's colleagues if they were found to be in touch with him. It was like something from *The Third Man*, and all be–cause a man had gone his own way and directed plays in the West.

That same man had been a Party sweetheart not so far back, and had enjoyed privileges and a budget that he would sorely miss in Britain, yet in a perverse way I envied Yuri. At least the men in grey recognised the power of theatre. After all, you can be dangerous to a government only if you are an effective force, and in Britain we were constantly made to feel irrelevant.

In Moscow I went to the Taganka Theatre, which Liubimov had run for many years. I saw a couple of his productions, a modern play based on a folk-tale and *Tartuffe*. Of the two, I preferred the latter and not just because I already knew the play. The older 'foreign' play gave Yuri more creative leeway. On other trips I had made to Eastern Europe, I had seen how censorship stifled new writing but how people became experts at working today's political message through a classical play. Throughout Yuri's *Tartuffe*, the figure of King Louis XIV sat enthroned on stage as a constant reminder to the performers of his fragile patronage, a connection which, I am sure, was not lost on the audience or the Party apparatchiks sitting smugly in their boxes above them.

Yuri's name had been removed from the programmes, but I was assured that the productions had not been changed. They were a stark contrast to his *Crime and Punishment* and also quite unlike one another. It was interesting to learn that he did not have just one hallmark style.

My trip had taught me how our theatrical traditions differed and had given me an inkling of the historical and political factors behind our separate evolutions. I had been told of a people subjugated by belief, who had merely swapped the icons around from Jesus to Lenin and back again (an idea which was pivotal to Liubimov's take on *The Possessed*). I had begun to learn their language and was just cottoning on to their subversive sense of humour. Most importantly for my immediate project, I had experienced Russian theatre *in situ*, and this gave me at least the A, B and C of Liubimov's performance vocabulary.

In true European fashion we had two months to rehearse *The Possessed*. Arnold Schnittke had been commissioned to write the score for the play and it was already on tape for us to listen to. From day one Stefan Lazarides's set was complete and ready for us in the rehearsal room, and after a hurried and rather pointless read-through, we were thrown on stage to flounder about, scripts in hand. The three walls of the set were made up entirely of strips of black elastic, strung vertically and each about four inches wide. At any point we could burst through them or fold away into them, leaving no trace but a slight tremble in the black. We could hang in them, get tangled in them, shine torches through them, ping them and ripple them. We could double the cast for a crowd effect by each holding a mask in both hands, poking them through the wall and jostling them up and down.

Apart from the walls, there was an upright piano on stage and other furniture was introduced as it was needed. There was no rehearsal schedule as such; we were all called all of the time and simply worked through the play from the beginning to the end. The opening scenes were gone over in painstaking detail and took many days. By the end of a fortnight, some people were wondering if they were ever going to get a go, but watching Liubimov at work was giving us more and more of a clue.

Yuri spoke to us through a female interpreter. We were told to listen to her but look at him. We soon got the hang of it; after all, we can all watch a film, listen to the soundtrack and read the subtitles simultaneously. Yuri had been an actor himself and would often physically demonstrate what he wanted us to do. This is normally taboo for a British director, but in Yuri's case the performance language was so physical that it was the most efficient means of communication. It was a good example of the outside-in approach. Mimic the outer form and then justify it internally, that way the motivation can still be very much your own. There is a good metaphor in there somewhere: you can obey on the outside but they can't control your mind. Or something . . .

Yuri would nitpick maddeningly over some exterior detail (actors had to imitate the exact leg swing and slow rocking motion of the guards that patrol Lenin's tomb, or practise to perfection that little speeded-up metronome wave that Brezhnev and his gang used to do from the Kremlin walls), but in other things he left our invention free. When it came to our individual characters, we were to read the book. Dostoevsky would tell the actor all he/she needed to know. That was Yuri's demarcation line. Beyond that he would give us only physical clues: this character *must* wear this Panama hat; that character must drink a glass of water like *this* and not like *that*.

My character, Maria Lebiadkin, was in the tradition of the Holy Fool, part comic, part pathetic, part imbecile, part seer. It was thought that the fool's wretchedness or simple-mindedness could bring the more corrupt and sophisticated nearer to God, or at least purge their souls through pity. I knew all this but it didn't help me play the part. Nor did the description 'mad' or 'cripple' help very much. All around me the rest of the cast were being encouraged to be as manic and eccentric as their wildest dreams, so how was I supposed to top them? I'd have to be madder than mad.

So it was not her madness I centred on but her delirious happiness. She loved God, her brother, Stavrogin, life itself – and her love split her open with a smile. I got the smile from the music. It set off an inner giggle which swelled to a sort of ecstasy. Once I had got the smile, her attitude and move-ments followed and led me on to her inner life, which in Maria's case was almost her only life. Dostoevsky describes her sitting motionless sometimes for eight hours on end just dreaming – not a thing one can capture easily on stage. Liubimov managed to give me space for some dreams, and also for the frightening moment when her adoration for Stavrogin turned to curses. Seeing Yuri looming out of the black, like a furious arrowhead poised to fly from the stretched elastic wall, gave me a vivid picture to copy. 'Anaa-thema!' he screeched at the bewildered cast. 'Anathema!' I imitated. 'No, no! Anaaathema!' 'Oh, I see, yes. Anaaaathema!' 'Yes, yes. Breelliant!'

Costume and character grew organically together in the rehearsal room. A built-up shoe gave Maria a lopsided dottiness, and an ill-fitting, threadbare jacket and floral skirt gave me her silhouette. Liubimov topped the picture with a red flower for my hair and added the idea that Maria rouged her face with the juice of a raw beetroot. (Everyone had their own particular moment of neurosis during the show, and getting a beetroot that would behave to Yuri's satisfaction every night, whether in Islington, Paris or Milan, was definitely mine.)

Maria lived in a tenement flat with her drunkard brother, who beat her daily. Nicholas Stavrogin, the nihilist anti-hero of the novel, had married her as a life-mocking gesture which she of course did not understand. All of this was revealed at a polite salon chez Madame Stavrogin, Nicholas's mother, where Maria had been invited as a pitied stranger.

We began rehearsing the scene and Liubimov placed me at the piano. Oblivious to the polite chatter around her, Maria started to punctuate it with little flutters over the keys. Then she got over-excited and thumped the piano harder, laughing like a reckless child. Although the actress in me knew this behaviour was out of order, and I was keeping half an ear out for key moments in the dialogue, Maria could have no such self-restraint, so in the interests of remaining in character I carried on. In a break in rehearsals Liubimov expressed his approval of what I had done, and I ventured my fear of upstaging some important speeches. He told me I need not worry. When I later saw the scene on video (Channel Four recorded the production), I realised he was right. Liubimov really did have some kind of directing genius. Somehow the audience heard what needed to be heard and saw what needed to be seen. I was in safe hands.

Schnittke's music was a major way into the style of the piece. The opening sequence was a choreographic depiction of a society falling into godless insanity, and while each of us groped embarrassedly for our individual ideas of what expressionism was, the music drove us on. It hit bass piano notes of nightmare, screeched frenzied strings, then calmed into a pool of melody and suddenly burst into a witty tango. We responded to it with that area of our imagination that only music can reach. It would conjure for each of us a different association, whether Eisenstein film, Viennese pavement café, Chagall painting, whatever, but the main thing was it was foreign, and that in itself transported us. Within days most of us had set aside our cynicism and our stiff British carapaces, and were surprising ourselves with our physical invention and fluidity.

I say most of us. While some threw themselves headlong into Yuri's world, others stood longer on the sidelines. For my own part, I saw it as another case of appropriateness, of freedom within constraints. Yuri had a movie in his head, and a hot line to Dostoevsky and the Russian people which we did not. Our best strength lay in going out to meet him and then somehow making the work our own. The cast of *Crime and Punishment* had complained of being puppets, but in their case they were expected to re-create exactly the performances of their Russian counterparts, who had made the show a great success in Moscow. *The Possessed* had never been allowed a production, so by comparison we were treading on virgin soil.

Yuri was indeed unbending on some details, but he welcomed our own inventions, which inevitably flowed freer as we became more familiar with the style. The process was infuriating at times and very confusing, but if at the worst we were puppets, so what? We could do the stuff we normally did for the rest of our lives. I had little sympathy with those who dug in their Method-acting heels. Why work with a director from another culture only to block his path with 'That's not how we do things round here'?

The question is, when is playing along called 'being a puppet' and when is resistance 'healthy British dissent'? The Almeida Company had assembled some of the least compliant actors in Equity for this job, and we managed to block some of Yuri's madder schemes (e.g. he seriously proposed sitting out front each night with a torch, signalling one flash for faster, two for slower!), but after that it was a case of each individual finding his or her breaking point. I think every one of us threw a tantrum at some moment, and we had a 'Bottle Chart' stuck up in the green room which registered how often and by how much each actor lost it. Some actors were off the map!

A sense of humour got us all through and this even became more 'foreign' as we took on some of the black madness of the piece. Nigel Terry, who played Stavrogin, passed me a piece of paper at the read-through. It was smaller than a birch leaf and on one side he had written in miniature, 'Maria Lebiadkin, Slum Dwellings, Minsk,' and drawn a mini stamp. I turned it over and read: 'Dear Maria, Sell the cow and bail me out. Yours, Nick.' When much later on tour Yuri invited us all to his Bologna home and sent a fleet of black taxis to collect us from the hotel, Nigel whispered to me darkly, 'We're going to be driven to an open field and shot.'

Yuri could take it all. He had a wonderful sense of humour himself, and he needed it. One day he came into rehearsals with a newspaper cutting sent by one of his Moscow friends. According to *Pravda*, Yuri Liubimov was dead. The vigorous man who now sat among us grinning demonically had apparently died an unrecognised pauper on the cruel capitalist streets of London.

It was hardly surprising that the authorities in Moscow had forbidden Yuri to do *The Possessed*. His visual concept was riddled with anti-Soviet imagery: banners, slogans and placards heralded every scene, and Peter Verkhovensky, the revolutionary zealot, was not even thinly disguised as Lenin. Dostoevsky's novel is sometimes known as *The Devils* and this notion of evil genius let loose on a nation possessed by their madness had very immediate resonances for a Russian audience. It is sadly ironic that in the West, where Yuri was finally free to put it on, that resonance was largely lost.

Lacking a strong connection with the meaning, the style was thrown into relief. It was the expressionistic mania of the production that was the focus of comment and reaction. Some loved it, some hated it. Some accused it of being dated, a throwback to the 1930s, but few understood that for Yuri the style was not a fashion choice but a necessity for conveying his meaning.

10

The Psychological Key

Meeting the Writer Half-Way

All well-conceived roles have psychological truth, but it does not follow that they are all unlocked with the psychological key. I hope Maria Lebiadkin had a psychological truth even though I approached her physically. Characters from Congreve to Coward have a believable inner life for all their comedy of manners, and Brecht's characters are not made two-dimensional because the actor keeps a certain detachment from them. The best route to Juliet may be through her language, you might get Richard III via his hump, and God alone knows how Shakespeare arrived at them, but hundreds of years later they totally pass the test of modern psychological scrutiny.

To be able to trust the playwright is half the battle. In the best instances the playwright has already done most of the psychological groundwork, and the actor has only to go half-way to meet him/her, rather than build the entire road alone.

Provided actors work honestly, they can be the best litmus test of the psychological truthfulness of a piece of writing. If a writer has made an unbelievable link between one moment and another for the sake of a neat plot or joke, or in order to be controversial or sensational, the actor will be quick to spot it. It is a question of survival. Trying to stretch the audience's belief every night in an ill-contrived scene feels a bit like walking a frayed tightrope over a plunging gorge. We need that bridge to hold.

The actor can eventually get to a place where he/she knows the character better than anyone, including the writer, but it is vital to hold on to an objectivity about where the character fits into the whole; to know when 'But my character wouldn't do that!' is a helpful insight or the voice of vanity or fear.

A Bit of Theatre History

What I call the psychological approach to character is probably the most commonly recognised and practised in this country, but 'twas not ever thus. I don't pretend to be a scholar, but as I understand it, it was naturalism which created the need for a psychological approach, and naturalism is a relatively recent phenomenon.

Theatre is a living art, so it is hard for us to understand the terminology of performance history. One had to be there. Every artistic 'ism' that hit the theatre was a dynamic reaction to the 'ism' that came before. Naturalism swept away what had become empty romantic melodrama, and in its turn was tested by symbolism. Brecht's '*Verfremdung*' (which literally means 'making strange', and which we know as 'alienation') threw down a challenge to a fatally complacent audience at a particular moment in history. Expressionism, absurdism, the Theatre of Cruelty and many other forms were experimented with and all for the same reason: namely to penetrate the carapace of the audience's ease, to implicate them in the way the world had turned out and to involve them in the possibility of changing it.

Theatre is a present-tense transaction. Its effect will always be relative to the times with which it interacts. In order to keep alive, the theatre has to resist the need for permanence and comforting answers. It should be like an arrow that never lands or a liquid that never sets, and our job is to keep chucking the arrow back in the air and keep stirring the liquid. Today's challenging innovation becomes tomorrow's hardened complacency and before you can say 'avant-garde', the guard is up.

Chekhov, like his creation Constantin in *The Seagull*, was impatient with the drawing-room realism of his contemporaries. Theatre had reached a dead end. When Hamlet exhorts the actors 'to hold . . . the mirror up to nature' he meant them to reflect the whole picture – the portrait in the attic as well as the pretty face in the glass that looked back at Dorian

Gray. But most of Chekhov's immediate precursors had taken Hamlet's instructions at surface level and the theatres were filled with expertly faked pictures of real life. These were jazzed up by incidents, love affairs, plots, scandals and deaths which entertained and passed the time, but afforded the audience no insight beneath the skin. Remind you of anything? This was the convention that Chekhov inherited and strove to break open.

First he tried symbolism, as in *The Seagull*, in which a creature is both itself and a poetic symbol by means of which a deeper meaning can be layered through the play. Unfortunately, the device seemed creaky and heavy-handed even in Chekhov's day and so he moved on.

He tried soliloquy, the practice of a character directly addressing the audience, which was hardly a new idea, but had fallen out of fashion with the ascendancy of naturalism. The naturalistic theatre aimed to create the illusion that the audience did not exist and that in their place was an invisible fourth wall to the room. This was obviously incompatible with the notion of soliloquy. When playing Chebutikhin in *Three Sisters*, Stanislavsky (Chekhov's actor-manager at the Moscow Art Theatre) worried about the old doctor confessing his thoughts out loud for the benefit of the audience during Act Three. 'How can I find a basis for doing on stage what I do not do off it?' he asked. If naturalism means we can do on stage only what we would normally do in life, then it is a very limiting dramatic form. Chekhov had come up against a brick fourth wall, but instead of bashing his head on it, he would find a way round it.

He honed and refined his plays till he had perfected the art of revealing a character's state through the smallest nuance, of making uneventfulness resonant and unexceptional people somehow heroic. He deliberately wrote about a class who were not Where It Was At, who had insight into their own irrelevance, but not enough vision to change it. On stage they seem to do nothing but talk, eat and talk about how they do nothing but talk and eat. With the benefit of a permanent acting company, Stanislavsky developed his new approach in order to keep pace with Chekhov's unprecedented demands. If nothing major is happening on the outside, the small details become paramount. Silence becomes active, and unconscious thought as important as the spoken text.

I am not about to sum up Stanislavsky's Method here, even supposing I could. His own books will tell you everything you need to know; after that it is all in the interpretation and application – a bit like the Bible really. This is not a totally facetious comment. In fact, I am quoting one of a group of drama students whom I met in Moscow while on tour with the Almeida production of Chekhov's *Ivanov* in 1997.

Stanislavsky loomed large in their lives, not least because he was an alumnus of their school. His portrait and photographs of ancient productions lined the walls and corridors. I provoked a heated discussion by pointing out that their mentor had become great by rejecting everything he had learned within those walls, and that maybe one of them would emerge as the next theatre genius by breaking Stanislavsky apart. I was playing devil's advocate, because during my earlier talk with the principal of the school I had sensed a religious reverence towards Stanislavsky and wanted to test how far it had trickled down to the students. What I found was a mixture of defensive fundamentalists and those who were more willing to adapt (hence the Bible comment).

That they were arguing at all was an advance on my previous visit to a Moscow drama school in 1984. Then I had sat in on a very regimented class of students all practising the same gesture, and I was struck by their silence and seemingly total deference to the teacher. Now the students were sitting any old how, bantering and giggling among themselves, legs draped over the backs of chairs, chewing gum and, most significant of all, uninhibited by the presence of their teacher.

It is easy to forget that Stanislavsky's ideas were shifting and evolving all the time, and were he alive today he would no doubt be a lot less dogmatic about them than some of his high priests. Like all great teachings in the theatre, his Method was designed to help the actor in a job that was difficult enough already without adding obstacles.

He devised a series of questions for actors in order to help them realise their imagined world. In answering 'Where have

I just come from?' they see in their mind the rest of the house, not just the three-walled room on stage. A question like 'Did I sleep well last night?' can provide the key to a whole scene. Stanislavsky's question 'What do I want?' can apply equally to the immediate and conscious (e.g. 'I want to stop my husband from leaving the room') as to unconscious motives which a character might well deny (e.g. 'I want to kill my mother').

Through concentrated and honest inquiry, actors can build an interior life for a character every bit as complex as their own, and will end up with far more insight into their character than they can hope to have into themselves. But Stanislavsky was not only concerned with the inner imagination, his was also a very physical teaching. He talked about 'the truth of objects'. Again working in the context of Chekhov's plays, where the putting down of a book or the stoking of a stove might be all that is happening visually on stage, that action towards an object becomes a vital means of expressing how the character is feeling.

A man burns with desire for a woman in the room. He cannot declare it so he reads a book instead. If she must not see his love, then to be truly 'life-like' the actor playing the man must not give it away to us. To signal it to the audience would be to break the pact of the fourth wall. But we do not show our feelings only consciously. In what we now know as body language, our subconscious can betray us, and Stanislavsky made his actors think about those physical betrayals. Maybe the lover caresses the back of his book as he blindly stares at the pages, thinking only of stroking his loved one's hair.

The 'truth of objects' had a more practical application as well, that of making the staged world as real as possible for the audience. A real samovar takes a real amount of time to boil, and enhances our belief in the scene. An overcoat should be lived in to the point where it takes on the shape of its wearer. Not only does this help the audience forget it's a costume, it also tells us something about the character. Does the eternal student sleep in his overcoat because he cannot afford enough bedclothes or does he hug it around him because he is in love with the image of his own poverty?

An object can be an unexplained vestige of a prior event, like the fork which is left on the garden bench in the last act of *Three Sisters*. Did that come out of an improvisation, Chebutikhin sneaking a snack perhaps? Or was it just a touch of playwriting genius? That fork, and Natasha's irritation with the sloppy bohemianism it represents, tell a whole story in a second.

Whether working from the outside in or the inside out, Stanislavsky got the actor to discover how their character stood, how they walked, how they shook hands and how rapidly they spoke. He encouraged the actor to 'live' their character morning, noon and night. They should walk the streets as their character, eat and probably even sleep as them, the idea being that when they stepped on stage one should not be able to see the join. This train of thinking has continued down the line through Lee Strasberg's Actors' Studio, from Brando to Hoffman and De Niro (who are among the few actors in the world with enough advance knowledge of a role and time to practise it).

With the development of cinema, it was no longer the actors' job to make the physical world look real, and this left them free to delve into the psyches. The trouble arises when Method acting is used as therapy and the director starts playing shrink. Too much immersion in a part leads to a loss of perspective, which is to lose the point. As they say to undercover cops, 'Your job is not to *become* a pimp, but to make people *believe you* are a pimp.' Just for a time.

'Why not just try acting, dear boy? It's so much less painful,' Laurence Olivier is reputed to have said to Dustin Hoffman, who had allegedly just run six times round the block in order to get the exact quality of breathlessness he wanted for a particular scene in *Marathon Man*. This might sound like a cynical cry to an idealistic actor, but there is an element of truth in it.

The other danger with the Method is that it can place too much emphasis on the quirks of one individual and unbalance the meaning of the piece. American movies have made a virtue of character- or star-driven plots, but Chekhov was writing for an ensemble where no character (even the title role) was predominant. The meaning of the play is shared, and laced through each character, so the actor has to perform a balancing act, keeping hold of his or her individuality while listening out for the chorus at the same time. The musical analogy is almost perfect. The composer's main theme is taken up by all the instruments. Each one has a unique sound and can express things no other can. The theme is changed, refracted, echoed and counterpointed, but only when all the instruments play in concert is its full coherence revealed.

A young actor in New York once tried to explain to me the divergence between our two countries' acting styles. He said that American acting is rooted in a film tradition, where scripts were like blueprints to be fleshed out by the actor. For this reason American actors had developed the art of being 'interesting' individuals whose watchable, gum-chewing charisma would carry the audience through the most insubstantial of scripts. We Brits, on the other hand, had been blessed with Shakespeare, Wilde and Stoppard, and could practise our classical concerts. I disabused him of a few generalisations, but thought he had a point.

Meanwhile, back in Europe, Stanislavsky's physical teaching still prevails in the attention to objects, costume and the exterior world. When I played Masha at the Barbican, an actress from the Moscow Art came backstage and criticised the way I drank from a bottle. I had done it deliberately because Masha wanted to misbehave, but that was no defence. 'Masha would not drink that way.'

When I worked on a film with Louis Malle, he talked little of my character but insisted that she always stroked things: trees, cats, a statue, the tablecloth. When I worked with John Berger and Nella Bielski on their play A *Question of Geography* and had to play a scene where I was arrested by Stalin's heavies and torn from my son, Nella's one contribution was to give me a white scarf to wear. It must be *that* scarf worn in *that* way and no other. I never quite understood it, but I recognised it. I had come full circle back to Liubimov and his physical clues.

Some Random Questions to Help Build a Psychological Profile

'How was my character as a child?'
'Where were they placed in the family: oldest, youngest, middle? Or were they an only child?'
'How do they think of other people, predominantly friendly or hostile? Why?'
'How do they think of the world, predominantly safe or unsafe? Why?'
'What is their overriding need, desire, fear in life? Why?'
'Of the other characters in the play, who do they most need?'
'How do they see their life, as tragedy, thriller or farce?'
'What would they be prepared to die for?'
'When, if ever, can they be bought?'

The important thing is to ask the right questions. Some characters are instant kindred, others are a total puzzle. For the former you can use the 'What if?' sounding board, as in 'What if I were put through that, how would I react?' or, 'What if I were living in that period of history, how would I behave?' But for characters whose *modus operandi is* totally different from your own, you have to make a bigger leap and learn to think like them. If you are nothing like your character, think of someone else you know who is. Using that person as a bridge, imagine them in your character's situation. How would they react?

In his book *Year of the King*, Antony Sher shows how he uses sketches to build a bridge to his character. First he draws the creature 'out there', based on a mixture of imaginings, associations or just other people he may know. He experiments with several images until they become more and more recognisable as a version of himself, exaggerated and distorted but possible. The exercise requires invention, study and an almost clinical knowledge of his own physique. Sher's illustrated stages of fusion are the visible equivalent of the more approximate and elusive process of internally moving from 'me' to 'him' or 'her'.

During that process we drift in and out of character. One minute we refer to our character as 'she' or 'he', the next as 'I', but at some unnoticed moment the membrane between our self and the other starts to break and we slip into their skin. This is the most mysterious mechanism in the acting process. Actors themselves cannot quite understand it and shy away from questions about it. If we could explain it, we could make it happen on cue every time. But just as we can suddenly slip into that skin, we can as suddenly lose it. The fear that we might not find it tonight, or indeed ever again, is the knife edge we have to play on.

Love in the Hot Seat

With his customary knack of pinpointing what is normally the private burden of an actor and bringing it into the open, Max Stafford-Clark used an exercise to help this transition from 'me' to 'her' or 'him'. We were doing *The Seagull*, in which every character is in love, and love is particularly dicey territory for the actor. Either we simply go through the acting motions of love and produce a generalised pretence, or we explore more deeply in the psychological murk and perhaps confuse our character's feelings for our own.

Recognising that the actor is and should be somewhere present in the character, Max encouraged us to own up to a composite persona and give ourselves a name which reflected this. For example, I might be Nina-Harriet, while Anna Massey could be Anna-Arkadina and Alan Rickman Alan-Trigorin. Then each composite persona was to stand before the group and describe their feelings for the loved one, who was in fact another composite persona sitting in the hot seat beside them. Where there was any natural chemistry we might as well acknowledge it and use it. After all, when it came to performance, we would be dealing with the person before our eyes and not a fiction on the page.

Each of us had a turn at the lover and the loved. The lover stood behind the loved one, circled them, knelt in front of them and, looking through the combined lenses of their character's and their own eyes, found things to love in them. Meanwhile, the loved one was cushioned from embarrassment by the padding of their double name. Thus I could say as Nina that I loved Alan-Trigorin's watching eyes, and Trigorin could praise Harriet-Nina's open face without Walter and Rickman getting into any trouble.

Turning such dangerously personal material into an up-front public exercise somehow took the curse off it and at the same time gave us permission to commit to a kind of love.

A Few Case Histories, Notes and Studies

The following are not to be seen as suggestions of how to play the parts, and certainly not as my last word on any interpretation. They are a record of my thinking at the time and are intended as illustrations of ways of approaching a part within the context of a particular production. Another point to note is that both here and elsewhere in the book I draw my examples more from the classical repertoire than from new plays. This is not a reflection of my preferences so much as an expediency. More readers will know what I am on about most of the time if I discuss *Three Sisters* or *Hamlet* than if I describe some new play that may have run only for a short season in a small venue.

MASHA KULIGINA (NÉE PROZOROVA)

Reputation: stormy, snobbish, self-centred, silly. Question for the player: How much does that reputation derive from past actresses who have played the part, and how much from the text?

Possible childhood profile: middle of three sisters. Neither respected eldest nor cosseted youngest. Craves attention and works hard to get it. Maybe this worked best with Daddy, so although not necessarily pretty as a child, she compensated by developing the art of twisting men round her finger. Needs male attention. What was mother like? Which daughter is most like her? Off which parental block is Masha a chip? The sister with the weakest sense of identity displays the biggest personality. That is her paradox. Romantic and idealistic yearnings. Married first in order to reinvent herself.

Frustration and dissatisfaction with her life lead her to blame others. She punishes them by imposing her moods, stirring up atmospheres. Volatility is the key. Don't iron out her contradictions, her complexity and restlessness. DON'T GENERALISE.

Most heartfelt pronouncements: 'There must be meaning, otherwise life is just weeds in the grass', 'I love that man', 'We must go on living', 'We know a lot of stuff that's just useless.' Differentiate between her self-dramatising and her true vulnerability. Find her moments of generosity and enjoyment. In what way does she love her sisters? In what ways are the sisters alike? Different?

In the play, there is a spectrum of attitudes towards certain themes – time, love, work, the possibility of happiness, the reason for suffering – and characters are placed along that spectrum, answering and counterpointing one another. How does Masha fit into the chorus?

How do the sisters help tell one another's story? That is, what can I learn about Masha by listening to Olga or Irina, and how can we elucidate one another's predicament? The sisters continually shift and swap their positions along the spectrum between hope and disappointment. They all at times expect a man to give meaning to their life and each gives up that hope at a different point. Olga gave up first and bravely settles for work, though her headaches give her away. Masha has settled ungraciously for a ridiculous marriage, but hope is rekindled by Vershinin. Does Irina's 'I'm already twenty-three and it seems to me I'm moving away from what is real and beautiful?', said in Act Three, help the audience retrospectively to understand Masha's moody silence in Act One? Does Irina make her choice to settle for marriage to the Baron because in Masha's story she sees the hopelessness of romantic love?

When, at the very end, they are all three stripped of these hopes, Masha has fallen the hardest. The other two have learned what it is to knuckle under and work. She becomes the youngest for a moment. Character difference is wiped away and life will begin from here.

Things I must know that Masha cannot know   What is the specific cause for each of Masha's moods? Moods are by definition non-specific. They are a protective fog round an unfaceable thought. Masha experiences only the fog, but I need to know what she is avoiding. Most dreaded possibility: 'I do not matter.' Could that be the unfaceable thought, the suppression of which is her mainspring motivation?

What is the significance of the Pushkin phrase Masha keeps repeating, 'A green oak grows by the curved sea-shore, and round that oak hangs a golden chain'? It disturbs Masha herself. 'Why does it keep going round and round in my head?' I must have some idea, though it remains in Masha's subconscious. When does she fall in love? Question: can we know in life the point at which we fall in love? Answer: no. At best we can remember the moment when we said to our-selves, 'I am in love', but the chemistry will have happened long before that. So how do I 'unconsciously' fall in love as Masha? This is a nitty-gritty acting question. All I can say at the moment is play the scene and be receptive.

Things I can agree with my fellow actor   When and how does the affair with Vershinin start? There are whole years between acts, what happens during them? Do Masha and Vershinin sleep together? The actors may need answers, but we should never make things more explicit than the writer intended them to be. Anyway, didn't Edith Evans advise a young actress, 'Always have a secret up your sleeve'?

HEDDA TESMAN (NÉE GABLER)

Daughter of late General Gabler. Treasured only child? Surrogate son and heir? Mother never spoken of.

So far mentioned   Trip to Norway. Discovery about father's bankruptcy and subsequent shame. Dropping-in and abstract work with Lindy Davies. Munch paintings.

Not so far mentioned   Article by Elinor Fuchs, 'Mythic Structure in *Hedda Gabler*', detailing how Hedda is not just a psychological portrait of a woman but also a mythic arche-type. Thea's name means 'goddess', the offstage red-haired 'singer' is called Diana after the goddess of the hunt, and Hedda is a corruption of Hela, the Norwegian version of Hecate. Maiden, nymph and crone (or the white, red and black figures in Munch's *Livets Dans*). Thea the childless and

Hedda the child-destroyer. Lovborg's vineleaves evoke Diony-
sus, and September, the time of the play, is both harvest and
the beginning of death.

Question: how does all this help you play the part?
Answer: regardless of whether I go along with Fuchs's theory,
it reminds me that any absolutely sewn-up psychological
explanation of the character is only part of it. I must con-
front or at least ask questions about my relationship to the
dark forces. Do they exist as a reality 'out there' or are they
just a magnetic pull within ourselves? As with the mask
work, I must be a channel for a force larger than myself, and
allow it at least to hang in the air.

Meanwhile, back on this planet, I happened on a
television programme about power in sexual relationships.
Interviewees explained how they lured and hooked their
bait, then moved on. The chase was all. 'So far, so what?' I
thought, until one woman, speaking to camera anonymously
from the shadows, explained that she had been raped by an
uncle when she was a child and that her predominant sense
of herself in the world was as a powerless victim. In some
compulsive way she felt she had to have power over her
lovers before they got power over her.

Something clicked. Don't worry, I am not going to suggest
that Hedda had been raped, but that woman's story helped
me identify a paradox I had come across in rehearsals.
Hedda's reputation as cold and powerful manipulator was
not squaring with my experience. The feeling of playing
Hedda was one of utter powerlessness. Powerlessness to
elevate her husband, to control her jealousy and – the
ultimate powerlessness – to stop a child growing inside her. I
did not yet know what in Hedda's nature or past life had
made her feel this way. I would have to invent a reason and it
would be none of the audience's business.

We do not just bring what we already know to a part; the
part teaches us things we may only have known in theory.
Through Hedda I understood how victimisers feel *they* are
the victims who must destroy before they are destroyed, and
that possessiveness and jealousy come from a deep feeling of
emptiness and empty-handedness. 'You have no idea how
poor I am,' Hedda says to Thea, caressing her voluminous

hair, 'and you are so rich,' as the caress suddenly switches to a vicious tug.

People have described Hedda as frigid, a woman repelled by sexual and bodily functions, but to me playing her she was a woman who felt only too capable of total sexual surrender, but was terrified of the loss of power/control that would have entailed. Hedda the 'cold manipulator' felt like a cornered animal lashing out on hot impulse against people and events that refused to go her way. The woman who craves 'the power to shape a human destiny' can get it only by destruction and death.

COMPARATIVE NOTES ON MASHA AND HEDDA

In some aspects these two are sisters, or live in the same compartment of my brain. To avoid being lured into an easy repetition of my performance, it is worth sifting through the sameness in order to clarify the differences.

Samenesses Both are the daughters of generals and feel defined by the prestige that brings. Being women, they have no status except through husband, brother or father. Their husbands prove failures (and in Masha's case so does her brother) and they take their frustration out on them. They both seek a romantic or heroic meaning to life, and only at the end understand that it is their own responsibility to create that meaning through their own actions rather than through their man's.

Differences Hedda is an only child, lacking the checkings and chidings of siblings. Neither has a mother living, but Masha does at least mention hers. Both fall romantically in love, but Masha ventures where Hedda fears to tread. Unlike Hedda, she hurts no one but herself (*pace* Mrs Vershinin I suppose, though she was already hurt). Hedda destroys herself at the point when she sees life most clearly. It is a moment of courage. Masha equally courageously faces a future threadbare of meaning and determines to carry on.

A TIP

Look for the fear. Fear is a great clue to psychological motive. Instead of judging your character as grasping or stupid or cruel, ask what they are afraid of. Some people shelter behind a seeming stupidity out of fear of not being liked. If a character seems blinkered, ask what they want to avoid looking at. Greed can be explained by a fear of deprivation, and I have already mentioned victimisers and their need to get in first. A studied wackiness may come from a fear of being ordinary, while an outwardly conventional person may be a misfit who is desperate to conform.

Apparent fearlessness can sometimes be understood as a flight from a greater fear. It was while doing research for a radio programme about women explorers that a penny dropped. I came across the diaries of Isabella Bird and was baffled as to what gave this diminutive Victorian invalid the courage to leave her Edinburgh sickbed for a life of bison hunting in the Wild West and tracking grizzly bears in the Rocky Mountains.

The nineteenth century was the great age for female pioneers and explorers, and yet it was the age in which female helplessness and invalidism were most romanticised. Was there a psychological connection between these apparent contradictions? Isabella Bird first sniffed foreign winds when at the age of forty she was sent on a cruise to improve her health. While travelling she discovered her own strength and her illness disappeared. As soon as she returned home it took over her body once more.

I began to notice other examples of plucky Victorian women emerging from a half-life of illness or nursing another's illness, and put together a theory that these Victorian sisters of ours would venture where the modern-day streetwise would fear to tread, not because they had no concept of the perils they might meet (though this was often the case), but because for them any physical danger was less terrifying than being stuck with a helpless body in an unexamined life.

OPHELIA (POLONII?)

Sometimes, when one role is offered hot on the heels of another, your imagination remains so steeped in the world of the last role that it spills over into the next. When Richard

Eyre asked me to play Ophelia to Jonathan Pryce's Hamlet at the Royal Court, he had just finished directing me in a film for television called *The Imitation Game* by Ian McEwan. This was the story of a young woman, Cathy Raine, who joined the army in the Second World War and was posted to the code-breaking headquarters at Bletchley. She was bright and well educated but soon realised that her talents were to be buried in menial tasks cleaning up after the Cambridge boffins. Her frustration and need to get near the centre of things resulted in her being imprisoned for the duration of the war as a suspected spy.

The piece was a brilliant exposé of patriarchal double standards, and before starting work on it Richard Eyre suggested I read Virginia Woolf's essay 'Three Guineas'. This was one of her last works before she committed suicide in 1941. It is an agonisingly relentless analysis of the patriarchal imperative to war and the way in which women collude with it. Woolf looked straight into the light alone and was burned up by it. At the end of *The Imitation Game* Cathy Raine has seen a similar light but lacks Woolf's tools to articulate it. Locked up, suicidal or tipped into madness, that was the fate of women who had they lived now would have been buoyed up by a tumultuous sisterly chorus.

With these things still churning in my mind, I started to tackle Ophelia. Fresh from *The Imitation Game* himself, Richard was also working on some kind of continuum of themes: patriarchal power, secrecy, corrupted love, the destruction of a woman. His version of Elsinore carried echoes of the corridors of Whitehall. Geoffrey Chater's patrician Polonius would have been perfectly at home in MI5, and to reinforce the connection he had played the witheringly steely colonel who had locked me up in *The Imitation Game*. Ophelia was to be no flibberty damsel, but an intelligent girl locked in her mind by the oppressive rules of the establishment.

The Royal Court's brief was to put on new plays or, if it did do any classics, to rework or reinterpret them as if they were new plays. Richard had wanted to emphasise the modern political play in *Hamlet*, and to this end he chose to eschew the supernatural element. His most controversial decision was to cut the part of Hamlet's father's ghost. The reason for this was that, unlike Shakespeare's audience, we no longer believed in heaven and hell as actual places, nor in tormented spirits trapped between the two. Instead of Hamlet's father's ghost being an outward manifestation visible and audible by whoever was on watch that night, he was to be understood as a projection of Hamlet's fevered mind. Hamlet was possessed by his father's spirit. When his father 'visited' him, his body writhed and contorted as if some alien creature had invaded him and was kicking at his sides. He belched the ghost's words from the pit of his stomach and gasped for air as his own voice recovered enough to answer.

Richard's 'modern play' approach helped ease me into what was my first classical role. Before I discovered John Barton and Cicely Berry (more of them when I deal with the language key), I could think of no other way to approach Ophelia than through her psychology. We had a mere three and a half weeks to rehearse, which meant that if I were lucky I would get about two shots at each scene before the run-throughs and technical rehearsals began. I was timid and still apologetic about taking up rehearsal time, so inevitably I did a lot of my work at home.

The most famous thing about Ophelia is that she goes mad. Richard had given me one major tip as to what he wanted, by telling me what he *didn't* want. He did not want 'mad acting'. I knew what he meant. For Ophelia her mad scene is an ungoverned artless release; for the actress playing her it can be a chance to show off her repertoire of lolling tongues and rolling eyes, in a fey and affecting aria which is anything but artless. That is the paradox of acting mad. The actor is self-conscious in every sense, while the mad person has lost their hold on self.

Generalised mad acting, being unhinged from any centre, leaves the actor floundering in their own embarrassment. The remedy for me was to find a method in Ophelia's madness, so that I could root her actions in her motivations (however insane and disordered), just as I would with any other character I was playing. Before playing Ophelia I had shared with many others the impression that Ophelia was a bit of a colourless part – that is, until she goes mad. I needed to find a unifying scheme that would contain both the 'interesting' mad Ophelia and the 'boring' sane Ophelia.

Suppose Ophelia is happily 'normal' until her lover rejects her and murders her father. Is that necessarily a cue to go mad? After all, Juliet suffered something of the kind when Romeo killed Tybalt, and although the idea tormented her she did not flip. I started to see that the seeds of Ophelia's madness had been sown long before the play started, by the workings of a cold, repressive environment on an already susceptible mind. I preferred this theory to the sudden – madness-through-grief idea which, together with broken hearts and walking spirits, seemed to belong in the theatre of Henry Irving or a Victorian poem.

In the little time available, I scoured the libraries for modern clinical accounts of madness and found much to latch on to in R. D. Laing's *Sanity, Madness and the Family* and *The Divided Self*. I am not concerned here with the pros and cons of Laing's approach; what interested me were his case histories of young schizophrenic women, and the mechanisms by which their families inadvertently contributed to their disorder. A latent schizophrenic tendency need not necessarily develop into madness, but certain triggers might set it off.

Here I found some uncanny Elsinore echoes. They always say Shakespeare can be made to fit any argument, but in this case I suppose it was just further proof that he knew all there was to know about human nature. If he had been directing me, he would no doubt have been impatient with my approach. 'Just say the lines, love,' he might have said. 'I promise it will work.' It was my own lack of imagination that needed to do more. So with Shakespeare, Laing and Virginia Woolf to help me, I built my little theory.

From some of my jottings at the time Family: father Polonius, brother Laertes. Mother is dead and no one mentions her. No known female companion. Only female role model known to be present in her life is Gertrude, who has too many of her own problems to be much help.

Speculation Little experience of love. Duty rather than deep love binds her to her father, and although her brother had been an affectionate companion in childhood, they have been brought up increasingly apart from one another. Her education, such as it is, has been mostly at her father's hands and of a deliberately unworldly nature, while her brother's education was a serious preparation for a public role in life.

Clues in the text   All in the name of loving protection, Laertes undermines Ophelia's trust in Hamlet and 'the trifling of his favour'. 'You must fear,' he tells her. 'Fear it, Ophelia, fear it, my dear sister.' And in case she still hasn't got it, 'Be wary.' Layer upon layer he adds, talking of 'the danger of desire' and her 'too credent ear'. On departing, Laertes charges her to 'Remember well what I have said to you,' and Ophelia replies, ''Tis in my memory locked, and you yourself shall keep the key of it.' Yet the very next minute, when Polonius pounces in with, 'What is't Ophelia he hath said to you?' she replies, 'So please you, something touching the Lord Hamlet,' and within seconds she is spilling it all out. So much for locked-up secrets.

To keep a secret is a means of preserving the self. It is proof to the keeper that they own a private self that cannot be reached. One of Laing's cases 'found it difficult to keep anything to herself because she talked too much and besides she thought people could read her thoughts'.

Further Quotes from R. D. Laing's Patients   One woman spoke of her father, who kept worrying 'that I should be kidnapped or some dreadful thing to happen to me. It's my own fault. He's got no confidence in me at all. I am always going to be led away by some crafty cunning bad man. He has put that into my mind, he has got that impregnated into my brain in some way.'

'I am not supposed to have an opinion because my opinion is bound to be incorrect, you know . . . perhaps my opinion isn't what you call reliable, perhaps in every way I am not reliable. I feel that I have to accept that I am not reliable.'

I know there is a danger in too schematic an approach to acting, particularly Shakespeare, and that I could easily have been carried off course by the sheer fun of theory-building, so I made sure that I took from Laing only what I needed, and relied on Shakespeare and events in the rehearsal room for the rest. The exercise was not about diagnosing Ophelia as a schizophrenic, but about gaining insight into the text. I started to hear the other characters' words from Ophelia's point of view, as traps and ambushes, and as means of controlling her mind.

'To thine own self be true,' Polonius advises Laertes as he sees him off on his travels, while in the same scene he tells Ophelia, 'You do not understand yourself.' Young men should learn to fend for themselves in life's battles, gaining confidence through experience, whereas women must be kept in fear and ignorance of their very natures.

Ophelia submits to another battering from Polonius: 'Do not believe his vows', 'Affection. Pooh. You speak like a green girl.' He asks her, 'Do you believe his tenders as you call them?', and to Ophelia's simple reply, 'I do not know, my lord, what I should think,' he answers, 'Marry, I shall teach you, think yourself a baby.' He does such a good job on her that by the end of the scene Ophelia has promised to reject Hamlet, send back all his letters and never speak to him again.

Other Shakespeare heroines have fought back under like circumstances. Jessica defies Shylock and runs off with Lorenzo. Rosalind, Imogen and Julia risk punishment and banishment in search of true love, but a lifetime of indoctrination, together with a particularly impressionable nature, ensures that Ophelia cannot resist.

From that moment on she puts herself entirely in her father's hands. Having been terrified by an encounter with the seemingly deranged Hamlet, rather than try to talk to him she rushes to her father and blurts out the whole story. Polonius in his turn reports everything back to the King, and all this culminates in the plot to test Hamlet's madness in which Ophelia is quite wittingly used as bait. Guilt, love, duty and, above all, terror confound her. Given this state of affairs, imagine the following exchanges from Ophelia's point of view.

Ophelia offers to return Hamlet's gifts.

HAMLET: I never gave you aught.

OPHELIA: My honoured lord, you know right well you did.

(*Which one of them is going crazy?*)

. . .

HAMLET: Are you honest?

OPHELIA: My lord?

HAMLET: Are you fair?

OPHELIA: What means your lordship?

HAMLET: That if you be honest and fair, your honesty should admit no discourse to your beauty.

OPHELIA: Could beauty, my lord, have better commerce than with honesty?

(*Holding her own pretty well; but then . . .*)

HAMLET: Ay, truly. For the power of beauty will sooner transform honesty from what it is to a bawd than the force of honesty can translate beauty into his likeness. This was sometime a paradox, but now the time gives it proof. I did love you once.

OPHELIA: Indeed, my lord, you made me believe so.

HAMLET: You should not have believed me . . . I loved you not.

OPHELIA: I was the more deceived.

This would be pretty devastating to most of us, but Ophelia is disintegrating fast. I am trying to convey something of the sensation of playing Ophelia, given the story so far.

When Hamlet suddenly springs on Ophelia, 'Where's your father?' the girl who cannot keep a secret feels transparent and replies, 'At home, my lord' a little too quickly. She has blown the cover, and now that Hamlet has seen through the plot, she is powerless to dissociate herself from its cynical perpetrators. She puts up little resistance as Hamlet brutally rejects her, in a scene played out mostly for the ears of her eavesdropping puppetmasters.

When everyone has left the stage, Ophelia gives us her one soliloquy, which ends with, 'O woe is me, to have seen what I have seen, see what I see!' The line has a similar ring to Isabella's in *Measure for Measure*: 'To whom should I complain? Did I tell this who would believe me?' The audience has witnessed the abuse of both women and is on their side, but the women themselves cannot be reached or helped.

They are sealed in the world of the play, with a knowledge which is too dangerous to share. The big difference is that Isabella has a gigantic sense of her self and her integrity, while Ophelia has virtually none. She has depended on Hamlet and her brother and father for what flimsy self-definition she has. The one has just denounced her as a whore, the second is abroad and the third is about to be murdered by the first.

I am not going to start decoding Ophelia's ramblings in the mad scene, because that is a task for each actress who plays her. How much does she know? Did she sleep with Hamlet? These and many other questions are up for grabs. The important thing is to work out your own private coherence and to have a strong intention behind each thing you say. However broken up your story, let each fragment come from a clear image. If there are 'unconscious' tics, let them come from a centred impulse. Inhabit your world, don't demonstrate it.

With a director who is sympathetic to your intentions, any demonstrating can be done for you by the production itself. Out of sheer embarrassment I never disclosed the details of my homework to Richard Eyre, but the tentative sketch which I brought to rehearsals gave him at least enough to go on. He picked up Ophelia's message, however faint, and helped to focus it physically. His greatest gift to me came in the shape of props.

The first was a bundle of Hamlet's letters upon which my grasp weakened as the play progressed. In the first scene I clung to them as if they were my faith in Hamlet, only to surrender them to Polonius as soon as he beckoned me to. In Act Three, Scene One, Polonius placed the letters in my lap like a photographer arranging a picture. He and Claudius have staged the scene, and the letters are Ophelia's props. She hands them to Hamlet, saying, 'My lord, I have remembrances of yours that I have longéd long to redeliver. I pray you now receive them.' As Hamlet departs at the end of the scene, he throws the letters in Ophelia's face and they scatter on the floor. Claudius and Polonius re-emerge from their listening post and discuss the scene they have just witnessed as if Ophelia were not in the room. She, meanwhile, crawls around the floor gathering up the letters as though they were the shards of her life.

The second prop that helped to tell my story was a bundle of blackened twigs. These were a memorable substitute for Ophelia's usual picturesque garlands. This not only added to her delusion but somehow helped to suggest a subversiveness, a sense that she knew something. 'Follow her close. Give her good watch, I pray you,' says Claudius. She is dangerous not just to herself but to the court. When I presented Claudius with a gnarled stick saying, 'Here's fennel for you and columbines,' it was no pretty gift but an accusation.

My performance fell far short of my aims, mainly because I was inexperienced and too inhibited to carry out all that I had planned at home, but I was totally supported by the production. Bill Dudley's set, with its secret panels and *trompe l'oeil* life-sized 'spies' lurking in the corners, together with a soundtrack of indecipherable whisperings, all added to the atmosphere of paranoia, and the chamber scale of the Royal Court suited my implosive rather than explosive version of madness.

But could I have been explosive if I'd wanted to be? That was the next question, put to me (in slightly different terms) by Trevor Nunn, who had seen my Ophelia and was sizing me up for the part of Helena in *All's Well that Ends Well.* He had appreciated the detail of my performance but, as he put it, could I preserve that detail *and* reach the back of the auditorium? (Bear in mind that he was talking main house at Stratford, not the cosy Royal Court.) Luckily for me, Trevor took the risk and over the next decade I joined in the effort to combine intimacy with projection, heightened language with naturalistic speech and verbal dexterity with physical strength that has preoccupied the RSC since it first began.

A Last Word on Psychological Logic

I confess to a weakness for seeing patterns and tidying up ends – a misleading habit when dealing with the human character. In 1997, while preparing to play Anna Petrovna in *Ivanov*, I followed up an introduction to a Russian Jew who was said to be a fount of knowledge on Russian history. I had

dipped into a two-volume tome on the history of the Jews in
Russia, and wanted to back up what I had read with my host's
more hands-on understanding. We met at his house for tea.

HW: I gather that in the 1860s there was a period of
enlightenment which gave the Jews more civil liberties
[Anna Petrovna, or Sara Abramson to use her real name,
would have grown up in that period], but then in the
1880s [the time of the play] there was a backlash, a
tightening up. Why was that?

MY HOST: There need never be a reason for these things.

HW (*gulp*): I see. I am just trying to work out why and how
Ivanov met and married Anna, only to totally reject his
actions later. He loved her once, and is more enlightened
than his provincial neighbours, but even he, when his
deepest rawest nerve is exposed, calls her 'you dirty Jew'.

Nothing from my host.

I suppose it could be because she is dying and everyone
is afraid of death . . .

Nothing.

I'm sure that is why Ivanov hates her. Her illness is an
accusation, a reminder of his guilt. Do you think the
Russians felt guilty about the Jews and that is why they
hated them?

MY HOST: Jews were always the aliens. On the Continent
they were 'revolutionaries'. In Russia they were 'counter-
revolutionaries' . . .

HW (*interrupting*): But . . . that's what I don't understand, because so many of the revolutionary leaders were Jews . . .

MY HOST (*with a not unkind laugh*): Again you are looking
for a reason. There never had to be a reason to hate the
Jews.

11

The Language Key

Beyond the Barrier

Our language is not really our own. It is an established tradition, a club we are forced to join in infancy and whose rules we agree to obey. It gives us a miraculous instrument whereby we can say a simple word like 'sun' and instantly transmit to someone else the idea of an inconceivably hot and unimaginably distant sphere of gases. If we can make language our own, we can bend it to suit our needs and even coin new words, but when language feels like 'theirs', it becomes a gag on the soul.

In some ways we are spoilt in Britain, in that our native language is also the predominant language in world culture. But this has been part bane, part boon to the British theatre. We have overrelied on 'our' words and often neglected the rest of our theatrical armoury. Robert Lepage, one of the world's greatest directors, has said that as a francophone being brought up in English-dominated Canada he saw language as an obstacle. In his case that 'obstacle' turned into a blessing, since his invention was forced to swim round it, exploring every other theatrical tool known to man or machine (and then some).

A great way to break the language barrier and stretch one's physical invention is an exercise I remember from LAMDA known as 'Gibberish'. This was the practice of substituting what was in the script with our own gobbledegook. The purpose was to release us from the constrictions of another person's words, to bypass 'meaning' and send us straight to a creative source we might not know we had. With Gibberish we could burst our civilised seams and see what else was there. Who were we when released from the conditioning shackles of our hereditary patterns of speech?

At LAMDA we invented fabulous hybrid languages (mostly based on soundtracks from Swedish, Russian or Japanese movies) which broke the mould of our familiar accents and tones. We rediscovered the infantile pleasure in making noises and letting them reverberate to the ends of our toes. But there came a moment when we wanted more. Gibberish had tapped a core energy, but because we could not really communicate we could not develop. We could get a rough idea across, but not the sophistications of a character's mind. We might have loved someone and wanted to describe that love. It may have been 'like a red red rose that's newly sprung in June', or have felt like 'a ride on a roller-coaster', but all we could say was *'Grosh roobly broo.'* We grew as frustrated as two-year olds. We had refound the *need* for words.

Help from the Bard

A false polarisation has developed between verbal and visual theatre. The best theatre thrives on a marriage of language and spectacle. Even Lepage needs words, and he and his cast work multilingual wonders with them. When it comes to Shakespeare, however, Lepage seems happier visually paraphrasing the ideas behind the words than working through the words themselves. Unfortunately, this is a pervasive trend among directors lacking Lepage's genius or his 'excuse'. These directors are usually perfectly at home with Shakespeare's language themselves, but patronise their audience with generalised visual concepts as a substitute for words. They pander to the audience's fear of language and thereby perpetuate it.

Shakespeare is not a bitter pill that must be sugared with fun and excitement. He is the master of excitement himself, but how are we ever to know that if we never get to taste the undoctored substance?

In my own case, a combination of hating the sound of my voice and not having had any particularly inspiring English teacher at school (the reason why many a classical actor began) made me a late developer on the Shakespeare-loving front. I was thirty before I came across Cicely Berry or John Barton.

These two people, with their combined and very different talents, embodied the guiding principle of the RSC (and this has nothing to do with that horrid idea of a house style). Cicely Berry, as voice director of the company, taught me not to listen to my voice but to feel it. She taught me that meaning is not just locked up in the literal translation of a phrase but lies in the rhythm, the physical sensation, the multifarious associations and echoes set up by a word which happen somewhere in our gut.

John Barton can be the classic absent-minded professor in many areas of his life, but in his work on Shakespeare he is that rare thing, a down-to-earth scholar. Of all sages he is the least dogmatic. He teaches us how to look for Shakespeare's 'hidden stage directions', because he recognises that what matters is how the language works dramatically. Textual analysis is fine and fascinating, but in the end what matters to the actor is, 'What out of all this is *playable?*'

That is not to say that Barton encourages shirking. Heightened language demands a huge leap and if we treat it like naturalistic speech, we jump short and fall flat on our faces. Take, for example, Cleopatra's line in her speech immediately following Antony's death: 'It were for me to throw my sceptre at the injurious gods; to tell them that this world did equal theirs till they had stol'n our jewel.' Cleopatra probably thinks of the gods as slightly senior cousins not worthy of their privileges. If we duck beneath the line or mentally paraphrase it to 'I'm jolly upset', we not only look idiotic, we also cheat the audience, let alone Cleopatra. The task is vocally and emotionally to match the degree of Cleopatra's grief (and that doesn't mean shouting).

So how do we try to match it? You can see that questions like, 'When have I felt like that?' or, 'What would I do if I were Empress of Egypt and my great love died in my arms?' are inadequate to the task. For a start, in naturalistic terms, most of us would simply howl. Words would not come easily to mind. But in a Shakespeare play you have to accept that the characters need to speak. Words can soothe grief, exorcise terrors, inspire armies, woo lovers or fend off madness. If you find the need behind Cleopatra's speech and see how the words work on her/you, the scene starts to unlock.

I have picked this sentence almost at random, knowing that anywhere in the canon I could find examples of how Shakespeare gives us not only the task but also the tools to fulfil it. But although I have never played the part, and although other speeches might have better illustrations, I will stick to this speech to make some general observations about character and language.

> No more, but e'en a woman, and commanded
> By such poor passion as the maid that milks
> And does the meanest chares. It were for me
> To throw my sceptre at the injurious gods;
> To tell them that this world did equal theirs
> Till they had stol'n our jewel. All's but nought;
> Patience is sottish, and impatience does
> Become a dog that's mad. Then is it sin
> To rush into the secret house of death,
> Ere death dare come to us? How do you, women?
> What, what! good cheer! Why, how now, Charmian!
> My noble girls! Ah, women, women, look,
> Our lamp is spent, it's out!

Suppose I were preparing to play the part and this was my first encounter with the speech. First, I would read it quietly to myself for the gist of meaning, then I would read it again and again, sometimes out loud, sometimes not, tossing it between my lips and my inner ear for any intelligence I can gather from the rhythm. Then I might play about with various games and exercises I have gleaned over the years. For instance, I would pencil in the iambic pentameter stress (i.e. di dum, di dum, di dum, di dum, di dum) and examine where the speech fits and where it breaks the meter. Why does it break? What effect does the break in rhythm have? This speech happens to fit the iambic meter pretty completely apart from two instances: 'All's but nought' and later 'Why, how now, Charmian' (that is, if you follow the most natural speaking inflection). For me, the first has the effect of crashing Cleopatra's system, as though she has run out of adequate imagery and resorts to the most simple statement of despair. The second break gives a staccato feeling of sudden waking to her women's distress, a gear shift from her imperial solo grief to a more tenderly shared one. The woman of 'infinite variety' can switch direction on a postage stamp.

Then I might play 'Find the Verb'. Quite often when you get in a muddle with a Shakespeare speech, when every word is important and you feel tempted to bash each one on the head, the solution is to stress the verb. The verb is the active word, the arrow that pulls everything else along in its wake. In fact, this speech is not complicated in that way, but it still might reveal something if I stress the verbs throughout: 'milks', 'does', 'throw', 'tell', 'equal', 'stol'n', 'become', 'rush', 'dare'. We actors often make the mistake of burying the verb, leaving a senseless sentence. So, in a fit of heartfelt passion, we might say, *'It were f' me t' throw my sceptre at the injurious GODS!!'* Sorry? Come again.

Next I might pick out any onomatopoeic words, any alliteration or assonance. These can be clues to a character's state, and they help bounce the rhythm along or momentarily hitch it up. I might use the 'th' in 'throw' as a plosive launch pad, and then use the 'r' to rev up to the long open 'o' which will carry Cleopatra's anger to the stars. I might toy with the 'joo' of 'injurious', the strange 'kw' in 'equal', the alliterative 'poor passion', 'No more but e'en a woman', the 'sh' in 'patience' and in 'sottish', the subversive 's' in 'sin' and 'secret', and see what they give me. (*Warning:* Too much luxuriating in sound for sound's sake leads to hammy acting, but as long as the words remain connected to an emotional centre, actors can be as operatic as they dare.)

Then I might play with cadences and rhythms. I would note where there are half-lines – that is to say where a line has a full stop in the middle and a new idea is kicked off half-way through: 'And does the meanest chares. It were for me', 'Till they had stol'n our jewel. All's but nought', 'Become a dog that's mad. Then is it sin', 'Ere death dare come to us? How do you, women?', and so on. This kind of breaking up of the sense as it is spread over the rhythm also requires the actor to hold on to that sense, suspending it over the edge of the line, letting it rest only at the full-stop.

In breathing and vocal terms this is known as 'carrying the energy through to the end of the sentence', which technically entails keeping your breath going strong till the last word.

Another common acting fault is to get so enthusiastic at the beginning of a sentence that you run out of steam by the end. Thus we get the opposite rendition of the line: '*It were for me to THROW MY SCEPTRE at the injurious gods.*' Such dying cadences, repeated often enough, are as good as a lullaby to an audience.

A major acting trap is to fix on a generalised emotion for a speech or even a scene and then get stuck on one note. If you attend to the details in the language and listen to the switches in rhythm, you will find that Cleopatra's grief comes in waves, each prompted and altered by the one that came before. Every actor will sense the speech differently, but for me, sounding it out at this early stage, there is a growing swell of anger building under the first three lines; then a sudden sharp buffet into the next thought, a large and thundering wave this one, which smoothes to a gentle reminder of who that stol'n jewel was. A black space. Then using words to clamber back out of the trough, an articulate fury against the virtue of patience, under which her own impatience is racing to reach the hard monosyllabic 'dog that's mad'.

One of Cicely Berry's exercises is to walk around the room as you do a speech and change direction at each punctuation mark. It is a great way of finding the specific impulse behind each thought and avoiding a generalised emotional wash. Don't take my word for it, try it. Start walking: 'No more, but e'en a woman,' (*about turn*) 'and commanded by such poor passion as the maid that milks and does the meanest chares.' (*Stop. Then set off in another direction with*) 'It were for me to throw my sceptre at the injurious gods;' (*sharp turn and on . . .*).

Another good game is to get someone else to heckle you as it were. They do this by calling out 'What?' intermittently throughout the delivery of the speech. For example:

ACTOR: By such poor passion as the maid that milks

HECKLER: The maid that *what's?*

ACTOR: The maid that milks And does the meanest chares.

HECKLER: Meanest *what?* Patience is *what?* Become a *what* that's mad? Ere *what* dare come to us?

ACTOR: Ere *death* dare come ...

HECKLER: Ere death *what* come ...

ACTOR: DA-ARE!!!

By this device, no word is taken for granted, and each particular image has to be found. The man who was the pivot of all the women's lives is a 'lamp' that is 'spent'. Death is a 'secret house'. When Cleopatra chides herself for lacking the passion commensurate with the crime of Antony's death, she surprisingly compares herself to a milkmaid.

Almost the most difficult acting problem of all is to allow a character to reach an unusual image in the blink of a thought. The momentum of the verse gives you no time to grope and yet if the image seems to come too easily it ceases to be believable. There are no easy solutions to this. The reason why your character needs to speak at that moment, the thoughts and images behind the words, and the speed with which they arrive at them must all be planted, absorbed and learned with the lines. That is why the often-asked question, 'How do you learn your lines?' is so gob-smackingly hard to answer.

To get back to John Barton's pragmatism, Shakespeare's text is full of acting aids which help the actors to learn their lines. It is an advantage that a line has a memorable metre, that there are distinctive metaphors and pictures to hang on to, and that, having noted an alliterative trick, you at least know that the word you are searching for begins with V.

There are many ways of learning lines and they are usually used in combination. Besides all the emotional and intellectual connections I have mentioned elsewhere, we use our visual memory (for images or the shape of a speech on the page), our musical memory (for cadence and rhythm), our physical memory (often our lips know the words, just as a dancer's feet or a pianist's fingers know what to do next) and our kinetic memory (a thought is linked with a move: e.g. when I am by the door I confess to the murder, when I cross to the window I declare my love for the victim).

For many actors, including myself, verse is much easier to learn than prosaic naturalistic speech. For one thing, conversational English gives us so many interchangeable alternatives.

Is it 'Do come in and sit down', or 'Please come in and take a seat', or 'Come in, won't you, and have a seat'? Not that Shakespeare does not frequently use everyday speech. With some roles, I have gone through the text highlighting the very naturalistic phrases to distinguish them from the heightened poetry. This was especially helpful with *All's Well that Ends Well* and in *Cymbeline*, where Shakespeare's style dots about. One minute a character is talking in dense conceits, the next they are asking what time it is. The actor should note those moments and emphasise them rather than iron them out. The one style offsets the other. It is a wonderful way of jolting the audience's ears and making them listen freshly.

As with any language which starts off foreign and becomes familiar with practice, after a few years at the RSC I could say, 'Go to, thou art a knave' or, 'Nay verily I trow' as if they were the most natural phrases in the world (though it was important to keep in mind that an audience takes a while to attune). At the other end of the scale there are passages of such ambiguity that they have baffled the best brains in history. An actor might be able to intuit the many layers of meaning, but we can only actually play one at a time. Our best bet is to go for the most actable one, say it with conviction and let all the other meanings hover in the air for the audience to work out.

When a character in Shakespeare switches from verse to prose or vice versa, it is an indication of a change of gear. The actor observes this and then rationalises the change in terms of the character's intention. In altering the form, the character takes charge of the scene at that point. It is fascinating to dissect a scene in terms of where the power sits at a given point, and how it is tossed back and forth between the characters.

It is the character who chooses whether or not to rhyme. When Romeo and Juliet first meet they consciously form a sonnet together. The audience will not be aware that the fourteen lines between lines 91 and 104 in Act I, Scene v, make up a perfect sonnet, but the two actors (provided that they have been lucky enough to have John Barton point it out) can use this secret and 'spontaneous' game to add an extra frisson to the scene.

I have said elsewhere that speeches are actions. When Macbeth persuades the murderers to kill Banquo (Act Three, Scene One), he manipulates them with a politician's skill, repeating to them their own grievances and planting the idea that Banquo is to blame for them. He rubs salt in their wounds and then works on their male pride to goad them to revenge. No weapons or physical coercion are needed, just propaganda and verbal blackmail.

Psychological logic will not unlock a scene like the wooing of Lady Anne by Richard III. It surprises Richard himself ('Was ever woman in this humour wooed?'). He is repulsive to her and her arch enemy, and yet there is a sexual charge in their verbal exchange. Richard picks up her spark, converts it and plays it back at her. He does it with the skill of a horse-breaker, and by the end of the scene, against her will and reason, she is tamed. By all means read the footnotes, but the only way to really understand the scene is to play it.

Evolutions

Look up 'character' in an etymological dictionary and you will see that it derives from various ancient words meaning to cut into grooves or engrave, from the ancient Greek word *kharakter* – a marking instrument, hence a graphic symbol, hence an attribute, a distinctive mark. The word as it is now applied to human qualities, mannerisms, personality and make-up evolved later.

Certainly the word 'character' in the sense of personality in a play did not exist in Shakespeare's day. He did not write, *'Enter Ophelia, late teens: a nervous blonde girl with suicidal tendencies.'* There was plot in which the actor played his or her part, and there was language which was nearer to action than it is now. For this reason an actress is less likely to be cast as Ophelia because she is the right age or because she looks Danish than because of her ability to work through language.

What came naturally to the Elizabethan player has become a specialised discipline to the modern actor. Most modern works require us to speak as we would in real life, often using words to water down or obscure our real meaning. In those cases, the actor's main task is to tap the more dramatic subtext behind the words. But there are also plenty of modern dramatists whose work is unlocked with the language key. Howard Barker, for example, has often been likened to the Jacobean playwrights. Through his extra-ordinary imagery he creates the atmosphere, even the smell, of another world. His language exposes the characters' viscera, so there is no need for a subtext. To play Barker, the actor needs all the imagination, vocal dexterity and physical energy that apply to any seventeenth-century play.

In Shakespeare's day the audience were tuned in to heightened language. It was part of the thrill. For them a soliloquy did not hold up the action, it *was* the action at that moment. For social, economic and historical reasons too complex to go into, classical theatre has become élitist. Large chunks of our potential audience are alienated by 'highbrow' language. But there is nothing intrinsically highbrow about Shakespeare. With more practice and less prejudice, anyone can get his message. Short-sighted education policies and exclusive ticket prices are not the actor's responsibility, but making Shakespeare clear and exciting for those that do get past those blocks is well within our brief.

The Pen is Mightier

In Elizabethan England, Shakespeare and his contempor-aries were known as poets, and that did not mean anything flowery or high-faluting. Get out that etymological diction-ary again. You will see that the word 'poet' came from the Greek *poiein*, to make or construct, and it developed to contain ideas of arranging, collecting and the creative act. Shakespeare chose his material and fashioned it well.

So trust his words; they will do most of the job for you. There is a joke about the actor who declares himself to be brimful of feeling 'if only all these words weren't in the way'. A Shakespeare speech is not a wall of obstruction, it is a gift. Suppose I am playing Juliet in the scene when she hears that Romeo has killed her cousin Tybalt. What amount of emoting could match, 'O serpent heart, hid with a flow'ring face! Did ever dragon keep so fair a cave?'? If my words are muffled with sobs, I deprive myself of the means of truly moving the audience. They will gather that I am in a bit of a state but they are unlikely to feel involved. It is not the actor's job to feel, but to make the audience feel, and in this case the words will do it.

The language will always be bigger than me, so to 'describe' my character in terms of a type is to reduce her. If I decide, for example, that Portia is a poor little rich girl or a spoilt racist, I limit her. I have then to stick to my generalisation all evening in order to demonstrate my theory. Any inconsistencies that do not fit my picture have to be ironed out. My character becomes predictable and the play is deadened.

If, however, I follow Shakespeare's score, I will find words that jolt the ear just when it has been most lulled. I will find images so unexpected that they force the imagination beyond the bounds of logic and comfortable reason. I will find rhythms which work at such a subliminal level that all I have to do is follow them and they will move the audience far more than I could do by emoting sighs and tears. All this because Shakespeare the poet knew a thing or two about making plays.

12

The Personality Key

'Crack me a filbert, Edward. I've had none.'
'Stab him! . . . Now! Stab him!'
'I can't be late. Am I late? . . . I've been waiting all day to escape.'

The above is a random selection of first lines of characters I have played. Given just these lines and no other data, something about the language and the rhythm gives you an instant sense of who is speaking. The playwright seems to have heard the character's voice and trapped it on paper, rather like Mozart is said to have done with his music, and the performer feels an instant trust. But what about those times when no such specific work has been done by the writer, when you are faced with a part that could be any old doctor, any old neighbour, any old girlfriend? In these cases the actor must invent a person out of nowhere. When combing the script yields few clues as to character, it is time to take the law into your own hands and impose a character upon it. In such cases the personality key is a useful last resort.

Some actors are already blessed with bags of personality and have a head start in such situations. They arrive at the read-through with a ready-made full-bodied character with which to enrich an otherwise nondescript role. Their personality may just be an accident of birth, but it is far more likely that it has been honed and polished over years. They have taken stock of their attributes and limitations and created a useful type out of these raw materials. This type is what they tout on the casting market, and with luck and some creative casting directors on their side, they can have a long and successful career. However, if like me your sense of your outer self is less definite, you are more likely to use your mimetic skills to borrow a personality from somebody else.

When I talk about personality I do not necessarily mean anything flamboyant, I am talking more about persona, the thing one presents to the world. The problem with an underwritten or non-specified character is one of arbitrariness. There are too many possibilities. You have some sketchy data about your character, you know how old they are, where they live, with whom, what they do for a living and even a bit about their aims, but how do they behave? Talk? Dress? They could be just about anyone. You try out some haphazard choices in rehearsal. You try out this accent and that, you imitate an acquaintance or, more dangerously, another actor who might better fit the bill. Suddenly you decide your character keeps bees, or has a secret fetish, anything to define them and pick them out from a generalised slur. This shilly-shallying can continue right up to the last moment and one is galvanised into some kind of decision only by the shock of being set before an audience.

Certain actors would find all of this quite incomprehensible. 'Just be yourself,' they would say. 'After all, they cast you in the part.' 'But I live with myself all day, why would I want to play me at night?' 'Well, you do anyway whether you like it or not,' the actor persists. 'I know that, but still . . .' I tail off. Neither of us is right or wrong, we are just different kinds of actor. There are actors who never change their image if they can help it, not even the parting in their hair. They are minimalists who have whittled their act down to the essential and because it works they see no reason to tinker with it. They know who they are and they know what their public wants.

To take a random example, Robert Morley presumably knew when he was cast in a role that roughly the usual was expected of him. With superb command over his own 'act', he could subtly vary the slant from endearingly oddball, via pompous to sinister, or whatever version of 'himself' the piece required, but the mould was essentially the same.

We are all a mass of contradictions, but some performers have managed to highlight certain aspects of themselves and suppress others to produce a consistent public persona. For my own part, I have been described on various occasions as wet, imperious, affable, eccentric, remote, vulnerable, clumsy, graceful, ugly and occasionally – with good lighting and a following wind – beautiful. I recognise that I can be a 'bit' of all of these things, but I have never made up my mind which particular strands of this ravelled muddle to cultivate. For this reason, when I am confronted by a part with 'Personality Required' stamped all over it, I am at a bit of a loss.

Actors like me hope to add up to more than the sum of our parts.

Personalities versus Chameleons

One often hears people complain that such-and-such an actor 'is always the same', as though that meant they were a lesser performer than the chameleon type who is 'different every time', but who can say which type of acting requires the more skill or affords the viewer the deeper insights into human nature? Playing yourself is harder than it looks.

Most actors want to hide in some way. Grabbing at labels for the sake of argument, let us say that the chameleons dodge recognition by altering their act each time, while the personalities hide behind a more consistent mask. It may be a What-I-would-like-to-be-seen-as mask, or a Side-of-me-that-I-daren't-live-out-for-real mask, but whichever the case the personality actor allows us to *think* we know them. 'Good old John Wayne,' we say, as though he were our buddy. The chameleon, on the other hand, hates to be so pinned down. Being a chameleon is not the quickest route to fame (casting directors find you hard to place and you are not easily spotted in the street), but it has many compensations, variety of work and a truly private private-life being the chief ones.

Chameleons are unhappy when called upon to be themselves in public; they are tongue-tied if asked to speak impromptu and hate the idea of opening fêtes. A chameleon cannot be told, 'Go on, do that thing you do.' In these situations actors with a familiar persona are better off. The audience greet them like old friends. They laugh at their jokes before they have reached the punchline.

As I have said before, I do not think one category of actor is better than the other – there are great actors and poor actors in both camps – and I don't think one can necessarily choose to be one or the other – there are extroverts and introverts in every walk of life. I have seen some top-notch performances given by bank managers, bus conductors, teachers and head waiters, while many (I would even say most) actors prefer to go about their business unnoticed. Sit in any waiting room or train carriage, join any crowd or queue, there may well be an actor in your midst. You would not know they were an actor and that is just the way they want it.

Using What You Have for Free

Even the most chameleon of actors is not the blank page that they would like to be. We all have our mannerisms and the physique that we have been dealt with. As we grow older, life's biffs and our own negligence stamp our bodies with various quirks – a slumped shoulder here, a pot-belly there. As we get older still, our necks shrink and our knees buckle – in short, our raw materials change.

Only a very few physical traits are inescapable or undisguisable. Short of painful surgery, nothing much can alter the length of one's legs, the set of one's chin or the colour of one's eyes. Even if I were to scrape away every other defining trait, my height, my square shoulders and my brown eyes would add up to something in other people's eyes, whether I like it or not. As one director put it, 'You have certain qualities for free, so concentrate on the things that don't come so easily.'

We have the choice to neutralise or emphasise our idiosyncrasies. An actor might make a fortune trading on his silly-ass weak chin, or he could broaden his range by growing a beard. A naturally burly actor might soften his tones and lighten his movements to avoid being typecast as a thug. With experience we learn more and more about the messages which our physical presence sends out to an audience. We can work with them or against them, but we cannot pretend they're not there.

Many directors (especially film directors) are nervous of this kind of self-awareness in an actor. We all have areas of innocence about ourselves and it is that territory which the camera can exploit. Some actors have totally lost that innocence and replaced it with technique. Their seeming spontaneity has been mapped out to the last nose twitch. It is a dangerous game, because only a handful of actors are skilful enough to fool the audience all of the time; besides, it can be a very short step between useful self-awareness and vain self-regard.

Getting to know how you come over can help you take criticism and save a lot of time. I remember a director complaining that a character I was playing looked miserable all the time. 'She is engaged to be married, for God's sake!' I had been peacefully thinking my character's thoughts, trusting that if I felt content I would look content, and to be so wildly misread was bewildering and hurtful. Thrashing around trying to understand the director and arguing, 'But I'm perfectly *happy!*' and, 'When exactly do *you mean?*' took up valuable time and didn't solve much.

Long since that occasion, I have come to terms with the fact that my face in repose tends to look sad or severe, and I try to counteract the downward tug of my mouth if and when necessary. Nowadays if a director criticises me for looking glum I can take it on the chin, as it were. I know what to do about it and am positively grateful for the hint.

The Personality Trap

I have recently arrived at a bit of a milestone. I have found a workable 'personality' which is near-ish to my own and which I am tentatively happy with. Out of the blue I was cast in a comedy series called *Unfinished Business*, and although I don't think the writers, Laurence Marks and Maurice Gran, knew me before writing it, the character (Amy) and I fit quite well together. This does not mean that we are like one another, that we would react the same way to events or that our lives are in any way similar – in fact, they are pretty much opposites – but to play Amy, I could use something akin to my own manner, rhythm, style and quite a lot of my own sense of humour. What is more, I enjoyed it, and believe me that is pretty unusual for someone of my chameleon tendencies. Maybe it's a kind of maturity, a belated coming to terms with myself. Still, I don't want it to become a habit or anything like that.

I was fortunate that the writers had given Amy a psychological roundedness which meant that I did not have to rely on personality to get me through. In a more flimsily written sitcom, where there is more sit. than com. and definitely more sit. than character, the personality key may be the actor's only lifeline. Likewise an actor who can bring a consistent well-loved personality to the latest indifferently written TV cop, vet or doctor will be welcomed with open arms. It is their flesh and blood that keeps the viewers viewing and the producers will milk them dry.

When one series runs out of steam, another is written as a vehicle for their talents. The actor becomes so identified with their character that the fans cannot tell where one begins and the other ends. I know of many successful TV stars who feel imprisoned in their mould and long to break out. In real life we outgrow our own images and projections and move on, so why shouldn't the actor do the same?

There are actors with such big personalities that they obliterate the part. The audience come out raving about their performance, but have not really seen the play. If the play is a much-performed classic, the actor might come up with a gimmick to distinguish their interpretation from those that have gone before. The gimmick gets the show talked about – 'Have you seen the Tattooed Macbeth or the Wheelchair Hamlet?' – and gives the critics a hook on which to hang their review. The gimmick goes down in history, sure, but what else do you remember?

There are parts which demand some unique personality ingredient, not because they are inadequately written or need a new angle, but in order to justify the effect they have on other characters and thereby the plot itself. If you cannot easily find these ingredients within yourself, go out and beg, borrow or steal them.

A Useful Game

You may know this one. You need a group of people who are familiar with one another and share a circle of friends and acquaintances. Someone (Player A) thinks of a person not present in the group, but whom everyone knows on about the same level (it is important that no one picks a close relative or partner, as it puts the game on an unequal footing). The object of the game is for the rest of the group to discover who Player A is thinking of, and they do this by asking a specific kind of question. For example:

'If your person were a country, which one would they be?'

'If your person were a musical instrument, which one would they be?'

'If your person were a kind of weather, which would they be?' ... which colour, which item of clothing, which meal, which architectural style, which household gadget, etc., etc.

The important point is not to confuse, 'Which painter would they be?' with 'Which painter do they most look like?' If the person always wears black leather, that does not necessarily mean that they would be the colour black, or be a thatched cottage just because they live in one. Some people are more consistent than others, but on the whole one gets extraordinary composites: for example, someone might be strawberries, Africa, a tepee, a Lotus Elan, Mickey Mouse and a Fabergé egg. So unique is this combination that if the game is played well, the group will end up in no doubt about the person's identity. This game is an antidote to the pronouncements of all those advertising executives, politicians, statisticians and so on who categorize people in terms of income bands and age groups, so as to make neat assumptions about their habits: band A buys brand X, type B votes for the Y party, age group C likes this sort of holiday ... Real people do not go quietly into their boxes, thank God.

Skinner's Voice

One of the most surprising bits of casting to come my way was the part of Skinner, the lesbian witch in Howard Barker's *The Castle*. The play was set in a fictitious early-medieval England, where the women in the community, led by Skinner, have established their own political system while their menfolk were away at the Crusades. When the men return, Skinner's world collapses. Her lover, Arm, returns to her husband, and the male principle is reinstated in the shape of a huge 'defensive' castle. Skinner murders the chief builder, is tried and then sentenced to walk the land with his rotting corpse strapped to her body. Love and rage buoy her up and she survives to become a worshipped icon and elected leader of the new order.

It was an enormous part and it required an enormous presence. Skinner was a charismatic leader (and I mean charismatic and definitely not charming). She was rough-hewn, fanatical and uncompromising. So why was I cast? I knew I had not been first choice for the part, and probably not even twelfth (one seldom is, and one shouldn't worry about it); the point was that I was going to have to play it, so how was I to reach her?

Skinner was part fish-wife, part priestess, part Amazon, so it was not much use going down the Who-do-I-know-who's-like-her? path. As I have indicated earlier, the most fruitful approach to Barker is through his language. Skinner's language was a strange mixture of raw poetry, gritty vernacular and subversive wit. I could hear her voice in my head. It had a gruff energy and a quality that struck terror into the soul. I opened my mouth to speak and Skinner evaporated. I had to find her voice.

Fortunately *The Castle* was an RSC production, so Cicely Berry was around to help me. I also had classes with a singing teacher to help lower my range. As unfamiliar sounds started to emerge from the pit of me, I felt a glimmer of belief and an embryonic Skinner-Harriet started to form.

So I arrived at Skinner's 'personality' through her voice. It led me to her rampaging wildness, to her self-mockery and finally to the pain sitting at the heart of her. To develop her qualities, I had had to override or blank out my own, but might that in itself be a link? Might not Skinner have had to reshape herself in order to carry through her task? Gentleness must be eliminated and ferocity must rule. Having created her own monster, she then could not put it back in the box. She has insight into this. When the keys to the castle are offered to her at the end, she at first refuses them, saying, 'I can't be kind. How I have wanted to be kind. But lost all feeling for it . . . No. (*She tosses the key down.*) I shall be too cruel.'

One run-through near to opening night, Skinner fell into place. When we had finished, Howard admitted his surprise. 'Where do you get it from?' he asked. 'Where do you get it from?' was all I could reply. Those are the great moments for an actor, when a character takes shape almost in spite of you, and you don't know how they got there.

It is alarming to meet the potential murderess in oneself, but I hope I have put her to bed till another such part comes along. Somehow the 'stranger' you first met becomes an extension of yourself that you did not know was there, moving and speaking in a way that is and is not you, even laughing with a laugh that is not quite your own. The new persona cannot be uncreated. You mined her from a deep place and now she is nearer the surface. You may never act her out again, but she remains lurking somewhere there, at the end of a phone line as it were, waiting for your call.

Icons and the Anonymity Paradox

From our most primitive days, human beings have needed to project their feelings on to public figures. High priests, witch doctors, kings and fools have all served this function in their time. We endow these people with wisdom, glamour and the power to destroy or create, whether they possess these things or not. They do not need to *be* the real thing, but their image must be watertight enough to make us *believe* they are. The pill and the placebo work equally well.

The latest evolutionary branch of this trend is in the cinema, which has spawned an entire twentieth-century panoply of icons, and catered for every shift in public taste from Rudolph Valentino to Woody Allen. Some are one-offs who just happen to click with the feeling of the day; others represent a universal type which is eternally in demand – the strong man, the beautiful woman, the ugly ogre, the wicked lady, the funny fat man.

Even icons alter with age. A gap appears where their younger selves once were, and even before the legend is dead the search for a replacement is on. If Hollywood cannot find 'the next Audrey Hepburn' or 'the next Cary Grant', it will try to create them, not realising that Audrey Hepburn cannot be

cloned. Of course, there was plenty of reinventing and pack-
aging involved in the creation of a Garbo or a James Dean,
but they weren't made up from scratch, the raw material was
pretty remarkable in the first place.

The trouble starts when the star wants a change of vehicle
but the public or the studio heads (which is chicken, which is
egg?) will not allow it. The fans don't want Clint Eastwood to
be a rapist or Goldie Hawn to be a bitch. It reminds them
that their beloved star is an actor and not a family friend, that
the persona they fell in love with does not in fact exist. Some
actors give in to the audience's demands and settle for the
power and healthy bank balance their popularity brings, but
for others even these compensations begin to pall. If they are
not to become bored, boring and bitter, they must break out
and risk losing their fans.

My view is that the audience should not be given in to all
the time. The market does not always know what it wants.
The greatest movies and movie stars have broken new
ground, providing us with things we never knew we liked.
The logical consequence of a totally market-led movie industry is that the whole world has to watch what the largest
demographic group of people want to watch. At the moment
it is American teens, and every cinemagoer in the world is
saddled with whatever their taste decrees.

The Hollywood-led market relies on the familiarity and
consequent bankability of the star. The star's name
guarantees a predictable range of performance. We know
whether he/she will be a goodie or a baddie, and the presence
of a star of each sex makes a romantic connection between
the two an almost one hundred per cent certainty (never
mind that the male star is in his sixties and the female is
thirty-three). Even the most versatile screen actor has a finite
package of mannerisms and over-exposure soon exhausts
them. There can be few surprises.

But what about those foreign subtitled films we see and
come out from reeling with admiration? It was not the
actors' names that attracted us to that Polish or French or
Japanese film. Hearsay or good reviews or the director's
reputation made us go and see it. We swear that the actors
were the best we have ever seen, and indeed they may simply

be much better than the stars we are familiar with, but couldn't a lot of their effect on us be down to the fact that we don't know them? This anonymity frees us to believe in them as the characters, to enter into and be changed by the story of the film. We completely forget they are acting.

Most of us don't bother to catch their names when the credits roll. We probably wouldn't remember them even if we could pronounce them. If we do ever see one of them again, we may have a glimmer of recognition, but (presuming the film is good) we will quickly be led into another reality and immersed in it.

That is the paradox. Popularity/familiarity can be the greatest obstacle to an actor's power to conjure and to change.

Naturalism ad Absurdum

Someone recently commented that as the characters in TV soaps are so convincing that their antics can hit the front pages of the tabloids, and we think of them as friends, how come people in Albert Square never watch *EastEnders?*

You Can't Beat the Real McCoy (*I Hope*)

Soon actors will not be needed, they say. It will all be done by computers. We will be able to watch virtual Humphrey Bogarts and hear Maria Callas's virtual voice till the cows come home. In our own homes we will be able to team Madonna with Clark Gable, make them walk on water and put words in their mouths. Terrific fun, but in the end what is the point? Haven't they understood that the closer the attempt at virtual reality, the further the real thing recedes? Where is Bogart's mind or Callas's passion? Computers may be a threat to bionic actors – those walking, talking special effects who are hired for their steely torsos and their ability to somersault off blazing buildings – but a virtual Bogart who doesn't choose his words and is not really *there* behind the eyes? I don't think it will ever catch on.

13

The Biographical Key

The biographical key is not really a key in itself, because in order to play the part of a real person, famous or not, alive or dead, you will have to try all the above-mentioned keys. Portraits, photographs and film archive footage of your 'subject', recordings of their voice, copying their clothes (or even perhaps trying on the real thing), writing with their pen, sitting in their chair, using false teeth to simulate the set of their mouth, all these will help you work from the outside in. Reading their diaries and letters, meeting their loved ones or, for those longer dead, visiting their birthplace or retracing their journeys, all these can probe under their skin. With the language key, you might latch on to some characteristic turn of phrase in their letters or diaries which suddenly brings the whole person into being. And in the case of the personality key, how much work you have left to do depends on how well you have been teamed with your subject.

As you research your character and retrace the playwright's steps, you will no doubt go off on detours and form opinions of your own, but guard against falling in love with your subject, and keep judgement at bay for as long as you can. If you do end up with a bias, is it compatible with the playwright's? If you think that Attila the Hun was maligned, you had better make sure you can get that across within the role as written, otherwise forget it. What is the style of the piece? Docu-drama? Brechtian musical? Eisenstein expressionism? As I said earlier, it is folly to work against the context in which your character is framed.

There is a breed of biographer who is always researching and never writes the book. They seem to live life through the person they are studying, almost substituting this vicarious life for their own. They can be very possessive of their subject and will brook no criticism. I came across one such, and it struck me that for all the mountain of facts he had gathered about his chosen alter ego, for all his assumed intimacy with the minutiae of his life, he was unable to communicate his enthusiasm. He could not make that other life light up for me. There was a lesson somewhere there. When do you ever know enough about someone to write the book or play the part? The answer is you cannot. At some point you have to lower your sights and decide which bit of their story you need to tell. Drama is not about facts so much as ideas. We are only really interested in another life for what it can tell us about ourselves.

So much of the actor's approach depends on their recognising the purpose behind the work – why the story is being told. For example, *Amadeus is* not so much a portrait of Mozart as the anatomy of an also-ran. It is Salieri who engages the audience directly, and it is his agony we feel. The actor playing Mozart is free to romp around the stage un-burdened by the need to portray genius. The play delib-erately points up the mismatch between Mozart's personality and his work, thereby removing the curse of so many bio-dramas, where an attempt to elucidate genius through per-sonality can only reduce and disappoint.

There is an in-built impossibility in any biographical performance, namely that you can never *be* that person, because they already are or have been themselves. So don't even try it. Treat it like any acting job. Use your imagination to meet the person half-way and admit that what you create is a hybrid.

Some Effective Hybrids I Have Known

Ben Kingsley/Gandhi, Prunella Scales/the Queen (at the curtain call I thought, 'Surely *she* doesn't have to take a bow!'), Jane Lapotaire/Piaf . . . But no, this cannot be a list. I will just single out a few cases which help me make a point.

When I was in the sixth form, the poet Stevie Smith came to give a recital at our school. Later in the evening she talked to a few of us in the headmistress's study, and I will never forget that voice, at once sing-song and tuneless, nor her schoolgirl hair caught up in a slide. Years later, I saw Glenda

Jackson play in *Stevie* by Hugh Whitemore. At one point when Glenda-Stevie was alone centre stage talking to the audience, I had a peculiar sensation: 'I've met you before, I wanted to say. Stevie Smith was dead by then, but the combined sensitivities of Glenda Jackson and Hugh Whitemore had as good as resurrected her. It did not matter that Glenda had a larger build than Stevie or a differently shaped face, she had selected some key Stevie features – the slide, the shoes – and captured her flavour, her essence. Glenda had somehow transcended her own mannerisms while retaining her actor's magnetism. In this way she had become an open channel, a medium for Stevie's words. I remember thinking that was a pretty good model for what an actor is supposed to do.

In the film of *The Elephant Man*, John Hurt went through a legendary ordeal in the make-up chair and somehow that was the right price to pay. It was a moving and amazing humanitarian film which taught us about ourselves by acquainting us with a freak. The fact that Merrick's physical deformities were so faithfully reproduced helped us to witness the unimaginable, giving us a privileged but well-supervised glimpse through the keyhole.

Without getting into the debate on the pros and cons of docu-drama, it is worth mentioning the responsibility that goes with playing with a real person's life. Although this rests mainly with the writer, the actor must bear some of it as well. If someone is long dead, few save other biographers and historians who regard themselves as custodians of the truth will be personally offended if you get something wrong. If, on the other hand, the person is recently dead, there may be relatives still living who would be hurt by an unkind portrait, or victims of the person's cruelty who might be equally hurt by a whitewash. Could you or should you find a way of counterbalancing the writer's view? If the person is still alive and not a public figure, can you justify the intrusion into their lives? If you get close to them how will it affect you? Or them?

David Edgar's play *Mary Barnes* centred on the story of one of R. D. Laing's schizophrenic patients, but it was *about* all of us, our relationships and attitudes in the 1960s. Another writer might have written a monkey-in-the-zoo piece which the audience could gawp at and come away from having learned nothing. Instead, David developed the play with the cooperation of Laing and Mary Barnes herself. Patti Love, who played her on the stage, met and befriended Mary, and has remained in touch with her over the years. She admits to having been frightened of Mary at first, not so much because of her 'madness' but because of her impressive height and strange speaking voice.

The Patti-Mary hybrid was perforce less physically daunting, but as a result of honest collaboration Mary's own message got through.

Impressionism versus Imitation

It is more important for an actor to communicate a person's spirit than to laboriously mimic them. I learned this lesson the hard way when for one night only I played Vita Sackville-West in a reading of the letters between Vita and Virginia Woolf. Eileen Atkins had compiled the programme and we agreed to semi-dramatise it – that is, we would read rather than learn the words – but in the interests of entertainment we would make a token gesture towards costume and set.

Eileen had 'lived with' Virginia Woolf for some time, having performed her own one-woman show, *A Room of One's Own*, but Vita was a relative stranger to me. I rapidly read Victoria Glendinning's book about her and soaked up some BBC tapes of Vita speaking to the nation in deep, rich, plummy tones about the gardens of England. After weeks of listening and repeating, like with one of those foreign-language tapes, I became quite convinced of my own transformation, though I never quite dared present it full-bloodedly to Eileen.

Came the day and we set off for Charleston Farmhouse, which had been the home of Duncan Grant and Vanessa Bell, and where we were to perform to a marquee-full of Bloomsbury devotees. We got changed in various bedrooms and loos and then met in the kitchen to approve one another's guises. Eileen looked wonderfully Virginia-like, with her thin, intelligent face and her pale-hued clothes. I had borrowed a bobbed wig and a hugebrimmed hat, and added a long wine-coloured jacket and skirt of my own. At the last minute I slung a string of pearls round my neck and we set off for the marquee.

I had been warned, but had somehow put it to the back of my mind, that Nigel Nicolson, Vita's son, was to introduce the programme. He started off by saying, 'I don't know which of these charming ladies is playing my mother but . . .' That was it. Her own son had not even recognised my emblematic silhouette. The whole architecture of my planned perform-ance collapsed. Gone was the noble stance and the booming voice, but the show must go on, and I clung to the raft of Vita's words. All the while. Nicolson sat two foot away from me in the front row. Never have ninety minutes lasted so long.

At the end of the performance we mingled with the audience in the beautiful summer night and I could no longer avoid meeting Nigel Nicolson. 'Splendid!' he cried (or words to that effect). 'You caught my mother's spirit, that was the thing.' Now I know he was bound to be polite, and I am not going to pretend that I triumphed, but it did dawn on me that even if I had been a complete Vita lookalike and sound-alike, I would not have convinced her son that his mother had come back to life. I stood a better chance of conjuring her spirit by standing back and letting her words speak for themselves.

The whole 'you cannot *be* them' quandary is never so apparent as when an actor is called upon to play a well-known performer. Although the emphasis of the piece is usually on the performer's offstage life, there are usually scenes where the actor has to emulate the performer's act. The best they can hope for is an admirable stab at it, but if any devoted fans expect their beloved to come back to life, they will be disappointed. They loved and followed a unique act and now see a pale imitation. In these cases the audience must be willing to suspend comparisons and go with the flow. After all, if any actor could be found who could dance exactly like Fred Astaire, not only would that actor not be 'any actor' for long, but there would be no need for Fred Astaire.

How many Hitlers have we seen on screen? We can play around with villains from distant history, but in the aftermath of Hitler's more recent villainy we are still in trauma and need to understand how the actual person came about. We have endlessly skirted around Hitler, countless books have been written and documentaries made about him, but the centre evades us. What new light if any can an actor throw on such a well-documented but still unfathomable man? Why should one actor's insights and speculations be more valid than anyone else's? They cannot be, and nor should we expect them to be. We can only marvel at their mimetic skills and look for the join in their wig.

Felicitous and Not So Felicitous Casting

Creative 'biographical' casting can deliberately exploit some parallel between performer and performed for the added dimension it may lend to the portrait. It was clever matchmaking that teamed Madonna with Evita Peron. The pairing of Gary Oldman with Sid Vicious was also inspired (mind you, we are dealing with a brilliant actor who can equally convince as Joe Orton, Lee Harvey Oswald, Beethoven and Dracula). When one icon plays another it lends an added layer of credibility, or an irony that the audience can enjoy. Sometimes an actor's stature derives from the parts they have played. Charlton Heston was built like a Leader of Men so he played Ben Hur. He was also built like a Michelangelo statue, which may have inspired someone to cast him as the artist (the heterosexual version needless to say). From hero to genius and then the sky's the limit. If Moses, then why not God? Why not Heston for President? But then who would play him in the film?

There is an intricate interplay between our physique, our psychology and the way we choose to present ourselves to the world. A prejudice sets up a vicious circle. The fat boy who is the butt of people's jokes plays the role to the full so as to keep his friends. The disfigured woman frightens people away, so in self-defence she decides to despise human company. Her derision shows in her eyes and she frightens more people away. The fact that you are small or tall, black or white, fat or thin in some way affects how you are treated and consequently how you behave in the world.

Unless you are prepared to gain three stone as Robert De Niro did when he played Jake La Motta, you will not know what it is like to live in a body other than your own. For this reason I was never satisfied with my version of Amy Johnson. While studying Amy's life, it soon became clear to me that I had been wrongly cast. Working backwards, I deduced that I had been chosen because I had recently played a quiet but plucky girl-next-door in *The Imitation Game*, and the producers thought those same qualities could fit my portrayal of Amy. But in my book there was a huge and essential difference. Amy was small and I was tall.

I could swot all I liked – read her biography, even loop the loop in a replica of her plane, meet her sister (who showed me the contents of Amy's handbag that had been washed up on the shore after her mysterious disappearance over the Thames estuary), watch hours of newsreels observing her voice, clothes and manner – but I believed I would never convince as Amy since so much of her persona flowed from the fact that she was petite.

I know the camera cannot tell how tall you are, but that was not the point. Amy's whole demeanour and inner drive had crystallised as a result of years of being treated like a fragile doll. She had needed a brittle toughness in order to prove she was as good as the boys. How could I put that across when, as a tall girl, I had developed in almost the opposite way? Like the gentle giant who used his strength sparingly in case he frightened people away, tall girls try to put people (particularly men) at their ease by playing down their height. They become the softie Labrador as opposed to the yapping tyke: Helena's spaniel to Hermia's vixen.

If I were to copy Amy's toughness without the bird-like frame that helped diffuse its force, gone would be the allure of the battling underdog, the ordinary girl making good. With all the rehearsal time in the world I would not be able to get behind Amy's big blue (yes, blue) eyes. No one else seemed to mind that I was such a different type from Amy, they were principally interested in her ripping good yarn, so

I settled for the considerable enjoyment of mucking about in planes and wearing nice frocks and abandoned all attempts to convince that I was her.

14

The Functional Key

How do you deal with a small part or a part whose only function is to feed – those parts which even the last-resort personality key cannot help much? Chances are most of us will have to play such parts a lot, if not most of the time. Theoretically a small part should be approached just like any other part, with the aim to be as three-dimensionally believable as possible. In practice, however, the text does not give you much to work on and the director cannot give you much time.

All stories, be they in films, plays or fairy tales, have their functional characters – the servant who rushes on to say, 'The king is dead', the plain girl at the ball who offsets the heroine's beauty. Shakespeare wrote hundreds of functional roles, those men with names like Balanius or Birenius who stand there telling one another what they already know in order to fill the audience in on the plot: "Tis ten long years, my good Birenius, since peace has blessed these goodly shores.' You know the kind of thing. Birenius/Balanius might be a deep and fascinating man, and in another story might occupy centre stage, but in this one he doesn't.

These parts are all take and no give. They help set the atmosphere and create the reality of the staged world. They throw the main characters into relief, feed their jokes and generally sacrifice themselves on the altar of the Main Theme. A leading role demands everything the actor has, but in return it gives back all that you put in and more. You reach beyond yourself and develop acting muscles you never knew you had. With functional roles it is the other way. You must chop off limbs, bite your tongue and squeeze your big expansive self into a tiny box.

So those are the facts and it is ultimately to your advantage to accept them. Suppose you are cast as the housekeeper who discovers her employer lying dead on the floor. You may have decided you are secretly in love with him and wish to ululate over his body, but the scene is not about your grief so it will not support you. By contrast, when the leading lady rushes on as his wife, the audience zoom in on her. What must she be feeling? How will she react? The actress only has to drop her handkerchief and stare blankly at the floor for the audience to do the rest. No one said it was going to be fair.

An actress friend of mine put her finger on something when she said she was fed up with playing the nurse, or the prison warder, or the receptionist. All she had to do was give information: 'His blood pressure is normal', 'It's the third door on the left.' Her main complaint was that these people had no relationship with anyone else in the scene, and it is through relationships that one develops character.

There are tricks to making a small part interesting for yourself. Michael Caine tells the story of how in his first small-part job the director complained that Caine did not seem to be involved in the scene. 'Well, I've nothing to say,' replied Caine. 'Yes, you have,' came the reply, 'you've got plenty to say, you have just decided not to say it.' Your character is the centre of their own play. If you sit firm within that centre and don't spill distractingly over the edge, you can have some interesting thoughts and contribute to the scene at the same time.

While watching a long scene, how often has your focus wandered from the speaker to take in the listeners in the background? Henry V can rally his troops till he is blue in the face, but if one of the soldiers is looking bored or staring into the audience, the illusion is shattered and Agincourt becomes a wooden O once more. Some directors have the knack of making every cupbearer feel important, and their efforts are rewarded by a fully involved cast. Watching those shows, you feel you could jump up on stage at any moment, ask the small-part player, 'What is going on in your head right now?' and know they would answer in character.

Paradoxically, a low budget can work in the actor's favour. Suppose a play has a cast of twelve characters but the company can afford only seven actors – true, five actors stay on the dole, but the lucky seven get to be used to the full. If they are not given the meaty main role, they make up for it by playing two or three smaller ones. In a larger company a different actor would be hired for each one of those small roles and would spend most of the evening getting bored in the dressing room.

In 1980, Trevor Nunn and John Caird applied many of the best lessons of low-budget theatre to the flagship RSC. Like a giant amoeba, their production of *Nicholas Nickleby* absorbed the talents not only of David Edgar, who had cut his story-telling teeth on the fringe, but also of actors who had been reared on the fringe and brought with them all the invention that necessity had mothered in them there. Actors switched from mobcaps to cloth caps to top hats in a trice. A rearing horse clattered in an ill-lit cobbled street thanks to a length of rippling black silk, two half-coconuts and some human neighs. A starving crowd pressed their noses up against the window of an eating house and within the blink of an eye became the guzzling rich inside. All done with lights and human bodies. No props, no clunking scene change, no live animals in the wings, and all the better for it.

Being a cog in a wheel has its rewards, and the more special the wheel the longer the cog stays happy. When I joined the cast for a revival of *Nicholas Nickleby* to play various urchins, milliners and street-criers, I had already experienced the joy of the production from the audience's point of view, and it was the memory of that joy that sustained me throughout the run. As I mingled in the stalls before each four-hour (or on some days eight-hour) performance, I wanted to say to the public, 'Don't look so worried. You are in for an unimaginable treat, and you are going to wish it would never end.' I could hardly wait to take my place on the stage and add my little dot of colour to the general canvas.

Some playwrights (or theatre poets) know how to tie every minor part into the major theme. The great Greek tragedians knew exactly when to bring the messenger on to paint the picture of the heroine's death. The actor playing the part can be the instrument and beneficiary of their genius. The Greek playwrights were concerned not only with the actions of the gods but also with the effects of those actions on the mortals below. They gathered those bit parts and also-rans into a many-headed chorus which had almost the most important function of all – namely to connect the audience to the plot through the voice of the Average Person. They pit their common sense against the wilful folly of the gods. They comment, argue and gossip, and generally keep the 'Will they, won't they?' tension alive. I reckon an actor could feel pride and pleasure in such a function, even while speaking in unison and stuck behind a mask.

Chekhov wrote many small parts but none was insignificant. That is because he was writing about a whole society. Every individual, however fleeting their appearance, throws light on some aspect of the world they come from. In *Ivanov* Anna Petrovna has very little stage time, but her appearances are so perfectly placed and she is so richly written that her offstage life is almost palpable. Even a tiny character like Ferapont in *Three Sisters* is given a moment where the sun whooshes on to his life. There is plenty to feed the actor's imagination, however frustrating it may be to spend most of the evening backstage.

But actors are not mugs. They will not be conned into believing a part is important when it is not. Not every writer is as generous or curious about all of humankind as was Chekhov. Some writers are really concerned only with a few individuals (usually representing some aspect of themselves) who thrash out the main argument of the play, occasionally supported by functional feeds: the complaining wife, the dumb girlfriend, the dull friend. Try as they might, the actors cast in these parts cannot believe in their character, for the simple reason that the playwright didn't.

It would be dishonest of me to pretend that even the best small parts do not eventually wear thin. There comes a time when sheer boredom gives you two choices: to either switch off and go through the motions like a zombie, or keep yourself interested by building up your part. In the case of a bad play, there are no acting rules. If you can find a way to get through the evening and give yourself a bit of fun into the bargain, go right ahead, I say. If you have the nous and the nerve to over-act and get the critics to notice you, bully for you. Let that butler trip up every time he comes on, give that maid a lisp and take it as far over the top as you dare. If it's a bad play, the audience will thank you for the light relief. In a good play, however, such antics are simply not cool. If you draw undue attention to your acting, you undermine everyone else's more subtle work.

The problem of playing a small or functional role in film or television is different. The advantages are that you spend days rather than repetitive weeks and months doing the job, get paid a lot more and might even be given star treatment for the few days on which your cameo role is involved, but the disadvantages are that the further your part is from the central plot, the more expendable you are. Even if your part is not cut, you may not be on camera for your big scene. The director might decide that it is the heroine's reaction the audience needs to see, not your face as you bring her the news. Your voice burbles on in the background while the camera lingers lovingly on her cheekbones. You are not of interest. It is a case of out of sight, out of mind. At least on the stage you are still in the frame.

Functional parts can teach you only so much, and many of those lessons are negative. Know when the play is *not* about you. Learn to *efface* your needs. Learn *not* to draw attention to yourself. Learn how *not* to get bored. At the curtain call you resent the beads of sweat dripping from the leading man's brow. When I was starting out they told me, 'Stand in the wings and watch. You will learn from the other actors.' But there is only so much you can learn from the sidelines. No matter what they say, you learn to act by doing it. It is by means of the leading roles and the responsibility attached to them that an actor matures, and there are simply too few of them to go around.

A Woman's Lot?

For social, historical and political reasons too complex to go into here (and no doubt familiar by now), it is the female actors who most often have to play the thankless supporting roles. This is not intended as a tired old whinge, but when it comes to functional roles an experienced actress will put up with them more readily than her male counterparts because she is grateful to have a role at all. An aspiring male actor can set his sights on any number of meaty leading roles and a career plan which caters for his every age. If he is not leading-man material, there are character parts galore to see him through his days. Of course there are failures, frustrations and unfairnesses, but however bad the men have it, the women have it worse.

For a short period of our lives within a narrow age bracket, and an even narrower definition of beauty, a woman can be a film star, but if she thinks that will sustain her for long she had better think again. Leaving the film world aside, what can an actress aspire to? Here and there there are sparsely placed pyramids with at their pinnacle an Electra, a Blanche du Bois or a Joan of Arc. Below them and still quite near the top, there are a few speciality niches that an ageing leading lady or character actress can carve out for herself and cling to if she is lucky. At the half-way point just above the pyramid's fat girth, the aspiring *ingénues* meet the ex-leads coming down, and from there onwards the slopes rush down to the enormous broad base of under-used and unemployed.

I have so far been one of the survivors (who are tiny in number when seen in the context of the profession as a whole), so it is not the sour grapes of personal disappointment that makes me angry to see actresses of huge capacity squeezed into stereotypes. These roles reduce rather than stretch us and, particularly if we have tried our hand at Shakespeare, we feel the difference keenly. We may occasionally take on the great male roles. but, like cross-racial casting, until the practice becomes widespread, it is bound to be more about the player than the play.

We may seldom have had the lion's share of stage time, but size isn't everything, as every woman knows, and we have learned to count the compensatory blessings of Shakespeare's scale. Then, just as we reach our emotional and technical peak, the path runs out. The heroines are married off and we face a long wait till we play some murderous queen or bitter hag. However powerful the language, the scope has narrowed.

Even if we can convince as Portia, Kate or Rosalind well into our forties, we have moved on from their preoccupations. There is more to life than snaring your man.

If we were men we could carry on practising the mighty words of kings, however long in the tooth. It is as though a female concert pianist were suddenly debarred from playing Beethoven at a certain age. She must put down the lid and go home. Occasionally she can earn a bob as a rehearsal pianist or accompanist, but her concert days are over. Come to think of it, though, that is not the right analogy, because the pianist can at least have the pleasure of playing at home.

This cannot all be laid at Shakespeare's door. He may have been a genius but he was also a man of his time. He and his contemporaries had an excuse for abandoning women after the marriageable age, but modern writers have none. It is no longer true to say that women's function in the drama mirrors our function in life. Women have made giant strides in the real world and drama has not kept pace.

This is not to say that in the last hundred years there have not been some wonderful female roles written by men. These writers did not choose to cast their beam on women out of some political correctness, but because they identified with them in some way. Ibsen and Shaw spoke through women of their own outsiderness, their own rebellion against the status quo. Tennessee Williams, Rattigan and Lorca spoke through women of their own forbidden sexuality. Unless male writers can identify with women, they will write them as objects – to be desired, owned or run from.

Over the last twenty years or so, women have been writing more and more of their own plays (and I do not mean only those worthy 'women's plays', where all the men are wimps and which do nobody any favours), but for all these steps forward there are many slippings back. The dominant white male culture dies hard, and at the time of writing the boys' play is back. In the real world the hitherto marginalised voices are grabbing the megaphone and swinging the spotlight round on to the black, the brown, the female, the old, the very young, the disabled, etc. On stage and screen we are still lagging behind.

There is no easy formulaic solution. If there were one, I would try it myself and write great parts for me and my friends. But we can't all be Caryl Churchill, and it takes more than wishful thinking to stir the creative muse. I know what will happen: there will be a marvellous burgeoning of complex roles for women in their forties just when my generation is hitting sixty. Well . . . Good!

Part Four

PERFORMANCE

15

Keeping It Alive

Second Nature

Imagine you are driving to work. You have your habitual route and you travel it at roughly the same time every day. Sometimes you arrive at work with no recollection of how you got there. The car seems to have driven itself. Since you passed your test and mastered the Highway Code, driving has become second nature to you and your car an extension of your own body. Only when the traffic or the weather is particularly bad, or when there is something wrong with your car, are you consciously preoccupied with the mechanics of your journey. You weave through lanes, change gear, give signals and judge distances almost automatically, dealing with everything that is thrown at you and never losing sight of where you are heading.

So it is with acting. After a certain amount of experience on stage, matters of breathing, timing, pitching to the audience become second nature. A new play is like a new route to be learned until all you need to know is where you want to go and you can trust the rest to happen. A new role is like a new car which needs breaking in until you no longer notice the smell of its leather and the seat has moulded to the shape of your bum. The rest of the cast, like the traffic, may take you by surprise, but for the most part they stick to the rules. For the first few previews you may need green 'L' plates, but by opening night you should be so on top of the material that you are free to respond to the moment. If all your preparation and rehearsals have not got you to this basic state, it is too late now. If you are still asking yourself, 'What would my character be thinking now?' you are not playing the scene. To continue with my driving analogy, you cannot be looking at the handbook and the road at the same time.

'How Can You Do the Same Thing Night After Night?'

Still sticking with that car route, no two journeys are quite alike. The A and the Z of your trip remain constant, but the sequence in between can vary from day to day. Yesterday a woman suddenly stepped off the pavement and you had to swerve to avoid her. Today a white van is on your tail. Last week there were roadworks and you found a new short-cut. One day you decide to set out a bit late just to get the adrenalin going, or dive up a side road on purpose just to vary the routine. In the same way, a combination of outside forces and one's own mood makes the challenges of tonight's performance different from those of the last.

There are three main determining factors as to how long you can sustain your night-by-night interest in a play: the play itself, your fellow players and the audience. Most plays take months to grow into, and the greatest ones can never be cracked. There does come a point when a production is all that it can be, but that is usually quite far down the line.

In the meantime, each player brings varying moods and states of alertness to the stage each night, and these subtly alter the quality of the game. On Tuesday we play well and take a great leap forward, on Wednesday we just miss it and take a frustrating six steps back. But the most influential and unpredictable factor in the 'keeping it alive' equation is the audience response, and it never ceases to amaze me how few theatregoers realise the effect they have on each show.

If You Can Hear Us, We Can Hear You

One night, when I was playing in *The Duchess of Malfi* at the Swan Theatre in Stratford, a woman in a bright red coat suddenly stood up in the stalls, undid her coat, folded it, twizzled round to place the coat on her seat like a cushion and sat back down again. The play carried on. A few minutes later, the same woman half stood up again, rummaged under her bum to readjust her 'cushion' and, after one or two bounces to check it for comfort, settled back to watch the play. Unfortunately, because she was now sitting higher up, not only did the person behind her have to shift and do a few 'tsk's, but her own lap was at a slope, which set her pro-gramme skidding down the silk of her dress; only a loud 'thwack' as her hand pounced on it could stop it racing to the ground. All this thrashing around had clearly made her hot, because from this point until the end of the play she used her mercifully retrieved programme to noisily fan the air.

At the end of the show I had visitors backstage. 'Loved the play. Marvellous, marvellous,' and all of that. But how could they have enjoyed it? 'What about that *woman!*' I protested. 'What woman?' they asked. 'That woman with the bright red coat and the programme! Didn't she put you off?' 'Oh, her. Yes,' came the reply. 'I'd forgotten her. She was a bit of a nuisance. But how come you noticed her? I thought you'd be too carried away.' I had to explain that, far from being carried away, actors were hyper-present.

To perform well we have to be in a state of alertness and sensitivity not only to our fellow players but to the audience's mood, and in 'listening out' to gauge the quality of their attention we cannot filter out the negative bits. One cough or sweet-wrapper rattle can throw the timing of a line or drown out a vital word. It takes only a few bored fidgets to under-mine the quality of concentration of the whole audience. They may not even be consciously disturbed, but sublimin-ally the actor-audience connection is derailed and the actors have to fight to get things back on course.

Who's Running the Show?

The old school of thought is that the audience is always right. If they are twitching they are bored, and if they are bored it is because you are boring. There may be a lot of truth in that, but theatre is a two-way deal and to a certain extent the audience gets out of it what they put in. The old school of thought did not have to take on today's TV habitués, those who sit back and say, 'OK, I've had a hard day at the office, the wife has dragged me here, so come on, entertain me.'

With an unresponsive audience some actors go into attack mode and force them to sit up. Others save their 'jewels', preferring not to waste them on unappreciative ears. By the same token, if we sense that an audience is picking up every little detail, we give them our all and more. Those are the nights when your character starts to fly. You may be grounded again the very next night but at least you have seen where you can go.

The general standard of a professional show fluctuates very little. Give or take the odd subtle variation, we deliver the same line at roughly the same pace with the same intonation at the same moment every night of the week, so how come it gets such a different response? One night we can barely control the audience's hilarity, the next we are met with a cautious silence. It cannot all be our fault. The fact that it is raining, that it is hot, that it is Thursday can corporately affect an audience, and singly each member brings with them whatever has been done to them that day.

The audience, the space and the actors create the event together. An audience can ignite scenes that never took off in rehearsals. It can also make sense of a character. When I played Viola in *Twelfth Night*, she did not come together until she met the audience. They alone knew her secret, so she could be her true self with them; with everyone else she must pretend to be a boy. The audience is Viola's only friend and her personality is subtly shaped by them.

There is no more terrifying moment than the first step into the glare of the lights on the first preview of a new play, and there is nothing so miraculous as that first laugh. They get it! Laughter is the most tangible indication of appreciation, so it can easily seduce you on to a purely comic route. The audience will encourage you and lead you on, but beware. The actor must remain in charge. If the audience has lured you into a comedy turn, later on in the evening when you want them to take you seriously, it will be hard to wrest your character back out of their hands.

I Could Do That

With acting, as with many skills, the bits that look difficult often aren't, and the really clever achievements go unnoticed. I may thrill to the spills of an acrobat which the acrobat finds positively routine, and take for granted some delicate manoeuvre which is the real challenge. The main difference between me and the acrobat is that most people can do what I do, at least a bit.

Because acting is one of the most watched crafts that there is, and, as with many sports, most people have had a shot at it, there are some strong opinions around. We are just lucky that those opinions are kept fairly discreet. Suppose theatre was like a football or tennis match with the audience bellowing, 'Gah! Look at that!' and 'What the **** are they up to?' while the critics spoke a running commentary: 'She missed that moment', 'Hmmm, a bit of a fluff there' and 'He's not on form this season.' What if we had to put up with that?

In sport a goal's a goal, and you can spot good footwork or a nifty pass, but there are no such universal criteria for good acting. In one sense good acting is simply effective acting – that which does something for the watcher. I cannot be a good actor if you do not think I am. But what works for one member of the audience can leave their neighbour cold. An actor's popularity is often more to do with chemistry than any objective standard, so that pronouncements like, 'So-and-so was brilliant as the cop,' challenged by, 'Nah! I thought he was crap!' could mean nothing more discerning than, 'I fancied him rotten' versus, 'Yuk!'

Even professional critics are more subjective in their reactions than they like to admit, often projecting their own prejudices and preferences on to performers, so that we end up learning more about the critic than we do about the show. Years of professional theatre-going do not necessarily make a critic any wiser as to precisely what an actor does, nor what exactly good acting is. Sometimes they confuse natural endowments with acting skill and write things like, 'So-and-so made a wonderfully lanky Andrew Aguecheek,' as though congratulating the actor on his choice of physique.

So popularity and critical acclaim are not necessarily proof of outstanding skill, and neither is financial success (since we are often paid most for the easy bits), so what should I go for? The answer is something to do with my own standards. Only I can judge the moment-to-moment choices of my game and that is the only aspect I can control. Anything else can be put down to chance or God's gifts.

The search for objective criteria or measurable public appreciation is a tail-chasing waste of time. The public (and I include critics) cannot and should not be dissecting the mechanics of your performance, because when you are acting effectively they should forget you are acting at all.

Let Them Come to You

It would be a dull world if we all acted in the same style and played by only one set of rules. Each person's criteria can change from time to time, and what we love in one context we loathe in another. My personal preference is for understatement, but if Dame Edna Everage were ever understated I should feel very let down.

The reason why I like understatement as a member of the audience is that it makes me feel I have discovered something for myself which the character did not want to let slip. A subtle player, whether of comedy or tragedy, seems to be passing a secret message to me personally in seat G23: 'Here, catch this if you can.' I feel involved and honoured, and I sit on the edge of my seat waiting for the next sign.

In comedy the actor lets you into that little space between him or herself and the character. You get the added pleasure of the double bluff. The actor pretends to be a character who is taking a situation very seriously and does not realise anything funny has been said. You laugh at the character, and at the same time a more or less conscious part of you knows that the actor hears your laughter, is rewarded by it, but is pretending not to notice it. The delicate filigree of 'I know that they know that I know that they know' adds layers to our delight.

Understatement is more rewarding for the performer also – a response earned without coercion is doubly gratifying. Much of comedy depends on the unpredictable dodging the predictable. You set the audience on a path of expectation and then trip them up. This often pivots on a sophisticated vision or idea, and if you give the audience too much help, putting on funny faces or voices and signalling 'Joke coming up', you will never know whether their laughter (*if* it comes) is a knee-jerk reaction to your mugging or a real appreciation of the line. If you plant the idea lightly and sort of turn your back on it, as though you don't expect the audience to laugh, they are more likely to do so, and when they do it will be proof of a miraculously speedy exchange for which we can all take credit.

There are few things so off-putting as comedians who announce their own funniness, or for that matter tragedians intent on displaying their own finer feelings to the world. We have all been guilty of such 'crimes' on occasion, and even though nine times out of ten they are caused by insecurity rather than vanity, they give the impression that we think ourselves more interesting, funnier, more pitiable than the character we are playing. It sounds a bit moral, but actors should know their place and not intrude on the audience. Ideally, the audience should see what is going on inside you without realising that you've *shown* it to them. Let them think they have caught you unawares.

Letting the audience come to you helps keep the evening alive. It makes the difference between a passive and an active audience. The actor senses when the audience is 'hooked' and from that point until curtain-down plays off every twitch at the end of the line. The audience also sense the connection, and a cycle of interaction is set in motion which changes us all. That is the aim anyway, and when it happens it is a lot better than watching telly.

At the Risk of Getting Serious

In Howard Barker's *The Bite of the Night*, the character Macluby tells the audience of a woman taken from the street and made to watch a play. She protests that she doesn't understand art, but she reluctantly sits through it. She understands some things and not others. She is shocked sometimes and mystified and occasionally amazed, 'laughing rarely, and always without knowing why'. At the end of the evening the woman says, 'If that's art I think it is hard work.' But Macluby tells how something had bitten her and she comes again with friends and then again, each time understanding different things, still 'laughing rarely but now without shame'. At the end, she tells her friends, 'That is art, it is hard work,' and one of her friends says, 'If you will I will come again. Because I found it hard I felt honoured.'

In Britain particularly we are quick to call anything slightly testing 'pretentious', and to equate 'serious' with 'boring' (something theatre should never and need never be). While I believe our anti-pretentious sense of humour is one of our greatest assets, humour can be lazy and glib. Some audiences will love you for not challenging them, but anti-intellectualism can be a bully. As Macluby says, 'It is not true that everyone wants to be entertained . . . Some want the ecstasy of not knowing for once, the sheer suspension of not knowing.' Some want to be disturbed; others want to be reassured. Most of us want both at different times. It is not always comforting to be taken 'out of yourself'. A play that confronts your fears and admits the ugly and discomforting can send you home far more uplifted than a hollow happy end.

Playing with Power

We have the words, we know what is going to happen next, we have been lit and beautified and we are in charge. For a few hours we are dressed in a little brief authority, but it is only borrowed.

When I played Portia at the Royal Exchange Theatre in Manchester, I remember resting on Shakespeare's words like a cushion of power as I took on Espen Skjonberg's Shylock across the gladiatorial arena (the Royal Exchange is set in the round). Espen is a Norwegian actor and a heavyweight, but Shakespeare had rigged the argument in my favour. I knew I would win in the end, but Portia wasn't so sure.

Before playing the part I got caught up in the academic arguments as to how much of the trial Portia had planned. As usual the answers were to be found in playing the scene. Portia's male attire gives her (and me) a second-hand power. She has been well briefed and has calculated for certain options, but if you go with the rhythms in Shakespeare's score, its pounces, swivels and switchbacks, it becomes clear that for the most part Portia is thinking on her feet. She does not know which way Shylock will go next and his demand for a pound of flesh is a bolt from the blue.

Shakespeare knew that the best fights need to be a close-run thing, and the thrill of such an equally weighted man-to-man match is something female actors rarely experience. No doubt Portia felt exhilarated too. At last she is able to exercise the speedy legal mind which (when I looked back on them) was evident throughout her earlier scenes. As a sheltered heiress in her Belmont ivory tower, she could enjoy only a petty sway over suitors and servants. Here in Venice she could maybe do some good.

With the laws of Venice on her side, she brings Shylock to his knees, but his suffering casts a shadow on her victory. She learns that power in the world has consequences. Act Five (which Henry Irving cut because his part had come to an end) is all about Portia's attempt to reconcile herself to an imperfect world. By sullying her own hands in the male world, she has finally earned the right to dish out judgements, and hers is a merciful one. A brief and borrowed power. A privilege. But how are you going to use it?

In Their Own Words

The authority of the English language is changing hands, thank God. In Shakespeare's time words were being new-minted every day, and now that invention and freshness are back on the city streets. All over the globe the cloth of the English language is being cut to fit people's needs. In this country, while the language of politicians and the media becomes blander and more vacuous by the day, the language in schools and on the street is developing faster than we can set it down. In London alone there may soon be as many street versions of English as there are postal areas.

Recently I saw a play called *Yard Gal* at the Royal Court Upstairs. It was performed by Clean Break theatre company, who work with women who have served time in prison. I sat in on an educational day of workshops and performance with a group of sixth-formers. They understood the language (Jamaica meets Hackney) and shrieked at the jokes, they sat forward in their seats and asked penetrating questions at the end. I felt like one of those Chekhov characters who say, 'Soon people like us will be forgotten', and like a

Chekhov character I didn't mind. Someone new had grabbed the megaphone.

Playing with Time: I

Think of a page of Mozart's music, an imagined beauty trapped in quill-scratched ciphers on a yellowing page. Think of that page copied and copied over the years until it finally arrives on the music stand of an oboist in a concert hall today. He lifts his instrument to his lips and by breathing down the tube turns those trapped bunches of dots on stalks into music. The beauty conceived two hundred years ago is released invisibly into the present-day air, and as you sit in the audience you feel that, give or take the odd slip that may have occurred in the Chinese whispers hand-down through the years, Mozart is speaking to you. This is one of the miracles of live performance.

It is difficult to find an argument that will win over those who need to know 'the point' of live performance, especially of the work of dead artists. 'Why should we spend money on such esoteric art forms?' But who made them esoteric, I ask? They are only languages which we could learn from an early age. Why should they be locked in secret hieroglyphics that only the experts can read?

Imagine Congreve's original manuscript of *The Way of the World*. It takes an expert to unravel the mesh of scrawl and turn it into legible words, but once this is done you find you can understand it. It is not such a foreign language after all. You marvel at Millamant's speech as she contemplates married life. So women felt like that in *those* days too!

Then you see it performed and a whole other layer is added. We engage with an actress as she connects with a character who was created by a man engaged in a dialogue with an audience from another time. We overhear their conversation and we ourselves are brought into the debate by the actress in our presence. She is a hotline from a world which knew nothing of anaesthetics, split atoms or air travel. We may patronise those quaint people from the past with their poor sanitation, but when it comes to affairs of the heart we have learned very little. So listen up.

MILLAMANT: My dear liberty, shall I leave thee? My faithful
solitude, my darling contemplation, must I bid you then adieu?
My morning thoughts, agreeable wakings, indolent slumbers,
adieu. I can't do 't; 'tis more than impossible. Positively, Mirabell,
I'll lie abed in a morning as long as I please.

Then she lays down her conditions. Her lover must allow
her:

> To pay and receive visits to and from whom I please, to write
> and receive letters, without interrogatories or wry faces on
> your part. To wear what I please, and choose conversation with
> regard only to my own taste. To have no obligation upon me
> to converse with wits that I don't like, because they are your
> acquaintance, or to be intimate with fools because they may
> be your relations. Come to dinner when I please, dine in my
> dressing-room when I am out of humour, without giving
> reason . . .

And so she goes on. It is humbling to note that women did
not find their voice yesterday, and that some of their most
eloquent speeches were 'given' to them by men. Listen to
Malory writing in the fifteenth century on behalf of Queen
Guinevere:

> 'For all of you, yea, you yourself Sir Lancelot, do think we ladies are
> prizes to be seized and owned like rings and ouches. But we are
> creatures of our own inclinings, even as you are.'

She and Millamant would probably have got on fine. If only
we were not always cutting the thread of continuity, we
might not have to keep reinventing the wheel.

Making Classics Modern

In Shakespeare's day actors wore their own sixteenth-century
dress even when playing ancient Greeks. It was understood
that the play was not about Then but about Now. When we
watch the latest production of a classical play, we are necessarily watching Now's take on Then, and it is our own
connection to both which gives the exercise its relevance.

The main channel for this connection is the cast. I recently saw a young mixed-race cast bring an obscure Restoration play to life for a young London audience. The play was not updated, transposed or in any other way tampered with, but because the actors had found their way through the 'old-fashioned words', clothes and gestures to characters they could identify with and a London they could recognise, they had taken the audience with them.

Updating a play has to be handled with care. It elucidates some themes but obscures others. Some plays need a leg-up and others are best left alone. If you do decide to update a play, the art lies in choosing which historical time or geographical setting is most appropriate for it. A notably happy choice was Bill Alexander's 1950s *Merry Wives of Windsor*. It is not a play which calls for much reverence in the first place, and left to its own devices can seem twee and unfunny. This version firmly placed it in the Ealing Comedy mould, which seemed to fit perfectly.

I myself was involved in another successful transposition, when Trevor Nunn set *All's Well that Ends Well* in the early 1900s. Forget the quibble that there would have been no King of France in those days; in every other aspect the play gained more than it lost. In a conventional doublet-and-hose version, it would be easy to miss the fact that this 'problem' play actually comes down on the side of class mobility, of merit as opposed to heredity, and of female emancipation. By associating the play visually with the worlds of Ibsen and Shaw, these modern themes were brought out.

Costume, Gesture and Language

So modernising a play does not necessarily make it more accessible to an audience. In fact, apart from some well-thought-out exceptions such as the above, a play's truth is usually best revealed in its own terms.

The lazily applied term 'costume drama' has created some misunderstandings. We do not wear period costume for decorative or nostalgic purposes, but because a character is part of a whole world and their mentality and predicament are intricately bound up with the customs of their time.

Particularly as a woman, I will get closer to understanding my character's predicament if I wear the sorts of clothes she wore and observe some of the manners she had to abide by.

I am already bound to speak with her words and that is made easier, not harder, if I hold my body as she had to do. I must sit, stand and speak differently if I am wearing a corset, or if my skirt trails along the ground. The fact that my character speaks in verse or *double entendre* implies a formality and constraint that are both reflected in and justified by the clothes she wears. If Millamant could dress in jeans and swing her legs over the arm of a chair, we would say, 'So what?' to her daring candour.

I remember seeing an interview with John Malkovich in which he talked about his part in *Dangerous Liaisons*. He said that he did not have much truck with learning fancy fan-work or adapting his posture to fit the period costume; after all, costumes were just clothes and you should not behave differently because you were wearing breeches rather than jeans.

I don't disagree with a lot of that. Fan language will be lost on most of us and costumes *are* just clothes to the character who is wearing them. But if you disregard the fact that your character lives in a world where people are compelled by custom to speak in code through fan-work, or (essentially in *Dangerous Liaisons*) indirectly through letters, a world where the fashion was to exaggerate the human form with pinchings and paddings, to crown young heads with grey wigs and to hide the ravages of smallpox under masks and make-up, if you simply slop about like late twentieth-century man, then your costume does look tacked on and out of place, and you look more of a pillock.

Umming and Erring

Umming and erring is the verbal equivalent of slopping about in an elaborate costume. I don't mean the conversational 'um's and 'er's. which can fit well with naturalistic speech, but those little giveaway signs that actors have lost their nerve with verse. Take a speech like Helena's in *A Midsummer Night's Dream*. It is very deliberately measured out in rhyming couplets, and it is through playing with those rhymes that you best arrive at Helena's self-deprecating humour. If I get cold feet I might kick off with: '(*Big sigh*) Haaah! How happy some o'er other some can be . . . I mean . . . Huh . . . Through Athens, um, I am thought as fair as she. Yeah. But what of that? Er, er, Demetrius thinks not so.' It is a common mis-apprehension that these 'naturalistic' grace notes will help you seem more 'real'. In fact they tend to have the opposite effect, drawing attention to the gap between you and your character and making you seem less real and more of a twit.

There are times when an 'um' or an 'er' can suddenly give a spontaneous jolt, but like so much else in acting it loses its power if over-used. 'If it works, use it sparingly' is a good general rule. In real life it is surprising how fast and fluently we speak and think.

Anyway, Shakespeare is full of his own 'conversation-alisms'. I will never forget Michael Bryant as Polonius on the Olivier stage suddenly stopping his own pedantic flow with, 'What was I about to say?' Then the most daringly stretched-out pause I have ever witnessed, during which all our hearts seemed to stop. Had he dried? What was going on? Then 'By the mass, I was about to say something!' Great ad-lib, we thought . . . if it is one . . . and then, 'Where did I leave?' It was so startlingly natural that I had to look it up when I got home. It was all Shakespeare and Michael Bryant had played it to the hilt.

And Another Thing

Talking of language and gesture, I get defensive when British actors are accused of not being 'Russian' enough for Chek-hov or 'French' enough for Racine. Are Russians or Germans 'English' enough to play Shakespeare? Apart from the fact that these playwrights make universal connections, and belong to all of us, we do one another's plays in translation, and it is the language that we speak that influences our behaviour more than is commonly understood.

Language and gestural language are integral to one an-other. I know many people who are bilingual and their whole body language switches automatically when they switch

tongues. What you cannot do is speak in the English idiom and tack Italian or Russian 'behaviour' on the top.

The language of a people reflects and frames the attitudes of those people. Translation from one language to another is not just a case of substituting like-meaning words, but of getting behind an entire habit of mind and body, born out of a particular history of existence.

Nowhere is this more evident than in the case of humour. I can now share jokes with my Russian teacher which a year ago would have left me mystified. We know that Chekhov thought his plays were funny, but we go wildly wrong if we try to jolly them up in an 'English' way. His humour came out of a national despair that we can know little about. So how can we hope to be 'Russian' enough to play him?

All I know is that there is no short cut to what lies at the heart of another people's language, and reproducing some cliché 'Russian' brow-beating won't get you there. Best to stop punishing ourselves for not *being* Russian and use our usual imaginative processes to find what deeply links us.

Regardless of what period or country a play is set in, on any given night the actor must have a living dialogue with a live audience. A British cast using an English translation for an English-speaking audience has to work within a framework of English rhythms and emotional gestures. We cannot and should not try to do *The Cherry Orchard* in Sheffield exactly as a Russian cast would do it in Minsk.

Pace

'Time travels at divers paces with divers persons,' as Rosalind says in *As You Like* It. I have spoken before of the actor's subjectivity and we are seldom so subjective as in matters of pace. If my personal clock is racing with adrenalin, I will sense that everyone around me is dragging. Pauses seem interminable and my energy goes into my boots. At the end of the show, convinced that we have put on ten minutes, I check the running time with stage management, only to find that the show played at exactly its usual length.

Yet sometimes we are proved right. It is hard to blame one individual, because we pick up the pace from each other.

Some actors are pace dictators. Their character pauses so much and speaks so sluggishly that you have to slow down your own character's reactions to justify not interrupting. For example:

PACE DICTATOR: *So* (*pause*), I am afraid to tell you . . . (*long pause during which* . . .)
YOUR CHARACTER (*thinks*): My son is dead! (*But you mustn't interrupt, mustn't cry, mustn't know that yet.*)
PACE DICTATOR: Your son . . . (*clears throat, looks around the room*) is . . . (*pause for 'How can I put this?'*) dead.
AUDIENCE: Zzzzzzzzzzzzzzzzzzzzzzzzzzzz.

When a scene is working it is like a tennis match. Players decide how to play each moment as each moment comes. Do I return your ball with equal force? Do I convert a hard serve to a soft drop shot? Do I lure you into a gentle rally and then win a point with a sudden wallop?

Some leading players misguidedly take on the entire responsibility for the pace of the show. 'I've got to keep the whole thing going,' they say to themselves, and in their anxiety they wrap themselves in a cocoon, blocking out any other actor's rhythm lest it should drag them down. What they have actually cut off is a source of inspiration and energy. When their own stamina starts to flag, they try to kick-start it with false bluster. The supporting cast feel less supportive by the minute. We do not have a conductor's baton to drive us along each night, so we must listen to each other and play jazz.

Pace and Space

Apart from the subjective inner clock, pace is also conditioned by space. If you are talking to someone two feet away you can be quite nimble with your tongue, but if you are shouting across the valley you need to slow things down: 'L–U–U–UNCH IS RE–E–EADYY!' (You also have to exaggerate the sing-song, which I can't do here.)

If you are sitting in someone's bedroom, talking to them while they pack to go on holiday, you pitch your voice to follow them around as they move from the bedroom to the bathroom, back into the bedroom and out into the hall. If they are out of the room, you automatically gauge how far away they are and aim your speech like an arrow out to them. Theoretically that is all that is going on when actors adjust their projection according to the theatre space. The difficulty is that the person you are talking to on stage may be only three feet away yet you have to be heard at the back of the furthest balcony. If it were a simple case of loudness, the actors would just shout at each other, but then bang goes the reality of the scene. That is why it is all about projection rather than volume, and projection is all about intention. If there is a clear intention behind a speech it will carry better than a shouted empty thought. I say this as though it were the easiest thing in the world, when in fact it is one of the hardest lessons for the actor to learn.

In an intimate theatre space, we rarely need to raise our voices above natural speaking level. We can take time to think thoughts, and trust they will be picked up as they flit across our face. We can open a newspaper, read it for a while, scratch our nose, mosey over to the window, stare out of it and still be interesting.

But that is only one style of acting. A large theatre not only allows more people to see a play but lends itself to all kinds of spectacle and stylistic experiment. If actors worked exclusively in small spaces, some important acting muscles would waste away. Besides, audiences like to vary the fare – they like a spot of Henry Irving now and then. There is a school of thought that feels actors on stage should be 'real' actors complete with histrionics, and leave the other subtle stuff for the screen. In my ideal world we should be able to do both.

For my first season at Stratford, my line of parts was distributed equally between the large Memorial Theatre and the friendly tin shack that was then the Other Place. The latter was preferred by most people, actors and audience alike, but perversely I was more interested in the main house. Like Everest, it was difficult and it was there.

The first big shock of the main stage was the energy level required. I felt that if I let myself relax for a second the scene would grind to a halt. I could not wait until I 'felt' right before I spoke my line. Why should the bus wait for my integrity? It could not and would not. So my integrity had to learn a few lessons.

First, my voice. Our voices are very personal to us. The vocal-emotional-psychological interconnection is a delicate mechanism. We get used to the sound we make and identify with it. I had always thought of myself as a small-voiced person. I knew I was technically capable of booming out over the audience's heads, but that did not sound like me. That was an acting voice. Cicely Berry cured me of this schizophrenia. She helped me develop my range and learn to accept it as mine.

Next, coping with the big stage. I found that if I turned sideways on to talk to a fellow actor, I cut off half the audience. They could not quite hear and felt excluded from the scene. If, however, I faced front and gave it all to them, I cut off my contact with the other actors and the scene. I learned to split the difference. That meant turning three-quarters on and 'sharing' my speech and face between actor and audience. It felt phoney at first, but a combination of practice and hanging on to my intention got me through.

Was all of this what people meant by an RSC house style? If so, I now knew it was born out of necessity not affectation. The space dictated it.

Space dictated pace and inflection too. The acoustics of the larger theatres demanded a sort of hiccup of delay around each line to give it time to register with the audience. It was a bit like chucking a boomerang out into the stalls, letting it hover a second and having to wait for it to return to you before you could throw it again. Nor were the acoustics good at handling sudden swoops or switches of pitch in the voice. Like a boomerang, the sound travelled best within a narrow plane.

As I write this, I can almost hear the protesting ghosts of Peggy Ashcroft and Robert Eddison, who together graced (the exact word) the Barbican stage in *All's Well that Ends Well*. These much-loved and much-missed friends and mentors of mine seemed effortlessly to project their subtlest thoughts and gentlest voices across the vast reaches of the stalls and beyond. They most certainly let the audience come

to them. Theirs was a technique built up over years of practice which few of us can emulate.

When we took *All's Well* to an old Edwardian theatre on
Broadway (sadly without Dame Peggy), we were told to
knock twenty minutes off the playing time. Trevor Nunn
convinced us that we could do this without losing one line.
We did a series of speed-runs. The point about a speed-run
(quite simply, playing the play as fast as you can) is not to see
how quickly you can gabble but to prove how quickly you
can think.

We did knock twenty minutes off the show and not a
word was cut. Over the year at Stratford and the Barbican, we
had accumulated minutes and favourite embellishments
which we clung to for safety and were loath to surrender. The
speed-run exercise taught me that these embellishments
were like barnacles on the bottom of the boat. They had
weighed us down and impeded our dash through the waves.

Swings and Roundabouts

From the performer's point of view, large spaces at their best
are exhilarating and energising. They give you a run-up to
big emotions and paradoxically make it easier to hide than in
a more intimate space where the audience quickly detects the
slightest phoney note and won't let you get away with it. In a
small space there is no run-up to the big emotions. You can
play safe and duck them, or you must leap from a virtual
standstill and risk falling flat on your face.

A small space can allow the actors to control the pace, the
atmosphere and the truth of the evening, whereas a large
stage can drown the actor in technical paraphernalia. When I
played Imogen in Bill Alexander's studio production of
Cymbeline, there was no scenery, just a few sticks of furniture, and the actors provided all the sound effects. The Other
Place was made even tinier by adding two more rows to the
front of the audience which enclosed the acting area in a
circle. There is something extra thrilling about doing Shakespeare at such close quarters. We could chat in verse and
whisper the poetry, letting it linger in the air a bit without
fear of losing momentum.

At one point, as Imogen, I sat on the aisle steps reading a letter and the person at my elbow would invariably try to read over my shoulder to check whether the words I spoke were really written there. Some nights, I would give them a little frisson and for no extra fee would subtly tilt the paper towards their prying eyes.

The down side to this intimacy is that such naturalism can set up impossible expectations. If the audience is encouraged too far into the 'this is actually happening' school of theatre, what about when somebody has to die? If the production has not set up any metaphorical dimension, bang goes the suspension of disbelief when the audience see the dead man's chest still heaving. But a prop corpse is not much help either. In *Cymbeline* Imogen has to wake up from a drugged sleep and find a headless corpse next to her which she assumes to be her lover's. For obvious reasons our headless corpse was not real but made of fibreglass or something, and it had a distinct curvature of the spine which caused it to rock if I so much as nudged it. All this two feet from the audience's nose.

Shakespeare had given me enough of a problem in that the audience knew it was not Imogen's lover lying there but her loathed enemy. They stand back from her grief and are merely curious to see how she will react. The opening lines of the speech were lovely to play as Imogen gropes her way into wakefulness. I could do all this as though unobserved. I could almost mumble, 'I hope I dream' through my sleepy-tongued voice. But reality eventually had to break through and there was no ducking out of the gnashing and wailing and obscure mythological references that Imogen goes in for. The audience politely sat on their giggles but I sensed their discomfort, and for all of our sakes I wished myself on a grand open stage where I could howl at the sky in peace.

The Georgian theatre architects got a lot of things right. At the Bath Theatre Royal, for instance, an actor can contact the back row with a whisper, and be large and heroic if the play requires. The trouble is that by modern standards the seats seem cramped and uncomfortable. In the latest luxury theatres, the audience sit in easy armchairs cooled by air-conditioning, but easy armchairs make for a laid-back audience and as for air-conditioning . . . It is a subtle rogue.

It creates eddies and air pockets, and its subliminal hum interferes with the actor-audience airwaves. Bring back ladies' fans, I say.

We are still waiting for someone to come up with a formula that will allow maximum bums on seats while providing great sight-lines and sensitive acoustics. They say you could hear a pin drop in the ancient Greek amphitheatre, and we haven't matched that yet.

A Word About Tears

Some actors can press a button and produce tears. They bite their cheek or think of a dead puppy, and they're off. If actors ration this gift and use it only when the context supports and justifies it, they can work wonders; but if they use it too liberally, it starts to look like begging for pity and something in the audience switches off. It is always more moving to see tears in the eyes of someone who hardly ever cries than in those of someone who weeps easily. In art as in life, tears are a currency which can be devalued with over-use.

Audiences do not like to feel manipulated. Their empathy has to be earned moment by moment over the evening. If they have not willingly suspended their disbelief by at least the interval, no amount of emoting and no string orchestra in the world will win them over at the eleventh hour. It all comes back to detail and living in the moment. Tears are no exception to the rule. Tears of frustration are different from tears of despair, tears of outrage or tears of remorse. This character weeps loudly and unrestrainedly, that one sniffs discreetly hoping no one will see. If tears are not rooted in the situation and character, the acting becomes dislocated and generalised, and generalisation is death to good theatre.

We actors get hung up on the idea of tears, because they are such a visible indication of feeling. I used to worry that when it got to the stage direction 'She bursts into tears' my eyes would be bone dry and the audience wouldn't believe me any more. In my anxiety I would put my character and the situation on hold for a minute while I pumped and squeezed and imagined loved ones dying. But my character already has the tears near the surface. She is fighting to stop them, whereas I am fighting to produce them, so my focus is diverted away from the scene.

In fact my best hope lies in staying within the scene and trusting the situation. If the actor enters each moment truthfully, the audience will not be looking for tears. They will see them if they want to even if there are none (and there probably will be by now anyway). Your truthfulness lets the audience in to do the crying for you.

Beyond Gnashing and Wailing

A Question of Geography was another play I did at the Other Place, but it had very different demands from *Cymbeline*. The play was set in the early 1950s in Stalin's Gulag. Dasha is living in forced residence in a town surrounded by a prison fence in the Magadan region of Siberia. She was originally arrested because . . . well, as my Russian friend said, there does not have to be a reason. The whole of the stage area is Dasha's room. In this room she cooks and eats real food with her guests, gives her man a real bath, in water that takes a real amount of time to boil.

When people leave the room Dasha is left 'really' on her own, and she talks to herself and to the people who are missing in her life. Her husband, who may be dead, is kept alive and brought into the space by her conversations with him. The audience are sucked into her reality as she populates the room. I knew that I must never betray to the eavesdropping audience that I was aware they were there. It was as near to film acting as anything I have done on stage.

The problem came on Tuesday nights. Tuesday night is bellringing night in Stratford-upon-Avon and the merry peal could be heard loud and clear through the thin walls of the Other Place. All very evocative – of Warwickshire but not Siberia. What should I/Dasha do? In order to be heard, I would have to shout above the bells and in so doing would shatter the atmosphere the audience have helped me to create. Dasha cannot hear the bells, so why on earth is she shouting? In any other show I would have said to myself, 'Don't be so precious. It's only a play. The audience need to hear you,' but something about this play took me the other way. Dasha is alone, so she does not need to hear her own thoughts spoken aloud. I decided never to raise my voice and speak only in the gaps between the bells.

By means of such quiet moments built up throughout the play, the audience became enmeshed in the reality of the room. In the final scene Dasha is rearrested. I can still see the spot on the floor that I stared at each night, listening to the rap on the door and saying to myself, 'This is really happening. This is really happening.' I could feel the audience's concentration like a laser boring into my back. It was as though they were folding Dasha's clothes with me and putting them into the suitcase. They seemed to step across the room in my shoes and kiss my son a last 'goodbye' with me, and when I left the room, they stayed behind with my son. If this sounds fanciful or, worse, boastful, it is because it is nearly impossible to describe the unusual power of this play.

Through an almost uneventful story, John Berger and Nella Bielski explored the very fundamentals of story-telling in the theatre: imagination, reality and the coincidences of time and place (or geography). The play looks at the ordinariness of human endurance. The people on stage are in the deep ice of their condition, but they are acclimatised to their environment. They do not complain about the injustice of their imprisonment any more than the fish in the sea complain of being wet.

The audience had had to submit to our pace, the pace of people with nothing to hurry for, and sit through the silence of a situation beyond words. In conversations afterwards, they often spoke of moments when they had wanted to get up and scream because we weren't. When we first rehearsed the play we too had wanted to scream, but our characters were way past that point, and the more we showed them trying to live a normal life the more shocking it was for the audience.

The characters saved their emotional energy, and the actors took the wisest course in also holding back. No amount of screaming and crying on their part could have altered their situation, and in the actors' case no demonstration of emotion could ever match the cause. So in a strange way the cast became acclimatised too. The play left the audience as drained and humbled as we had been when we first performed it, but eventually we could switch off quite easily and would beat the sad, slow-moving audience out of the building and, only a little guiltily, rush off to the pub.

Yet however harrowing the play, it was not depressing. Because the actual physical world of the characters is bleak, they survive by developing their spiritual and imaginative muscles. They tell one another stories and keep dead loved ones alive in their imagination. In stories our lives can be caught between a beginning and an end and examined. The meaning of your story depends on which slice of life you look at, how you show it and where you put the end. If you end Dasha's story where she is carted off to prison, it is comfortless, but when you are told that Stalin was to die within the year, things look different.

Playing with Time: II

How do you put the unimaginable on stage? When the South African lawyer Albie Sachs was arrested in 1963 and held in solitary confinement, he did not know when his sentence would end. Under the 'Ninety-Day Law', he could be held indefinitely without trial, because although he had to be released after ninety days, he could be rearrested two minutes after leaving the prison gates and endure another ninety days, and so on. Sachs wrote a diary during his ordeal and, as he wrote, he did not know when or whether he would ever be free. He was writing a story that had no end in sight, and although within the diary he speculates about it becoming a book or play, I should imagine that the possibility felt as remote as the moon.

Three years later Sachs left South Africa a free man and his diary did indeed become a book, and in 1978 David Edgar adapted *The Jail Diary of Albie Sachs* for the stage. Since then, in studio theatres up and down the country, audiences have witnessed Albie's story retrospectively and in so doing have salvaged some sense from his otherwise senseless suffering. That is not to say that we have been doing Albie Sachs a favour; it is the other way around. He went through something which but for an accident of birth and geography we might have had to go through too. He was imprisoned for beliefs which we take for granted. By vicariously undergoing his trial as watchers at a play, we have been able to test our own beliefs and fears – 'Would I crack up under such pressure?', 'Would I betray my mates?' – in safety.

But how can you re-create Albie's aloneness when his theatrical 'cell' is surrounded on all sides by banks of sympathetic listeners? The play is interesting and eventful. Stage time passes between Albie's conversations with his jailers, interrogations and his attempts to keep himself sane and entertained, which have something of the same purpose for us. In reality, such incidents were rare highlights in an otherwise uninterrupted solitude. How can a play convey the seeming endlessness of real time, or the distorting tricks time plays on a disoriented mind? How can you hope to share this experience with an audience who know that the play is approximately two and a half hours long and that they will soon be home to relieve the baby-sitter?

In a brilliant scene, Sachs/Edgar attempts to address this paradox. 'Albie' talks to the audience from his cell and tells them of the play he plans:

ALBIE: At first it was a book. But books are flat, controlled . . .
I wanted something more immediate, more active, more alive.
So it had to be a play.

And so he continues to describe it until he hits the obstacle:

ALBIE: But . . . the real problem is to show just what it's like, in
isolation . . . to people who are not alone, because they are
together, watching, as an audience, my play.
Perhaps the best thing is . . . for me to come out, to the
audience, and say, my day is sitting staring at a wall, now I am
going to make you sit and stare, you mustn't talk, or read your
programmes, look at other people. For three minutes, you
must sit and stare.
And then, perhaps, they'd know.
Just what it's like.

We each sat silently for three very long and very lonely minutes. And then there was an interval.

Postscript

Several years later, Albie Sachs was the victim of a car bomb and lost an arm and the sight in one eye. It was decided to stage *Jail Diary* as a benefit performance to raise money for a specially adapted word processor for Albie. In the play there is an unseen character, the occupant of the neighbouring cell, who communicates with Albie by whistling snatches of Dvořàk through the walls. The importance of this thin thread of air is summed up by Albie when they have their first musical interchange: 'Oh, whistler, you have turned me into we.' As the play goes on and the two continue to communicate in this way, Albie builds a mental picture of his companion, and so do we.

At the end of the benefit performance there were many speeches and tributes, and then Albie himself got up. How strange it must be for him, I thought, to have watched 'himself' on stage, to be able to compare the reality with the stage version, to remember that totally private, unsharable time when what was happening today would have been inconceivable.

Albie Sachs stood among us intimate strangers and invited a person from the audience up on to the stage. A middle-aged African woman crossed the floor to meet him and the two of them embraced. Then Albie told us how they had met for the first time during the interval that evening, and how the woman had approached him and shyly introduced herself. 'I was the whistler,' she had said.

Nothing Works Every Time

Kicking off the play in the right state is crucial. It is difficult to catch up if you start off unprepared. For some parts I do a long voice warm-up, for others I just drink a cup of tea. If I am playing a bold extrovert character like Lady Croom in *Arcadia*, I need to wind up the extrovert in me, hanging out in the canteen or visiting dressing rooms until I have become suitably boisterous and am raring to go. For moody broody characters like Hedda Gabler, I usually keep myself to myself and listen to something wild and deep on my Walkman.

When I am playing several characters in repertory, there is a sort of if-this-is-Tuesday-it-must-be-Viola element to contend with. People sometimes wonder how we manage not to get confused between one character and another. I don't really know how, except that the routine for each play is slightly different, as are the casts involved. The geography in the wings varies according to the play, and for each one there is a different array of props on the table. At the very least you have half an hour sitting in the dressing room before the show to focus on the part, but it sometimes takes only the slipping on of a wig or pair of shoes to bring the whole thing back.

You are in the wings about to perform. The homework is done and now everything depends on your here-and-now state of body and mind. Your nerve keeps slipping away. How to hang on in those last few minutes? Deep breaths, of course, and it sometimes helps to recap a potted version of the story-so-far from your character's point of view. The most important questions to ask are 'What do I know?' and 'What do I want?' Having thus wound the character up, you can let them go into the scene and hope to find out the rest on stage.

In an ideal performance, our characters' moves and speeches should be prompted entirely by what happens that night on stage, but the reality is that most of the time we do not reach that Zen state and need to plot in more triggers of our own. A voice in your head has to mutter little prompts in your ear: 'Remember you love him', 'Remember you don't suspect her yet.' You must keep them simple, as this is not the time for labyrinthine thoughts.

Some things cannot obviously be triggered by the here-and-now of a scene. They seem to come out of left field. Suppose my character is sitting in her kitchen, listening to a friend's tale of woe, and suddenly remembers she has to collect her kid from school. Where do I get that memory jolt from? During rehearsals I played around with ideas. My friend moaning about her husband makes me think of mine, then of the children. 'Oh, my God, the children!' I visualise a little girl alone in the school playground. 'Maisy! I've forgotten to fetch her from school.' Or whatever. When it comes to performance time, I must whittle all that down to a key trigger, perhaps the sight of a kid's painting on the kitchen wall. Real thoughts happen in a glance.

But triggers have a habit of slipping about and changing over a run. Suddenly a trick doesn't work any longer and you have to rethink. One night the sight of my husband's yellow bow tie sets off my impulse to murder him, when up until then it had been the way he hummed under his breath. The imagination does not work to order and our best bet is to embrace that fact.

Many actors have little superstitions and dressing-room mascots to help them cope with the whims of the Muse, but for me they just make things worse. It would only take one thing to go wrong for me to fly into a neurotic panic: 'My teddy fell off the shelf! It's going to be a terrible show!' If any actor boasts of a foolproof ritual, they are lying. In my experience nothing works every time, and wouldn't it be boring if it did?

Never Desert the Ship

The actors depend on one another all through the evening. If I act badly I make the other actors look bad and vice versa. If Actor A playing the tyrant is not convincing, then Actor B will not be believed when he cowers at his feet. We all contribute to the stage reality and help one another play our parts. When in doubt, listen to your fellow actors and look into their eyes. Only when there is nothing going on there should you fall back on your own devices.

I deeply admire actors who are prepared to look ugly and be disliked for the sake of a play. Out of hours they may disapprove of their character as much as the audience does, but on stage they totally inhabit the part and brave whatever flak comes their way. The more unflinchingly honest they are, the more human the character. There are no monsters, only human beings. Monsters let humanity off the hook.

One of the hardest things to cope with is standing on stage in a situation you do not believe. It is possible to lose your faith in a play or production, but you must still your critical voice and never let your loss of commitment show. However crass the play, however awful your character or however unconvinced you are by your fellow actors, there is nothing worse than signalling to the audience that this is how you feel. It is just not theatre cricket.

Off stage you might be able to share your deadly secret with a judiciously chosen friend, but be very careful not to infect the rest of the cast. That is unless you sense that they secretly feel it too and would be greatly relieved to find they are not alone.

However, just let an insensitive outsider criticise the play and you rush to defend it. Whatever you truly think of it deep down, you still have to get up there every night and do it.

Playing with Time: III

I am playing Nina in *The Seagull*. It is five past eight in the evening. At approximately ten past, Nina must rush on stage in a flurry of anticipation and half laughing, half crying, say, 'I'm not late, am I? I can't be late.' From eight o'clock I have been waiting in the wings like a racehorse under starter's orders and as soon as I hear my cue, not a second earlier or later, I will set off on the course that must be run until the curtain comes down. At ten past eight I must be ready in Nina's light heart, but only as she is feeling at that point in time. I must push to the back of my mind the knowledge that by the end of the scene she will be in love with the man who is going to destroy her. All I need to know is that I long to be an actress, that tonight I will perform for the first time a play written for me by Constantin, the boy who loves me, and that in the audience there will be a famous actress, Arkadina, Constantin's mother, and her lover and guest, the famous writer Trigorin.

At about ten past nine that same night, a week has passed and Trigorin is about to leave. On cue, not a moment earlier or later, I must be ready in Nina's reckless heart as she seizes a moment alone with him. It is now or never. 'I've made up my mind . . . I'm going on the stage . . . I'm throwing everything up to start a new life. I'm going away, same as you – to Moscow. We'll meet there.' Trigorin slips an address into her hand and then kisses her long and hard. That kiss takes place at approximately nine fifteen and, as it lingers, it fends off future tragedy. I must surrender my own insider information to the heady now-ness of Nina's desire.

The lights fade and the audience stirs and murmurs, the stage management race into their scene-change routine and the lights go up on Act Four. Two years have passed in five minutes. The scene is Constantin's study. It is a stormy night and in the distance through the window we can just make out the skeleton of Act One's wooden stage, with its torn curtain flapping in the wind. As the act gets under way, the audience learns that Constantin is now a writer, that Masha still loves him, that Sorin is dying and for that reason the family is being summoned around him. His sister, Arkadina, is due to arrive any minute with Trigorin, who is back by her side. Nina is mentioned. She did become an actress but her career has been full of trials and disappointments, and no one can quite agree whether she has any talent or not. She had a child by Trigorin, who soon abandoned her, and the baby died. Then someone changes the subject.

While the audience is being filled in with my/Nina's story, I am getting thinner under the stage. By that I mean that with the help of some cheek shadow and some darker, looser clothes, I am trying in the five minutes available to me to reproduce what two years of heartbreak would have done to Nina's appearance. As for her inner heart, that is a lot trickier. I can only feed the facts of her story into my imagination. I cannot experience it, though some of her memories are mine too: Constantin's play, the first meeting with Trigorin, that kiss. Is not my own past just a story I tell? Do I have to relive each moment in order to recall it?

As I change under the stage (I prefer to remain in contact with the play rather than break my concentration in the dressing room), I toss my thoughts between Nina's time and my own. Tonight is Tuesday and I am not quite the same as I was on Monday. If I let it go, my imagination will wander up different paths today from yesterday. When I go on stage, it can be only now, not a re-creation of last night. I can give only the performance I am giving, not some other one I might wish to give. I plug into a combination of my physical state and Nina's thoughts. Her thoughts alter my state and the rate of my breathing.

I focus on Nina's story. Why has she come back? What does she expect? What does she want? I picture her wandering round the lake. I try to put me in the picture and feel the cold, slicing rain. I clutch at fragments before they slip away and other ones swim into view. (Well, you know what it is like trying to force daydreams into line.) Extraneous noises and my own nervousness distract me. Some things help, some hinder. I hear Constantin playing the piano and it feeds me, but I must filter out the sound of the backstage tannoy.

Nina's story brings tears to my eyes. Hers or mine? I'm not sure but I use them anyway. A few lines into the scene Nina will tell Constantin that she has just visited their old stage and that she cried there for the first time in two years. Her eyes still sting with those recent tears and the slightest trigger can set them off. On Chekhov's cue 'She sobs', a dam must burst commensurate with the tragedy she has had to bear. Tears for Nina are a luxury. In this momentary haven with a man who loves her, she can give in to them, before shoring up her heart again to face the world.

But that is still to come. As I sit under the stage there is a race against time. I know that at approximately five past ten, when my cue comes, not a moment earlier or later, I must walk on stage already centred in Nina's broken heart, ready to play each moment as it comes.

You know that bit in *Twelve Angry Men* when Henry Fonda asks the jury 'not to think of a white horse'? I am reminded of it as I prepare to go on stage. Nina must not know what I know, that Trigorin is in the house. She may suspect it, and deep down wants to find out if she's right, but I must be ready with her uppermost thoughts and tuck my knowledge away. When Trigorin's voice is suddenly heard inthe next room, I cannot be taken by surprise, but if I stick with Nina and what *she* is conscious of each minute, at least I won't anticipate her shock.

[225]

Between approximately five past and a quarter past ten, I/ Nina ride the course of the play on stage. I know when Nina will leave and that Constantin will shoot himself. I know what he will say to me and what I will reply, but somehow I must enter the head of Nina, who knows none of these things. In this half-world between her truth and mine, I must listen and breathe and think on my feet. I must create an illusion of spontaneity, a possibility that the outcome might be changed.

At approximately ten fifteen I kiss Constantin goodbye and take Nina's whole future off stage. What becomes of her now is immaterial. I have a drink of water in the wings and breathe myself calmly back into this Tuesday night in London. In a few minutes' time I will join the cast on stage and take my bow. I can smile happily because I am no longer Nina, and anyway she will be young and hopeful again at eight fifteen tomorrow.

On a prearranged date one Saturday night, we will not be required to do the play any more. We will no longer be able to cheat time. At approximately ten fifteen I will walk off stage to face my own future and never be Nina again.

When the Part is Over

For some weeks you have known the date of that last performance. It is like having advance notice of the end of a relationship. Then inevitably the day comes around and you are doing the show for the last time. You linger in moments you have hitherto taken for granted or skated over. You try to bottle every feeling and burn each image on your mind's eye like a photograph that can be taken out at will and lovingly looked at. Before you know it you have spoken your last word.

Half an hour later you cast a final look round the dressing room to make sure you have left nothing behind. You pause a moment and whisper a sentimental 'Goodbye' (if you are me), but who are you saying it to? Where has your character gone? She is not in the costume lying folded in the skip like a limp ventriloquist's dummy. She is not beneath the wig plonked roughly on the wig block. Nor is she in your own eyes any more as you check your make-up in the mirror. Your make-up for the last-night party. Heigh ho and off you go, you fickle thing.

A character stays with you like the memory of a friend or lover you have moved on from. Once in a very blue moon you may have to meet them again. When I recorded *Hedda Gabler* for the radio eighteen months after playing her on stage, I dreaded getting involved with her again. I didn't want to revisit the dark places she had led me to. Besides, I had been living quite happily without her; perhaps I wouldn't be able to rake up any feelings for her. In the event it was amazing how quickly I fell back under her spell, and it was quite reassuring to find that it was all still there but slightly different.

Naturally the relationship with a film character you have lived with for only a few weeks does not bite so deep as a character you have played for months or even years in the theatre. I recently rather saddened a film producer on my last day's filming by saying, 'Sybil is dead.' To me the character's life was over, but in the film world she hadn't yet lived. By the time she starts her 'life' in the cinema, I will be far away.

Ephemera

The theatre feels like one of the most ephemeral of art forms when you are taking part. You can see your telly and film career on your video shelf, but all you have left of a theatre piece is the programme, some photos and perhaps some reviews. Yet for all this, of the remarks that come my way I hear, 'I will never forget that play' or, 'I can still see that moment when . . .' far more often than I hear, 'I will never forget that film/TV show.' I think that is because, at its best, live theatre involves the audience at a different level than anything recorded. When we sit in the audience we don't just watch a fait accompli, we are part of the event. We remember the play as a personal memory. It is something that happened to us.

And Tacked on the End . . . the Curtain Call

These are organised at the very last minute before the first public performance. You have had three exhausting days of technical rehearsal and have miraculously got through the dress rehearsal. All you want to do now is crawl away to get nervous and be sick in peace. But suddenly, 'Can we rehearse the curtain call, please? Full cast on stage.'

So which is it to be? Is it the Who's Best Walk-down? Or the We All Love One Another Spontaneous Rush-on? The Musical Rouser? (Bit of a cheat, this last one: however mediocre the performance, you can usually trick the audience into Uplift mode with a good tune.)

Personally I find curtain calls the most toe-curling part of the evening, and they can be equally toe-curling to watch. Among the huge variety of individual bows, there is the Donald Wolfit-style curtain-clutching, 'I've been through hell' mode; the scowling, 'I know you don't mean it, I was frightful' mode, which can easily look like, 'How can you be so undiscerning?'; or the 'After you. No, no. After you' type, who really means, 'I know they're really clamouring for me, but I'm going to pretend to be humble.' You can try and emulate the Eastern European Earnest or resort to the 'Go home, all of you. Some of us have got pubs to go to!' However, the 'Let's clap the audience, they've been a jolly good bunch' is usually saved for when we mean it.

I usually settle for a simpery smile while my toes curl, but I have had a few goes at the 'Operatic diva', which I didn't pull off very well. I was lucky enough to play narrator to the French opera group Les Arts Florissants and travel all over the world with them. I must say people make a lot more fuss of singers than they do of actors. I got quite jealous . . . of myself too. As narrator I enjoyed roughly the same status as the soloists, which meant bunches of glads and hoots of 'Bravo!' as I took my solo bow. My toes curled so far, I'm surprised I didn't fall over.

16

Acting on Film

Chalk and Cheese

People often ask actors whether we prefer theatre or film and TV, which to me is a bit like being asked whether I prefer being cool or warm. Warmth is good after you have been out in the cold, and a cool room is heaven on a baking-hot day. Similarly, because acting on film and acting on stage are almost opposite but complementary activities, I long for the one after too much of the other, and vice versa.

Here goes with some generalisations:

> On stage the actors have more control and responsibility.
>
> On film the pace, focus, context and emotional temperature are mostly down to the editing, and out of the actors' hands.
>
> On stage the actors project their energy outward.
>
> On film the actors contain their energy behind the eyes.
>
> On stage the actors can sense, hear and dimly see the audience, and get a response immediately.
>
> On film the actors cannot conceive of the abstract impersonal millions out there, who will watch the film in the future, so they forget them and play to one 'person': the camera.
>
> In the theatre actors are often paid a pittance for doing eight shows a week for months on end.
>
> In a film actors can get paid very silly sums indeed for a few weeks or days.
>
> Stage actors can be in only one place at a time and their performances have a limited run.

Film actors' performances can be seen simultaneously in hundreds of places many times a day, long after the actors are dead and perhaps for centuries to come.

On stage the actors remain life-size throughout the show.

On film the actors are like Gulliver, a giant one minute and a dot the next.

On stage the actors have to keep the audience interested when they are just crossing the room.

A film cuts out the boring bits.

On stage an unknown actor might be offered the lead if he or she is the best person for the part.

On film the lead will be offered to the star who is currently big at the box office, whether he or she is right for the part or not.

In Britain many actors work in all the media. For an American actor that is more difficult. With the film industry based on the West Coast and the theatre world more centred on New York, it is physically very difficult to straddle both camps.

What tends to happen even here is that actors get put into slots. If someone is seen a lot on TV, they are offered more TV, and the same goes for film and theatre, with the added complication that theatre takes up so much more of the actor's time that they are seldom free for film. Crossing from one medium to the other often entails putting yourself deliberately out of work. Sod's law then sees to it that all those telly offers you had to turn down because you were on stage suddenly dry up. You cannot hold out any longer so you take the next stage play that comes along. So it's back to square one, if you're lucky, and back on the dole if you're not.

Since film and theatre exercise such opposing acting muscles, we worry that we might no longer be capable of 'crossing over'. Unnecessarily cautious directors and producers compound the situation. The casting agent suggests so-and-so for the lead in a low-key film. 'No way!' says the director. 'He played Captain Hook in that rowdy pantomime, didn't he?' as if the actor would be unable to refrain from leering and twirling his moustaches in the film. 'How about so-and-so for Major Barbara?' the casting office asks the theatre director. 'Never heard of her,' comes the reply. A video is sent. 'Yeah, she's great, but she's got a Geordie accent.' 'I think that was just for that film.' 'Yeah, well. We don't know anything about her. I mean, has she ever done anything on stage?' There is common sense in some of these worries, but a lot of them are hogwash.

Good actors will adjust their performance to fit the frame. They will quickly absorb any useful tips and then apply their usual powers of observation and communication to whatever the task. We can all fall into protectionism, mystifying our jobs to make ourselves seem more special, but it is in everybody's interest to spread the talent around. I admit that there are such things as effortless beauty and screen chemistry, but there is much else besides which can be picked up by common sense. As with everything, you learn most by doing it.

In my own case, the lower the budget the more I have learned. This is because, for some of the reasons listed above, I have had bigger parts (ergo more responsibility and more time on set) in low-budget or television films. The more you hang around on the set the more you overhear the director and crew plotting the next shot, and the more at ease you become with the camera crew the more questions you can ask, and the more you understand about the camera, with its different lenses, frames and movements, the more relaxed you become in front of it. If you come in for only the odd day on a big film, you have a stand-in to do all the waiting around for you and you spend most of your day in your caravan getting nervous or bored. By the time you have got the hang of how the director works, the job is almost over.

Rehearsing

Film acting is less about preparation and more about responding on the spot to the demands of each day, and as no two days are alike we cannot build up a system that will work from one job to the next. Also, because no two jobs are alike, I can only really talk about mine.

In my experience, you have a great conversation with the director when you first meet, and then maybe a few more over the phone, but from the moment filming starts you seldom speak. The director of a film has to be like an army general. They must keep an eye on every department, not just what is happening in the frame, and whenever there is a break they are on the phone, in a meeting, watching rushes or planning the next day's shoot. They rely on you to have taken on board what was discussed at your initial meeting, and you rely on them to tell you if you are doing anything wrong. That's about it. Most of the rest is homework, beauty sleep and hoping you will be on form when the cameras roll.

For some film jobs you are lucky enough to have a short period of rehearsal, but this is mainly for the director's benefit, to rehearse camera positions and plan cutting points. You can use this time to bond with your 'instant' family or 'instant' passionate lover, and to sniff out what the director is planning. I usually find it impossible to act full out at this point. You tend to be rehearsing only bitty little thirty-second scenes, which seem uneventful and pointless in isolation, particularly on a marked-up rehearsal-room floor. You do the same scene over and over: doorbell rings, walk to the door, open it, mumble, 'Oh, it's you', and camera leaves you behind as it follows your guest into the room. 'Can we do that again please, just for the timing of the walk?'

I like to think I cotton on quite quickly to what the director wants to see, but I do remember one time in an atmosphereless pre-fab, rehearsing a scene where I was supposed to find a dead body on a rock. In the middle of the room was a pile of coats representing 'rock', and time after time, on 'Action!', I paced out my path to the rock, called to the heap of coats, 'I say! Are you all right?', knelt down to examine the topmost coat and gasped.

'Cut! Let's do that again, shall we?'

This went on for hours. I knew the director intended to shoot the scene from the top of a cliff and from down on the beach, and that there would be limited hours of daylight and even more limited time when the tide would be right. I also knew that there would be a problem with my footprints in the sand – there could be only one lot of prints, so only one take. I understood all that, but what more could we learn from rehearsing here with this silly pile of coats?

'Let's try again,' the director sighed. 'And I do think you would react a little more. After all, it's the first time you've seen a dead body.'

'It was, about two hours ago,' I mumbled sulkily.

So that was it. He was worried I hadn't got it in me. I promised that I would be all right on the night and at last he let me go. There are some things that shouldn't be over-practised, shock and surprise being two of them. When I did do my one take, a combination of a buffeting wind, a pre-carious rock and an effectively made-up 'corpse' produced that spontaneous reaction the director had been searching for.

The Jigsaw Lid

Everyone knows that films are shot out of sequence and back to front. This is mainly dictated by locations: this stately home is free only in the first week of November, that busy London street can be cleared only between seven and ten a.m. on Thursday of week five, we can shoot in the college only out of term time, and so on.

Because of all this, one of the most useful things you can do with your time before shooting begins is to go through the schedule with a fine-tooth comb, working out what scenes you will do in what order. If the story-line is A-B-C-D-E-F-G the shooting order might be D-F-A-B-G-E-C. The schedule gives a general summary of each scene for the whole crew, but you need to do your own version with the details specific to your character.

In scene C my character meets a man and falls in love. In scene D she runs a bath and the phone rings. It's her boss detailing a new assignment for her. On day one, when we shoot scene D, I will be so caught up with getting to know everybody's names, worrying if the director wants to recast, managing the quirk in the bath tap that the props guy has pointed out, I might easily forget that I am in love and that when the phone rings I hope it will be Him. I have barely met the actor playing the man of my dreams, and not having shot scene C where we fall in love, it is not yet part of my memory. The director will not mind, or even notice, that I was not thinking of my lover as the phone rang, but I will. In film it is the specific detail of your thoughts that creates the depth of your character and keeps the audience interested.

That is where planning your private acting agenda comes in. Think of the A-G sequence of the story as the completed picture on the lid of the jigsaw box, and of each scene as a piece of that jigsaw. You plan the detail of each scene constantly referring to the overall picture, so that when the jigsaw is broken up, you can commit to the minutiae of each piece in the confidence that it will all make sense when it is placed back in sequence in the edit.

The jigsaw system is particularly helpful with detective stories. When Edward Petherbridge and I teamed up as Lord Peter Wimsey and Harriet Vane, we had a hell of a time keeping hold of the plot. Detective writers mete out their information very strategically, and we would have become as befuddled as the viewers had we not kept track of What We Knew So Far, in which scene. No good giving suspicious stares at the murderer before you even know he was at the scene of the crime.

A Small World

Frances Carr knew next to nothing about the plot she was caught up in. In 1983, I was over in Ireland shooting a six-part thriller for Channel Four called *The Price*. Frances was a millionaire's wife who, together with her daughter from a previous marriage, was kidnapped by an ex-IRA cowboy. They spent four weeks imprisoned in a windowless cellar, not knowing when or whether they would ever see daylight again.

For *The Price* my jigsaw picture had to be very sketchy. Frances received tiny snippets of information via her hooded kidnappers, who told her only what they wanted her to know about their negotiations with the outside world, so she could never be sure what was true. To begin with she was kept apart from her daughter. Was the girl still alive? Had she been released? What day of the week was it? What time of day? If

Frances was given an extra egg for breakfast one day, did it mean her captors had triumphed in some way and were in a generous mood? Was this good news or bad for her? The plot of *The Price* was fantastically intricate. Frances's husband, Geoffrey (played by Peter Barkworth), was caught up in a web of conflicting interests. Bankers, PR men, kidnap insurance brokers and the police in the North and the South all tugged him in different directions, and to add to the mix his wife had given him such hell during their brief marriage, one wondered whether she was worth rescuing at all.

I decided early on that it was best not to know any of this, or at least to try and forget it, in order to get nearer to Frances's perspective, so, having read the script only once, I took the reckless step of throwing away any scenes that did not directly involve my character. Since the plot divided cleanly into the kidnap scenes and the 'outside world' scenes, the actors from the two groups rarely met or socialised together back at the hotel in the evening, and this all helped sustain my 'ignorance'.

On average a television film unit aims to shoot five minutes of the plot per day. This works out at roughly six to eight pages of script, so that on *The Price*, for example, a whole morning might have been spent on someone coming into my cell, setting down a tray, saying a few words and leaving. When hours are taken up on minutes, minutes can seem like hours. We break for elevenses thinking it is tea-time. We leave the hot set in search of fresh air and daylight and find it has been raining all day and it is already dark. These distortions of perspective were helpful steps into Frances's world.

Thanks to Peter Ransley, the writer, I had seen some video tapes of interviews with kidnap victims and I began to understand how Frances might become more emotionally attached to the kidnappers with whom she shared her shrunken but actual world, and upon whom she directly depended for her life, than to the increasingly dream-like figures from her past.

But Frances was no straightforward victim. In the first episode, Ransley shows her as a manipulative and somewhat dysfunctional prick-tease who is given to lying. He pushes her beyond the merely emotional into a sexual connection with her captor. Do we believe her when she tells her daughter that she is doing it for them? Do we believe her at the end when she tells her husband she is expecting his child? He certainly has his doubts, and she relishes them as a kind of revenge.

When Frances returns home after her ordeal, a seeming normality is restored, but she cannot come to terms with her husband's complacency. At a dinner party held to celebrate her safe return, she gets a hint that he has done some sort of a deal. She is not sure what, but she realises that he has played with her life in order to save his business.

She and her daughter have been emotionally scarred for life, she herself has had a finger amputated, the kidnappers have lost their lives for a cause, however wayward, and here is Geoffrey triumphant. He has lost some sleep perhaps, but no money – his business has made back all it shelled out and more. Could he have acted earlier to ransom her? Who was the victim and who the villain? Having deliberately 'forgotten' the intricacies of the kidnap negotiations, I could see things only from Frances's point of view. The nature of the filming process allowed me to indulge in such partisanship. In a theatrical ensemble it would be less healthy, if possible at all.

Another Perspective

The 'kidnap team' spent four or five weeks stooped and crouched in a damp basement, getting more and more tired and fed up with the cold (and with catching one another's colds). Luckily we were shooting in story order, so I could allow natural wear-and-tear to affect my appearance. My nail varnish chipped, my nails broke, my hair got greasier and my clothes got shabbier as Frances's did. But at the end of a day of pretend trauma, I could scrub myself clean in my Dublin hotel, order up room service and relax in front of the telly.

One night on the news I heard of the very real kidnap of supermarket millionaire Don Tidy. From then until his release I was haunted by the story and taunted by the spurious nature of my job.

To Plan or Not to Plan

Because there is so much sitting-around-and-waiting time on a film set, you might spend all day gearing up to a five-line speech, going over and over it, planning every inflection until the whole thing becomes meaningless. On the page the script reads: 'JANE: Well, I never thought I'd see you again. But then, I don't suppose you expected to see me. You haven't changed. I didn't like your face then and I still don't now.' By the time you get on set, the speech trips cleverly off your tongue, but you feel like an automaton.

In order to retrieve some spontaneity, it is helpful to remember that as far as your character knows, she has not come to make a five-line speech, but simply starts with the impulse to say, 'Well, I never thought I'd see you again.' Having said that, she finds the need to make her next comment, which, together with any other external stimuli on the set, prompts the next phrase, and so on. It takes some nerve to trust that your brain will respond thus on cue and under pressure, but when it works it is well worth the risk.

The scene I am perhaps most proud of in *The Price* I did not plan at all. I had made a common mistake of skipping over the scene in preparation because there were no lines to learn. Those scenes are often the NAR (No Acting Required) scenes – the car chases or the tricksy aerial views, the bits which are thrilling for the technical team but can be very dull for us. (It works the other way round when there is a lot of acting and rather straightforward camera moves.)

All I had to do was sit in the back of a chauffeur-driven car and be ambushed, dragged out of the car by four hooded gunmen and thrown into a van. Easy. It was the end of a five-month shoot and I had nearly exhausted my screaming and emoting supplies; it was up to the others now. The chauffeur had to do the driving. The crew had to work out the mechanics of the roadblock and see that the car window shattered when a bullet went through it, killing the chauffeur stone dead. All I had to do was react.

By the time I realised that it was in fact Frances's most emotionally naked moment in the film, it was too late. The camera was about to roll and I just had to trust that something would happen. And it did. Perhaps because I was exhausted, I was relaxed, and film acting is about relaxation. On the cry of 'Action', I was right there in Frances's panic, blurting out her unscripted words. I quote this incident because for me it was so rare. To an old hand at film acting it would probably have been no big deal.

You Can Never Plan for the Weather

It helps to know what the director has in mind, but quite often the director is not sure what they want until they see what they've got. That is their prerogative, and a lot of the greatest strokes of genius are achieved in the editing room. Often on location something catches their eye that was not in the plan. Some accident of light or shadow, or the spontaneous intrusion of a passing old man, inspires a whole new set-up; a torrential downpour on the last day on that location forces us to shoot indoors.

When I worked with Louis Malle on *Milou en Mai* in 1989, I needed as much time as possible to practise my French. At the beginning of the shoot I spoke decent schoolgirl French at a rather halting pace, but by the end I was pretty fluent. Trouble was that as per schedule we were to shoot the exteriors first and then go indoors, and most of my major speaking scenes took place out of doors. Sod's law.

Still, there was always the cellar scene. This was a scene in which Michel Piccoli and I go to fetch some wine from the family cellar and linger down there a bit longer than is strictly necessary. The camera tastefully leaves us with a tantalising hint of what might go on, as it cuts to another scene. Louis had told me early on that the cellar scene was one of his favourites. I had better get it right then, I thought to myself, but that's OK because we are not doing it for some while.

What I had overlooked was that the scene was marked down as a 'Weather Cover' scene. That meant that if ever the weather failed us, there were some interior scenes we could switch to at the last minute. August in Toulouse and I thought I was safe, but no. Down it plopped just after lunch one day

during week two, and the murmur went up, '*On fait la cave.*
On fait la cave!'

Now, one of the best things about a French film is, as you
can imagine, the lunch. Trestle tables spread with white
cloths are laid with carafes of red and white wine at either
end. Not being an habituée, I tend to fall asleep after
drinking wine at lunch, so I normally steered clear and drank
water instead, but on that day, when I heard those dreaded
words about 'la cave', I rushed to the eating area, and, thank
God, the caterers had not cleared the wine away.

I wanted to loosen up, that was all, but on a hot day with
a nervous stomach the effect was a bit too drastic. With my
guilty secret, I braved the cellar stairs and attempted a
straight line to my mark. As if to test me, there was a camera
track laid down on the floor, and I was convinced that the
whole crew had guessed I was pissed and were holding their
breath to see if the uncool anglaise was going to trip.

We rehearsed the scene. Michel Piccoli strode over to one
of the wine vats and filled two glasses from the tap. As he
handed me my glass he whispered to me off script, '*C'est du
vrai, hein?*' Of course it would be real! Why hadn't I thought
of that? You don't fill genuine wooden wine vats with Ribena,
do you? How many takes did we do? And how much wine
did I sip? I have no recollection, officer.

A Paradox

When you speak a foreign language, you are acting. When I
speak French, I subconsciously imitate a French person. I try
to think like them and I adopt their gestures, even to some
extent their sense of humour. Louis had written his idea of a
certain type of Englishwoman, but he had written her in
French so she seemed French to me. She was not the clumsy
'Parlay voo' cliché we think they think we are. She was a
sensuous hippie, a free spirit who passed joints around and
thus helped liberate an uptight French family.

For Louis, Lily had a charm that was connected to her
Englishness. I would never understand what that was, and it
was best kept that way. However 'French' I became to my own

ears, for Louis my whole demeanour – accent, etc. – was that of an Englishwoman. I was English, so at least I need not worry about that bit. My job was to concentrate on relaxing, and in my book that meant getting better at French.

All I Gotta Do is Act Naturally

When we were rehearsing a scene on the second day of the shoot, Louis Malle's cameraman took me aside and, thinking he was being helpful, told me I looked tense. 'For the camera you must be relaxed,' he proffered. I explained that I was only looking strained because I was struggling to keep up with Louis's instructions in French (thinks: 'I have made a film before, you know. I may not speak your language perfectly, but I'm not stupid and now I'm really unrelaxed!').

The cameraman continued to offer advice until, bit by bit over the shoot, I won his trust, if not his admiration. He told me that in France there was more segregation between film and theatre actors, and that when he had heard I was from the 'Royale Shekspire Compagnie', he had assumed I knew nothing about film.

Well, I didn't much. I had just picked up a few pointers. I had been told that all you have to do is think and the camera will pick up all your thoughts. The trouble is, it not only picks up what you want to transmit, it also betrays your weaknesses and fears. When I used to go riding as a child, I was always told, 'Don't be nervous. The pony will sense it and play up.' You start to get nervous about getting nervous, and that is how it can be on film.

They say that for film you must behave naturally and not act at all. Fine, but to achieve the effect of naturalness we are often called upon to do some extremely unnatural things. I am walking along a clifftop in mid-close-up with not a care in the world, looking romantically out to sea. That is the impression. In fact, I am wearing a harness attached to the wheels of a jeep in case I am carried over the cliff by the gale-force wind, and I am picking my feet up like a dressage pony so as to avoid the rungs of the camera track.

I rehearse a scene where I describe how I lost a baby and can never bear children again. The director is sensitive to how difficult the scene is and allows me to find the most comfortable position from which to play it. I decide I cannot look the other actor in the eye. I lean on the windowsill and look outdoors, and this leaves me freer to underplay the emotion. The story is strong enough without my having to milk it. I can look out at the fields and rest my gaze on the horizon. I can take my time. I can act naturally.

The director then brings the crew in to see what we have worked on and to fit around it. Soon they discover a hitch. It is five-thirty in the evening and the outdoor light is changing by the minute. They will have to put up a wall of white polystyrene to bar my view of the fields. Bang goes that faraway look. The curtain by the window is casting an ugly shadow on my face. Could I just stand six inches back from the ledge? 'But then I can't lean on it,' I point out. 'Well, it would help us if you could just stand there a bit back from the window.'

When we finally shoot the scene, I stare at the polystyrene panorama and deliver my speech a foot back from the window, feeling as awkward as a lampstand. I feel grumpy and unconfident, and anything but natural. However, months later when I see the finished film I have to admit that the lighting is beautiful. It catches the mood of the scene and almost plays it for me. I still felt cheated, though. I was sure I could have done it better if I had leant on the sill. But then, with an ugly shadow across my face, who would have focused on my story?

It is easy to overlook the fact that the Just Act Naturally guideline contains the word 'act', which can refer to spontaneous behaviour or to the artificial replication of that behaviour. The actor's skill is to pretend something is happening when it is not. Besides the usual acting requisites of emotional recall and imagination, 'natural' behaviour quite often entails cool, detached study. What does a person look like as they walk down a street with no thought of being watched? How does a person behave when they walk into a strange room for the first time?

You might decide that because the room is new to your character, you will try to open the door the wrong way, pushing instead of pulling it. Sometimes the same idea is inspired by a happy accident on the first take. Whichever way you arrived at it, for take after take you must re-create this 'spontaneous' mistake, and because you cannot know at the time which take will finally reach the screen, you must treat each one as if it were both the first and the last you will ever do.

We have a third eye hovering above us which minutely monitors our act – ' too much', 'too little', 'phoney' and so on – and twiddles the knobs accordingly. I am alarmed sometimes at how busy that third eye can be in real life, whether watching one's own reactions or those of other people. I was caught in the middle of a street brawl once and stood mesmerised by the sheer speed of it, mentally making the note, 'Mask of aggression and mask of fear are indistinguishable' until someone whisked me out of the path of a flying bottle.

We store these little moments up in case they should come in handy in some future acting role. That way if we have to pretend we can at least pretend accurately. Nor should we be ashamed of such artifice. If it is in a good cause, it is an honest deception.

At One Remove

As a general rule, one is more often cast to type on film than on stage. There are obvious reasons for this. The camera will see through a heavy disguise, so why not find a guy who really looks the part? Because films take up less of an actor's time and pay more than the theatre, casting departments have a far bigger pool from which to choose. But looking the part and being like it are completely different things, and this presents a difficulty when it comes to acting naturally.

I have spoken about approaching characters that are far from you, how you can fix on someone you know who is like your character and think, 'How does *he or she* walk, smile, talk, express fear?' For a theatre play there is time to grow into your character during rehearsals, but with film, although you may have mapped the character out in your head and settled on a 'look' with the wardrobe and hair department, it cannot all come together till your squeaky new shoes have been broken in and your new voice, walk and manner have been tried out in situ and in interplay with other characters.

Some film directors (notably Mike Leigh) devote a large percentage of time to exactly this problem. The actors spend months researching a real life that is at several removes from their own and growing into their skin. However, as most film schedules cannot wait for your character to gel before they start to roll and as there is no short-cut for the actor, when that camera zooms in on you on your first day on set you feel as nervous as a conman in a lie-detector test. You cannot act naturally, because then you would be you. So how does *she* behave naturally? There is nothing for it but to commit a semi-stranger to celluloid and hope you will quickly meld.

The Loss of Innocence

Some of the most memorable and moving performances I have seen on screen have been given by children. This is usually because they are not consciously trying to be touching or interesting. The camera can catch even the most artful children unawares. Adult actors may not like it, but we are also taken unawares, and more often than we think. Those off-guard moments are sometimes the truest and the best. We must be prepared to give everything up to the camera, and although experienced actors cannot actually recover the innocence of a child, we would do well to emulate it.

I know the camera is watching me, but I must behave as if it is not. The tiniest thing can betray my self-consciousness. A man has been following me in the street. I have let myself into my flat and bolted the door. I hear the lift outside whirring into action, then the doors slide open and closed, and I hear stealthy footsteps and a floorboard creak just outside my front door. I am not really alone, because there is a film crew tucked away in the corner, and I am not really afraid, because the intruder is being played by a very old friend. There is no way the camera can capture real fear on my face, I simply have to pretend. It is what I am paid to do. I should be perfectly capable of reproducing the symptoms of fear through imagination, observation and scrupulous honesty applied to both.

When I hear stories of directors terrorising actors before a scene and claiming that the look they caught on camera was more convincing than anything that acting could achieve, I wonder if it is more than my actor's *amour propre* that feels insulted. It not only shows a lack of respect for the actor's craft, but also shows up the director's inability to bring out a good performance in a more civilised way.

Strong Support

Quite apart from actors being chameleons and personalities, there are characters who divide that way too. Part of the interest in playing a character like Hedda Gabler is that she seems to display a different persona to each character with whom she interacts, and you have the stage time to act out all her contradictions, leaving the audience their own time to try to work her out. If by contrast you have only a tiny cameo role who appears maybe twice, once near the beginning and once near the end of a story, it is best to settle on a few memorable characteristics which you display consistently each time you appear. This way the audience remembers which one you are, and you benefit from being remembered.

Most good writers build this in and know how to make supporting parts memorable. I was doubly blessed in this way by both Jane Austen and Emma Thompson when I played Fanny Dashwood in *Sense and Sensibility*. Then I was blessed again by the costume and wig designers, who more or less created Fanny. All I had to do was climb into her formidable armoury of crinolines, feathers and fans, move about and say the lines.

But perhaps the most important contribution to my performance was made by Ang Lee, the director. Emma and the producers had cleverly decided that for a British cast doing such an English piece, a foreign eye was needed to direct. Otherwise it risked falling into a more conventional Heritage slot. In his previous films, Ang had proved himself to be a brilliant observer and capturer of human relationships and family rituals. His main preoccupations – love, marriage, greed, hypocrisy – were universal and if he could so deftly slice to the heart of Taiwan family tussles, might he not be able to transpose his talents to Jane Austen territory and give us all a refreshing outsider's take on it all?

The gamble was brilliantly pulled off. Ang is not a man of many words and I think we were quite shy of one another to begin with. We had never had a long discussion about Fanny and, after all, we could each consult the book (although Emma's version of Fanny was slightly altered). What Ang did instead of talk was to ask each actor to fill in a questionnaire with some straight biographical questions about our characters, and some more psychological or speculative questions: for instance, 'If your character were alive today, who would he or she be?' This was a brilliant device with a two-way benefit. Ang got a crash course in English social history and found out a bit more about us, and we got the usual advantages of research plus the reassurance that Ang knew who our characters were.

As I have said before, it is unusual for anyone but the leading players to get much time to talk to the director once the shoot begins, but on this occasion Ang's little questionnaire removed any big need to talk. We had had a discussion based on my essay (I found myself writing in sub-Austenese, which in itself helped build a bridge to Fanny), at the end of which I felt total trust that Ang had understood what I wanted and would help me achieve it.

Fanny had to have her consistent hallmarks – her dress style, her lapdog as fashion accessory, her snooty look and cut-glass tones – but Ang gave little glimpses into third dimensions, a hint of sadness or a moment of nakedness. His editing and Chris Coulter's lighting surpassed anything I could do alone in bringing Fanny to life, and most importantly they did not underline her too much.

When we came to shoot the final wedding scene, we started by rehearsing the procession out of the church. As instructed, a mobcapped crowd rained confetti over us as we walked down the church path. After we had practised several times in order to find the best camera position, Ang came up to us and explained that, because we were rather bunched up, he could not always see what we were doing. Who was chatting? Who listening? Who laughing? I had quietly been playing with the idea that Fanny, who is feeling upstaged and thoroughly sour about the wedding, walked down the path in a bad-tempered silence, nostrils aloft and batting the crowd's confetti off her shoulders with an impatient hand. I demonstrated this to Ang and he made encouraging noises.

In the final cut, there we all are spilling out of the church in front of the flag-waving crowd, and as we continue down the path lightly glimpsed over someone's shoulder is Fanny fastidiously brushing confetti from her shoulder and wrinkling up her nose. If Ang had made more of it (in a close-up, say) it would have been embarrassingly overstated; as it is, it is there for anyone who might catch it as an added little something to smile about. So it was throughout the film. I did not have to push to get attention and so I relaxed, and this gave Ang more choice of material to pick up if he wanted.

By the Way . . .

Why is it that as one gets older the parts get nastier? At least it is usually so for women. It is deeply dyed in story-telling tradition from ancient Greece to Molière and still goes on today. From Snow White we graduate to the Wicked Stepmother, from Nina to Arkadina, from Ophelia to Lady Macbeth. In films in particular, as a woman gets older she usually gets vainer, sillier, more narrow and more bitter. Nine times out of ten, hers is merely a functional role offsetting the beauty and sweetness of the heroine – that is when she is in the frame at all.

But am I bitter? Hey, no. Since older actresses cannot be choosers, let's look for the compensations. Bitches can be more fun to play than insipid *ingénues*. Everyone loves a character who dares to be disliked, as we ourselves do not. And besides, they often get the wittiest lines and the most eye-catching frocks.

Film Can Do It for You

I have found that even my best-laid plans are like a paddle against the rapids. They help to make me feel I have some command over my performance, but flexibility and pride-swallowing have proved the most essential qualities to cultivate during a film. Often you chart your little course between A and G only to find that in the final edit scene E has been cut. That was the one scene where you showed that your character had a sense of humour, or knew about her husband's affair. These details were important to you, but they are not central to the story. Film develops its own narrative logic in the editing room, and I must take it on the chin if my scene is sacrificed to the newly shaped beast.

Cutting can also do you a favour. A screen close-up can be more eloquent than a fifteen-line speech, and any sensible actor would rather cut the speech than risk overstatement. In a stage play, the audience can choose where to look. During the main character's tirade they quickly flit to the servant in the background or the old aunt or the son, just to see what they are making of it. Our eyes can assimilate all this information in a trice. With a film, the camera (alias the director) decides what is interesting and when the audience should look at it. If I want to underline a moment on stage, I leave a little extra time around it, or make some gesture to draw the audience's eye, but on film the camera does the underlining for me. I just have to sit and think, and as the camera zooms in to a close-up, my thought becomes supremely important.

On stage the actor has to provide all the momentum – the variety of pace and mood to keep the audience with them. On film that is out of our hands. Incidental music, real locations, unusual camera angles and varied lighting can make us look good, or make the situation exciting, funny or sad.

In the early days of Soviet cinema, the director Lev Kulyeshov demonstrated how much of the actor's performance can be achieved through editing. First he projected on to the screen the close-up of an actor's face wearing a neutral expression. Next he cut to a shot of a plate of hot food and then back to the same close-up of the actor. The same face that had seemed expressionless seconds before now seemed to twitch with hunger. Next Kulyeshov showed footage of a dead body, before again returning to the close-up. This time the actor's face seemed clouded with grief. The last cut-away was of a beautiful woman, and when the camera looked back at the actor's face the audience saw it light up with lust. The actor himself had seen none of these things. His performance was created in the cutting room. Moral of the story: you can act your little socks off, but there is nothing to beat a blank face in the right place at the right time.

Money for Jam

In case you think I'm saying film acting is easy, let me remind you of a few tasks: finding and keeping hold of a relaxed energy throughout a long and broken-up day; having laser-sharp concentration ready on cue; summoning up the patience and flexibility needed to cope with the fact that you never quite know when that cue will come. These demands are no easier or harder than the demands of theatre acting, they are just different.

On film the actor's task is almost imperceptible to the naked eye. I once overheard one of the sparks (electricians) on a TV drama muttering furiously under his breath, 'Actors get paid money for jam.' I nearly swiped him on the jaw. Standing there with arms folded on beer belly, raking in probably twice as much money for jam as me! Admittedly, the actors *seemed* merely to be sitting round a table eating and talking all day, but anyone in the business should have known that meal scenes are notoriously complicated and time-consuming to shoot, and the actors were in fact having to repeat the same small scene from sixteen different angles, and make it look spontaneous every time.

I wasn't expecting praise from the man, any more than he was expecting me to congratulate him on his lighting rig (or whatever it is he does – OK, the ignorance was on my side as well), I just hoped for mutual trust that we were each pulling our weight. At least when he was at work, you could see his muscles strain and his body perspire, but our efforts of concentration and patience are necessarily invisible.

Ready for Action

It is my first day on location playing Amy Johnson. We are to do the scene where she touches down in Darwin, Australia, at the end of her record-breaking flight. For Darwin read a grey windswept airfield in Northamptonshire. I have been made up and kitted out and am about to be introduced to 'Jason' (a replica of Amy's airplane of the same name). I am led round the corner of the flying-club building and there I see . . . a small green tin bath with wings. My stomach turns over. In 1930, aged twenty-six and with nothing but a school atlas to guide her, Amy had flown alone for 11,000 miles in that!?

The director and I have agreed not to rehearse and to try and get a spontaneous reaction in one take. The crew work extra hard to make sure nothing goes wrong. Meanwhile, I sit in my open cockpit and try and recall what I have read of Amy's story. I remind myself that I have been alone for days and am not used to people. I try to picture flying blind above the clouds over jungles and being forced to land in the desert during a sandstorm, weighting down my plane with sandbags and clutching my gun as I listen to the howling desert dogs, wondering if I will ever get out of there alive. All of a sudden a voice says, 'So where do you come from, Harriet?' One of the crowd has decided to chat. I probably look like I could do with cheering up. 'London,' I manage to snap out between my falsely smiling teeth.

Hold on to that mood. Think of your triumph. You've made it! The first woman to do it!

'Oh, yes? And which bit of London would that be?'

'Sorry? Oh, the west.'

Back to the clouds and the juddering wind beating my face. But I can't concentrate. I have been stand-offish to the poor man. He was only trying to be friendly. I look at him and manage a watery smile; but suddenly I can see all the BBC anoraks, the camera, the boom, and the flats of Northamptonshire. Cut it out quick. Australia! Australia! It's hot. You've arrived. You're exhausted. Phew! Just made it.

'OK, stand by to shoot, everyone . . . Sound running. Mark it. Scene 127, take one. Action!'

I cut Jason's engine, climb out of the cockpit and walk unsteadily towards the reception committee. I've done it! I've done it! 11,000 miles. All those people. Disbelief, terror, relief, exhilaration. It's all too much. I can't open my mouth, but I have to make a speech. As I grope for the lines, the effort is real. The crowd applauds. 'Cut!' Not bad.

'Great!' says the director. 'Print that one.' (*Pause while someone whispers in his ear.*) Yes, what is it? (*Another pause while director and camera crew get in a huddle.*) 'Sorry, folks, we'll have to go again. I'm afraid you, sir – ' pointing to my chatty friend ' – I'm afraid you were looking straight into the lens.' To look into the lens is like waving at the audience: 'Hello, Mum. We're making a film!' We did it again, and again, and probably again – I don't remember, but spontaneity had bitten the dust.

A French Adventure

It is frightening when a dream comes true. As a teenager I would sometimes slop along the London streets dragging a stick against the railings and, putting on a French pout, I would mumble cod French phrases under my breath. I was in a Truffaut film and woe betide any staring passers-by or traffic lights that interrupted my flow.

In 1989 I met Louis Malle at the Dorchester Hotel to discuss the possibility of my being in his next film. As I sat across from this engaging modest man, images from *Les Amants*, *Le Souffle au Coeur* and *Au Revoir les Enfants* flashed in my mind. Louis only once referred to my French: 'I hear it is impeccable.' 'Well, a bit peccable,' I gulped, while inwardly thanking Patsy Pollock, the casting director, for bluffing on my behalf.

After that meeting I heard nothing for a good three weeks. My agent rang and said, 'I think we'd better face it, we'd have heard by now.' I begged her to double-check. Louis was hunted down. 'Of course she is still in the running. But would she mind coming to Paris to meet Michel Piccoli?' Would I mind!

In Paris things got serious. 'We speak French from now on.' I remember sitting in a restaurant between Louis and

Michel, staring at a hill of butter shaped like the Matterhorn and thinking of Michel in *La Grande Bouffe*. I was tongue-tied. I couldn't remember the French for rehearsal, let alone the Italian for ceiling.

I returned to London in despair. I'd blown it. I'd had a *Purple Rose of Cairo* experience: they had momentarily come out of the screen to meet me, but I could never go back with them . . . I was wrong. The next day Louis phoned from Paris: 'We'd love you to play the part.'

If you're going to be in a French film, let it be a truly French film, and *Milou en Mai* was a French film *par excellence*. It was set in 1968, and so its atmosphere was similar to those classics that had fuelled my teenage fantasies. Both off screen and on there was much emphasis placed on The Meal. From the first read-through at Jean-Claude Carrière's house in Pigalle, sitting round a white-clothed table bedecked with silver coffee pots and mountains of croissants (so unlike the BBC) to the scene in the film where we discuss revolution over piles of freshly caught crayfish, to the careful choice of restaurant each night, to the picnic scene under the trees . . .

Unlike most male English directors I had come across, Louis was interested in every little detail of make-up and dress, and conducted lengthy trials in the studio at Joinville before we set off for Toulouse. A man's shirt must not be *this* pastel blue, but *that* pastel blue. My own costume was mostly borrowed from an ex of Louis on whom he had partly based the character.

In France I found that standards of aesthetics and performance were inextricably bound together. A beautiful woman was *'douée'* (talented), a good take was *'très jolie'*, a bad bit of acting was *'pas beau'*. I found myself adjusting my own standards of good screen acting to include this aesthetic dimension. Perhaps it was not enough merely to think the right thoughts and act naturally. But then neither is it enough to be ravishingly beautiful but blank. The best screen acting is a combination. Some people are born knowing how to tilt their face to the light. On cue as the cameras roll, a kind of suffusion of watchability flushes through their skin. Add to that a certain intelligence and a minimum of acting instinct and wow! It was a humbling discovery.

For nine weeks I had the privilege of living in Louis Malle's dream. During rehearsals over the first two weeks he created a believable family out of a very disparate cast: from Paulette Dubost, who had starred in *La Règle du Jeu*, to modern screen 'anti-stars' like Miou-Miou; from veterans of the Comédie Française like Michel Duchaussoy to local people (Louis's own neighbours) who had never acted before, to children and donkeys and dogs.

We spent six days out of seven at the old house La Calaoué and it sort of became our home. The stables and outbuildings were converted to editing and screening rooms, to offices, make-up, wardrobe and catering. Our dressing rooms were rooms in the house, where we could retire to gossip but never feel far from the action. We could hear *'Silence partout!'* from the window and tiptoe to watch the scenes we weren't in.

Louis did not talk much about what was going on in the characters' minds; he concentrated on what could be seen, and curiously even more on what could be heard. Often in rehearsal he would close his eyes and listen to check that the 'music' was right, and it was the sound man more than the cameraman whom he consulted after each take. Inauthenticity is perhaps more easily detected with the ear than with the eye.

Speaking French from morning till night, I felt perpetually at one remove from my familiar self. There were days on end when I was like the dunce of the class, struggling to keep up. Louis had a very precise comic sense, and his rigorous choreography and insistence on certain rhythms of text were very exacting for me. However useless I felt I suppose I was flattered that he applied the same standards to me as to everyone else. As if to reward me now and then he would invite me to a meal *en famille* with his wife, Candice Bergen, and this English-speaking interlude would restore my confidence and sense of self.

When I see the film now I have a strange dual sensation. On the one hand, I see a classic French movie depicting a strange foreign world; on the other, I see the filmed highlights of a summer I once spent. The *Milou* experience forms a wonderful kink in the landscape of my memory. There is a huge spill of dappled sunlight on the map of 1989, an eternal picnic under the trees. It dwarfs so many other memories. It was a gift that dropped out of the sky and into my lap, and I don't know whom to thank.

If

I have no film career as such, but I am lucky enough occasionally to take part in a film. There is a difference. The powers that be in the film industry see actors not just in terms of how well they can act but as a potential investment. Even were I the greatest actress alive, there are simply not enough roles for older women to warrant an investment in my career. If you cannot be seen in a prominent role at least once a year (and a good role in a good film, remember), you cannot build a fan base that will guarantee your bankability.

> If there had been a film industry in this country when I was in my twenties . . .
>
> If fringe theatre had been less interesting . . .
>
> If television had not been of such high quality at that time . . .
>
> If I had been unquestionably beautiful . . .
>
> If by the time the British film renaissance came along I had not been in my forties . . .
>
> If there were more grown-ups running the big studios . . .
>
> If more of those grown-ups were women . . .
>
> If I were fatter . . .
>
> If I were thinner . . .
>
> If I were Scottish . . .
>
> If I were a bloke (of whatever age or shape) . . .
>
> If I had met Woody Allen . . .
>
> If things had been different . . . blah blah blah.

I carry on counting my blessings and hoping for that one brilliant all-embracing role. Me and a few thousand others.

As If It Matters

BY WAY OF AN EPILOGUE

I went to Disneyland once and joined the queue for the Space
Mountain ride. Imagine an extra-steep rollercoaster which
travels in the dark! No spying the track ahead and preparing
your stomach for the dip, just the blind shock of a drop, and
the odd surprise slap in the face with a wet flannel for good
measure. The queue shuffled forward and at regular intervals
along our route we saw exit doors with notices advising those
with weak hearts or faint spirits that it was not too late to
chicken out. At each of those opportunities I felt my ghost
feet rehearse their escape while my real feet followed the ones
in front.

All the way through one's career there are signs saying, 'It
is not too late to chicken out', 'The world won't mind if there
is one actor less.' Anyone I have known to 'chicken out' has
done so out of great courage and common sense. The rest of
us carry on, partly because by now we are not good for much
else and partly because we have come so far and invested so
much in the choice, it would seem like some sort of betrayal
to pull out. The world may not need me, but what about that
pact I made with my younger self? I may have forgotten quite
what it was that she believed in, but don't I owe it to her to
keep going in case I glimpse a reminder along the way?
Besides, the Big Break could be around the corner at any
time. One might be the next Arthur Lowe or Joan Hickson.
In this profession it is never too late to become a star.

Choices were easy when you started out. You had everything to learn, so any job was a good job. Then, as contacts
led to other things, the crossroads began to appear. There
would be perhaps two clearly marked roads to choose from,
one with a sign reading, 'Small part in strange film. Presti-
gious director', the other pointing to 'Lead part in interesting
play. No money', and still others marked simply, 'Unforesee-

able possibilities'. No time to ponder. Eeny, meeny, miney, mo – which hand do you want?

You know that each fork in the road will lead to other forks, which may in turn lead to the Job That Was Made for You, or even the Person Who Was Meant for You, and you know that by choosing one route you may be cutting off these chances for ever. No one can help you to make your decisions. 'Listen to your instincts,' people say, but when you come to think of it, why should your instincts know? 'What made you choose that job?' people ask you years later. They seem not to realise that your choices were always limited by a) what shows were in the pipeline at any given time, and b) whether anyone wanted you to be in them.

There are parts I wanted to play but never did, and now the moment has passed – not just because I am too old for them in looks or years, but because I have emotionally moved on from the position that once linked us. These are like love affairs I never had. I just know we would have got along, but either we never met or we were introduced at the wrong time. So you let them go. A bit like life really.

So where am I now and what next? The best and the worst thing about this job is that you can rarely predict where you will be in six weeks' time, let alone six months'. Sometimes the view ahead is peppered with crossroads and choices, at others it is an empty wilderness challenging you to lay down your own track. At times the decisions are easy, either because you are so broke you must take whatever comes or because it's one of those rare but wonderful occasions when an offer is simply perfect.

I have lost the grandiose swoop of ambition that I started off with, and in its place there is a more modest mission which is hard to define. It has something to do with faith. Faith in the resonance of details; faith in the discernment of the public.

This faith is fed by conversations, in particular with young people, who seem to be rebounding from all the hype and seeing and hearing for themselves. The market has been telling us for some time that 'serious' theatre is moribund, and its audience is exclusively middle-aged and middlebrow.

Young people are said to be interested only in fast-moving sex and violence, and bored by anything that is remotely difficult.

First, it is no crime, I hope, to provide for the tastes of people over forty. Second, if theatre is moribund, how come there is no let-up in the stream of young entrants into playwriting competitions each year? How come, despite even less financial encouragement than in my day, new fringe theatre venues are opening all the time? How come I sat last year among young audiences for Beckett and Ionesco who seemed totally at ease with these 'difficult' plays?

There are audiences for action-packed blockbusters and there are those who are as interested in the fragile nuance of human interaction. There may be many more of the former than the latter, but I do not believe these groups are mutually exclusive or can be broken down into straightforward categories of age or class.

Jennie Lee, Labour's famous Minister for the Arts and herself from a Scottish mining family, recognised that 'a measure of the nation's self-confidence is its willingness to develop creative intelligence in its people'. The returns on such an investment in people can never be demonstrable in strict market terms. The artistic achievements of this century will be remembered for their impact on ideas rather than for whether or not they made a profit. It is worth remembering that the most influential Englishman of all time wrote plays for a living, and that people from all ranks could understand and afford to watch them.

Art is not intrinsically élitist. It has become so through hundreds of years of deliberate appropriation by a particular class as a weapon for social exclusion. It has been adopted as a badge of fine feeling and social superiority by people who often lack both, and their posturing has helped obscure the real attractions of art and fuelled distrust of art lovers in general.

Sadly, nowadays we have inherited less of Jennie Lee's legacy than of the market-led cynicism of the 1980s. Too often we see pundits and politicians who set the agenda for education and the arts adopting a faux-populist stance in public while furtively nurturing their true tastes in private. Instead of pandering to the prevailing prejudices, they could use their platform to turn opinion round.

But the most persuasive argument against prejudice is experience. That is why it is so important to make the arts geographically and economically accessible. In Britain the very words 'art' and 'culture' have become so loaded that I need to explain my terms. I am talking about activities which expand the individual's creative imagination, challenge the status quo and enhance the individual's sense of participation in the world. I am talking about activities which have the potential to breach differences, overcome ignorance and, above all, to combat boredom. It is boredom and disaffection, even more than economic deprivation, which lie behind so much crime and cruelty in our society. It is stress and emotional isolation which cause mental breakdown, drug abuse and poor performance at work. Is it so fanciful to link the state of our arts with the spiritual welfare and overall health of our society?

By exposing young people of all classes to a thrilling work of art or by allowing them to experiment artistically themselves, chances are they will find things less difficult, less irrelevant and therefore less boring. Broaden the base of the participating talent and you might broaden the base of the audience. I long to see a stage, screen or orchestra whose make-up reflects the multicultural reality of our society, with an audience to match.

It takes only one bad experience of theatre to put a person off, so we must be as good and as exciting as we can possibly be. For this, we need government investment in training (this includes the regional theatre seedbeds, where we develop that training) and in experiment which might produce the great work of the future.

So that is the more modest goal I have adjusted to. It used to be 'Change the world', now it is 'Don't be boring'. If I at least try to follow the latter, I stand a chance of contributing to the former. It all comes back to faith. A lot of the job of the actor is to believe and make others believe. Wishful thinking is of no use to anyone, but faith can make a difference. At any rate we may as well act as if it might, just in case it does.

CV

CV

PRE-DRAMA SCHOOL, worked as ASM on the world première of *After Magritte* by Tom Stoppard and *You're Free* by Henry Livings, both for Interaction's Ambiance Lunchtime Theatre

1970–73   trained at LAMDA

1973   Common Stock Theatre: *Tales from Whitechapel; Watch the Woman* by Olwyn Wymark and Brian Phelan

1973–75   Duke's Playhouse, Lancaster: roles include one of Beauty's ugly sisters in *Beauty and the Beast*; title role in *Huckleberry Finn*; Elizabeth Proctor in *The Crucible* by Arthur Miller

1975–77   touring with 7:84

1977   touring with Paines Plough Theatre Company: Cecily and Prince Edward in David Pownall's *Richard III, Part 2*

1978   touring with Joint Stock Theatre Company in *The Ragged Trousered Philanthropists*

1979

THEATRE   Jane in *A Fair Quarrel* by Thomas Middleton and William Rowley, directed by Bill Gaskill for the National Theatre; various roles in *Fears and Miseries of the Third Reich* by Bertolt Brecht, directed by Nikolas Simmonds for the Open Space

TELEVISION   Clarice the maid in *Rebecca* for the BBC; Cathy in *The Imitation Game* for the BBC

1980

THEATRE   Ophelia in *Hamlet*, directed by Richard Eyre for the Royal Court; Dawn in *Three More Sleepless Nights* by Caryl Churchill, directed by Les Waters for the Soho Poly and Royal Court Upstairs; Edward/ Victoria in *Cloud Nine* by Caryl Churchill, directed by Max Stafford-Clark for the Royal Court; Madeleine Bray and others in *Nicholas Nickleby*, adapted by David Edgar from the novel by Charles Dickens, directed by Trevor Nunn and John Caird for the RSC at the Aldwych

TELEVISION   Varya in *The Cherry Orchard* by Chekhov for the BBC

1981

THEATRE   Lily (Nina) in Thomas Kilroy's Irish version of *The Seagull* by Chekhov, directed by Max Stafford-Clark for the Royal Court

1981–83

THEATRE   season with the RSC at Stratford-upon-Avon, Newcastle upon Tyne and then launching the Barbican Centre, playing Helena in *A Midsummer Night's Dream*, directed by Ron Daniels; Constance in *The Twin Rivals* by George Farquhar, directed by John Caird; Winnefrede in *The Witch of Edmonton* by Thomas Dekker, John Ford and William Rowley, directed by Barry Kyle; Lady Percy in *Henry IV, Parts I and II*, directed by Trevor Nunn (London only); Helena in *All's Well that Ends Well*, directed by Trevor Nunn (also toured to Martin Beck Theater on Broadway, New York)

1983

FILM   *Reflections* by John Banville, directed by
Kevin Billington

TELEVISION   Amy Johnson in *Amy* for the BBC;
Frances Carr in *The Price* for Channel
Four and RTE

1984

THEATRE   Julia in *The Lucky Chance* by Aphra Behn
directed by Jules Wright for the Women's
Playhouse Trust at the Royal Court; brief
tour of Yorkshire mining communities
with 7:84 roadshow *The Enemy Within*

FILM   *Turtle Diary*, screenplay by Harold Pinter
from the novel by Russell Hoban,
directed by John Irvin

1985

THEATRE   Maria Lebiadkin in *The Possessed* by
Dostoevsky, adapted by Richard Crane,
directed by Yuri Liubimov for the
Almeida Theatre and European tour;
Skinner in *The Castle* by Howard Barker,
directed by Nick Hamm for the RSC at
the Pit, Barbican Centre

FILM   *The Good Father*, screenplay by
Christopher Hampton from the novel by
Peter Prince, directed by Mike Newell

TELEVISION   *The Possessed* for Channel Four; *Refuse to
Dance*, documentary about Howard
Barker

1986

THEATRE   Masha in *Three Sisters* by Chekhov, directed by Paul Unwin for Bristol Old Vic

TELEVISION   Harriet Vane in *Lord Peter Wimsey* for
the BBC

1987

THEATRE Portia in *The Merchant of Venice*, directed
by Braham Murray for the Royal
Exchange Theatre, Manchester

1987–89

THEATRE season with the RSC at Stratford-upon-
Avon, Newcastle upon Tyne and the
Barbican Centre, playing Imogen in
Cymbeline, directed by Bill Alexander;
Viola in *Twelfth Night*, directed by Bill
Alexander; Dasha in *A Question of
Geography*, by John Berger and Nella
Bielski, directed by John Caird; Masha in
Three Sisters by Chelchov, directed by
John Barton (London only)

1989

FILM *Milou en Mai*, screenplay by Louis Malle
and Jean-Claude Carrière, directed by
Louis Malle

TELEVISION Sheila in *Benefactors* for the BBC; Cat
Lady in *They Never Slept* for the BBC;
Mrs Pankhurst in *La Nuit Miraculeuse*,
directed by Ariane Mnouchkine for
French TV

1989–90

THEATRE season with the RSC at Stratford-upon-
Avon, Newcastle upon Tyne and the
Barbican Centre, playing title role in
The Duchess of Malfi by John Webster,
directed by Bill Alexander

1991

THEATRE Biddy in *Three Birds Alighting on a Field*
by Timberlake Wertenbaker, directed by
Max Stafford-Clark for the Royal Court

TELEVISION · Charity in *The Men's Room* for the BBC;
Giulia in *Ashenden* for the BBC

1992

THEATRE · revival of *Three Birds Alighting on a Field*
at the Royal Court

TELEVISION · 'The Day of the Devil': part of the
Inspector Morse series

FILM · *The Hour of the Pig*, written and directed
by Leslie Megahey

CONCERT · narrator for Les Arts Florissants' concert
tour of Europe and USA, performing
Purcell's *The Fairy Queen*

1993

THEATRE · The Woman in *La Musica* (*Deuxième*) by
Marguerite Duras, directed by Joseph
Blatchley for the Hampstead Theatre
Club; Lady Croom in *Arcadia* by Tom
Stoppard, directed by Trevor Nunn for
the Royal National Theatre and UK tour

TELEVISION · 'The Most Beautiful Dress in the World'
for *Bookmark* for the BBC; Dorothy in
The Maitlands for the BBC; Rachel in
Hard Times for the BBC

CONCERT · *Medea*, a piece for actress and orchestra,
performed at the Queen Elizabeth Hall

1994

THEATRE · revival of *Three Birds Alighting on a Field*
at the Manhattan Theatre Club in New
York

TELEVISION · Charlotte in 'A Man You Don't Meet
Every Day' for *Without Walls* for Channel
Four

1994–95

THEATRE   Karen in *The Children's Hour* by Lillian
Hellman, directed by Howard Davies for
the Royal National Theatre and UK tour

1995

THEATRE   Anna in *Old Times* by Harold Pinter,
directed by Lindy Davies at Wyndham's
Theatre (and Maly Theatre, Moscow)

FILM   Fanny in *Sense and Sensibility*, screenplay
by Emma Thompson from the novel by
Jane Austen, directed by Ang Lee

CONCERT   narrator for Les Arts Florissants' concert
tour of Australia, Japan and USA,
performing Purcell's *The Fairy Queen*
and Charpentier's *Le Malade Imaginaire*

1996

THEATRE   Claire (and various children's voices) in
Sweet Panic, written and directed by
Stephen Poliakoff for the Hampstead
Theatre Club; title role in *Hedda Gabler*
by Ibsen, translated by Helen Cooper,
directed by Lindy Davies for the
Chichester Festival Theatre and UK tour

TELEVISION   Mildred Blades in *A Dance to the Music of
Time* for Channel Four

1997

THEATRE   Anna Petrovna in *Ivanov* by Chekhov,
directed by Jonathan Kent for the
Almeida Theatre (and Maly Theatre,
Moscow)

FILM   *Keep the Aspidistra Flying*, screenplay
by Alan Plater from the novel by George
Orwell, directed by Robert Bierman; *The
Governess*, written and directed by Sandra

Goldbacher; *Bedrooms and Hallways* by
Robert Farrar, directed by Rose Troché

TELEVISION   *Ivanov Goes to Moscow,* documentary for
Channel Four; Amy in *Unfinished
Business* for the BBC

1998

FILM   *Onegin,* adapted from poem by Pushkin
by Michael Ignatieff and Peter Ettedgui
and directed by Martha Fiennes

TELEVISION   second series of *Unfinished Business* for
the BBC; *Norman Ormal,* written for
Harry Enfield by Craig Brown for the
BBC; 'Time to Go' for *Dalziel and Pascoe*
series for the BBC

1999

THEATRE   Celia in *The Late Middle Classes* by
Simon Gray, directed by Harold Pinter at
Palace Theatre, Watford and tour; Lady
Macbeth in *Macbeth,* directed by Greg
Doran for the RSC at the Swan Theatre,
Stratford upon Avon

TELEVISION   Queen Morag in *Leprechauns* for
Hallmark Productions and NBC

2000

THEATRE   Lady Macbeth in *Macbeth,* as above,
continuing at Stratford, then touring to
the Globe Theatre, Tokyo, the Young Vic
Theatre, London, and the New Haven
Festival, Connecticut, USA; Sonya in
Life x 3 by Yasmina Reza, directed by
Matthew Warchus for the National
Theatre and Old Vic

FILM   *Villa des Roses,* directed by Frank van Passel

TELEVISION   Film of *Macbeth* for Channel 4.

2001

THEATRE   Julie Cavendish in *The Royal Family* by George S Kaufman and Edna Ferber, directed by Sir Peter Hall, at the Haymarket Theatre, London

TELEVISION   Pamela in *My Uncle Silas* for Yorkshire Television

2002

THEATRE   Beatrice in *Much Ado about Nothing*, directed by Greg Doran, for the RSC at Stratford-upon-Avon, London and Newcastle upon Tyne; Paige in *Dinner* by Moira Buffini, directed by Fiona Buffini for the NT Loft space

TELEVISION   Title role in *George Eliot: a Scandalous Life*, directed by Mary Downes for BBC Arts

2003

THEATRE   Lori in *US and Them* by Tamsin Oglesby, Hampstead Theatre

TELEVISION   Virginia Woolf in Peter Akroyd's *London* for BBC Arts; Mary Wollestencraft in *Mary Shelley*, directed by Mary Downes for BBC Arts

FILM   Margot Maitland in *Bright Young Things*, directed by Stephen Fry

RADIO WORK includes *Romeo and Juliet, Never in My Lifetime, A Cruel Madness, Rhyme or Reason, Buddenbrooks, The Perfect Spy, Radio Cars, Macbeth, Benefactors, A Winter's Tale, Arcadia, Rebecca, Medea, Sherlock Holmes, People Like Us,* Cocteau's *The Human Voice, Hedda Gabler, The Heat of the Day, Villette, The Heart of the Matter, Ivanov,* and *Cyanide at Four O'Clock*

CONTRIBUTIONS TO OTHER PUBLICATIONS include
Players of Shakespeare, Vol. 3 (Cambridge University Press);
Clamorous Voices (The Women's Press); *New Theatre
Quarterly*, Vol. IX, No. 34 (Cambridge University Press);
Renaissance Drama in Action (on playing the Duchess of
Malfi, Routledge); *Mothers by Daughters* (Virago); and
Macbeth for 'Actors on Shakespeare' (Faber and Faber, 2002)

Index

[271]